WORKING ABROAD

THE COMPLETE GUIDE TO OVERSEAS EMPLOYMENT AND LIVING IN A NEW COUNTRY

31st EDITION

JONATHAN REUVID

PPP INTERNATIONAL
redefining / standards

KoganPage

LONDON PHILADELPHIA NEW DELHI

Publisher's note

Every possible effort has been made to ensure that the information contained in this book is accurate at the time of going to press, and the publishers and authors cannot accept responsibility for any errors or omissions, however caused. No responsibility for loss or damage occasioned to any person acting, or refraining from action, as a result of the material in this publication can be accepted by the editor, the publisher or any of the authors.

First published in 1977
Thirty-first edition 2010

120 Pentonville Road	525 South 4th Street, #241	4737/23 Ansari Road
London N1 9JN	Philadelphia PA 19147	Daryaganj
United Kingdom	USA	New Delhi 110002
www.koganpage.com		India

© Godfrey Golzen and contributors 1977, 1979, 1980, 1981, 1982, 1983, 1984, 1985, 1986, 1987, 1988, 1989, 1990, 1991
© Kogan Page and contributors 1992, 1993, 1994, 1995, 1996, 1997, 1998, 1999, 2000, 2002, 2003, 2004, 2005, 2006, 2007, 2008, 2009, 2010

ISBN   978 0 7494 6111 9
E-ISBN   978 0 7494 6112 6

British Library Cataloguing-in-Publication Data

A CIP record for this book is available from the British Library.

Library of Congress Cataloging-in-Publication Data

Reuvid, Jonathan.
    Working abroad : the complete guide to overseas employment and living in a new country / Jonathan Reuvid. -- 31st ed.
        p. cm.
    Includes index.
    ISBN 978-0-7494-6111-9 -- ISBN 978-0-7494-6112-6 1. British--Employment--Foreign countries--Handbooks, manuals, etc. 2. Employment in foreign countries--Handbooks, manuals, etc. I. Title.
    HF5549.5.E45G64 2010
    331.702--dc22
                               2010016040

Typeset by Saxon Graphics Ltd, Derby
Printed and bound in Great Britain by MPG Books Ltd, Bodmin, Cornwall

I'm not looking for a cheap health plan.
I'm looking to pay less for a great one.

Whether you're putting your feet up or they're never touching the ground, you'll discover there's no place like back home for great British health cover.

We have a range of award-winning International Health Plans to suit every need and our prices* are lower than you might think – just put us to the test…

To save on your international health cover call AXA PPP healthcare today on

+44 (0)1892 550817 quoting reference **WA2006** or visit
www.axappphealthcare.co.uk/wa

PPP HEALTHCARE

Contents

Individual country profiles can be found on the Kogan Page website.
Weblink: www.koganpage.com/WorkingAbroad10
Password: WA29006

Introduction

THE JOB OUTLOOK FOR UK EXPATRIATES

British expatriates are still highly regarded abroad and their salary rates are competitive against labour recruited from the United States and most Western European countries which joined the European Union (EU) but not the 12 since 30 April 2004. The global recession from which the North American and most European countries are only now recovering hit the job market internationally, and the overseas job markets for British knowledge workers and managers remain tough, although US and European contractors still turn to the United Kingdom to recruit some skilled workers for both their short- and longer-term projects overseas at rates of remuneration not necessarily below those demanded by their own nationals. This type of contract is normally lucrative for the UK national and has the added advantage that the contractor frequently provides good living conditions and contractual benefits. Inevitably, this kind of job opportunity dwindled in 2009 and may not revive before 2011.

The ability to earn significant salaries overseas when appointments are on offer, together with the chance to avoid UK taxation that is expected to rise steeply from 2011, sounds like Utopia. However, the expatriate worker is faced with a new set of problems. Many of these will be outside the work assignment itself and will involve their family and social life. Working abroad requires a substantial adjustment in attitudes towards work and life in general. The ability to adapt to the new environment is absolutely essential, together with a willingness to make the best of things as they are in the new surroundings. Attempting to change that environment to your accustomed way of life is doomed to failure and will cause the resentment of the host country.

Lucrative overseas employment can solve many problems and may seem like the answer to a prayer. But it also creates human problems that may result in broken marriages, ruined careers and disturbed children. In accepting a job overseas you are taking a considerable risk and you should calculate how big the risk is in your particular case. Very often you will find that there is a direct correlation between risk and reward. For example, working for a major international company in Saudi Arabia, with the benefit of a more secure environment at work and company housing, ought to carry much less risk than working for a Saudi company. The rate of pay offered may be very different, with the Saudi company offering much higher pay, but without the security and facilities which a Western employer would provide. However, even working for a multinational company will not stop or cure all the problems caused by working overseas. Cases well publicized in the media confirm that it will also not give workers immunity if they break the laws of the host country; nor, as we are all too well aware, does it provide immunity from acts of international terrorism.

People work overseas for many different reasons and are motivated by so many different things. It is difficult to believe anyone who says that money is not one of the major incentives. The duration of overseas employment is also varied. Some people just want to work a one- or two-year contract to help pay off the mortgage, to produce the capital to start a business, or in the case of UK citizens, to avoid a reduced standard of living during the likely period of austerity from 2011. Others engage in a series of shorter-term project assignments, often hopping from one country to another. However, such short-term contracts attract many applications and usually tend to be taken up by 'permanent expatriates' – those people who have spent much of their working lives abroad and migrate from one assignment to another.

The risks of working overseas for extended periods were enhanced by a Court of Appeal decision (24 January 2004), which said that rights contained in the 1996 Employment Rights Act were designed to cover 'employment in Great Britain'.

The unfair dismissal rights of expat workers has been a grey area of employment law, particularly since a section of the 1996 Act was repealed without replacement more than three years ago. Hitherto, judges had ruled that employees working abroad should be able to pursue unfair dismissal claims in the UK if their employment had a 'substantial connection' with Great Britain, a much looser interpretation, which the Court of Appeal said that it did not accept.

Increasingly, though, employers are looking to replace expatriation with short-term assignments, often to train suitably qualified local nationals on the job, or even commuting to locations, where practically possible. This trend is particularly noticeable in the emerging Asian countries, such as China and India, where there is an abundance of well-educated personnel with high skill levels. New technology has encouraged such changes and the introduction of 'virtual assignments' has meant that professionals can manage projects from their own country, with regular visits to their international office. While this might avoid the problems traditional models of expatriation face – such as the upheaval of family and home – an entirely new set of problems arise, such as the burden of frequent travel.

Career development is another common reason for working abroad and is particularly important for those working in multinational and international companies, government bodies, banks and organizations with large export markets.

An expatriate returning to the UK faces as many adjustments to life and work as they do in going out to an overseas job. Picking up the threads of a career in the UK can be extremely difficult and overseas experience is not always regarded favourably. Employers with no previous experience in overseas work themselves may think that you are returning from a very alien environment with outdated technology and human relations practices no longer acceptable in the EU, and doubt your ability to cope with new technology and life in the UK. In reality, there is little or no job security for returning expatriates, even in favourable economic conditions, as Stephen Gill explains in Chapter 4.

Recruiting organizations need to find workers who can perform a specified job in an overseas environment. It is easy to find candidates who can do the job in a British environment but only a small proportion can survive and succeed overseas. Their second task is to ensure that any applicant they select is aware of all the problems and difficulties they are likely to encounter in the country where they are going to work. They do not want the candidate to be surprised by conditions when they arrive, resulting in a premature termination of contract. This is bad for the individual and may affect their future employment prospects. It is bad for the company since it is very disruptive and involves them in substantial replacement costs. It is also bad for the recruitment agent since it undermines the confidence of the client company, which can turn totally against the idea of using British workers.

Given that you have decided, after careful consideration of your family and your career, to find work overseas, you will need to identify the best way of achieving this, and to decide in which overseas countries you wish to work. Working in the Middle East is very different from working in Africa, which is also poles apart from working in the United States, Europe or Asia. Carrying out research on your host country before departure will help, and the resource section (contained on the Kogan Page website) will help get you started on this. However, more often than not it is not until you arrive in your new home that the differences in work and home environment, and whether or not you will be able to fit in comfortably, will become apparent.

CHANGES IN OVERSEAS JOB MARKETS

The overall number of jobs for UK expatriates declined significantly over the 20 years up to 2008. Before that the jobs most affected were for unskilled, semi-skilled, clerical and administrative workers, many of which are now filled by workers from South East Asia and the Indian sub-continent where wage rates are much lower, or outsourced where possible to the same locations. However, even high-wage professional jobs have now migrated to low-cost countries where educational and skills standards are high as a result of the trend towards global outsourcing in service industries.

This trend has been strongest in IT services, particularly in call centre activities related to commercial and investment banking and other service industries where there is a high usage of information technology systems management and data transactions. India, with its pool of well-educated, English-speaking workers, is at the forefront of these developments, together with Australia, Malaysia, Singapore and, increasingly, China. South Africa, too, is offering opportunities for offshore relocation. As the migration of white-collar work moves up the value chain from call centre operators to occupations such as equity research, accounting, computer programming and chip design, there is a clear threat to domestic UK jobs employing those skills. There may be limited short-term opportunities for British expats in setting up and managing these service facilities but salaries are unlikely to be more than 10–20 per cent above current UK rates. Of course, the ability to avoid tax and deductions from salary and the receipt of free accommodation and other benefits may still make such contracts financially attractive. Other movements in overseas job markets have taken place nearer to home. On 1 May 2004 the EU was enlarged from 15 to 25 members with the long-awaited accession of Cyprus, the Czech Republic, Estonia, Hungary, Latvia, Lithuania, Malta, Poland, Slovakia and Slovenia. More recently, on 1 January 2007 the accession of Bulgaria and Romania increased EU membership to 27. At one level opportunities for British managers in professional firms and foreign-invested enterprises are declining as local management skills and experience grow. However, for those seeking employment or considering a change of residence to any of those countries, the level playing field of EU membership that applies in terms of employment law and social services should make relocation possible if income differentials are accepted.

So far, the traffic from the new EU member states, notably Poland, has been largely one-way. Well-educated and skilled nationals from those countries take up work in the UK to gain experience and to enjoy the benefit of higher wages and salaries before returning home to work there. Although the return traffic is said to be on the increase, this temporary migration did nothing to increase job opportunities abroad for British citizens.

Today, it is questionable just how level the playing field may really be for UK nationals applying for jobs in other EU countries. With unemployment having soared everywhere, it is difficult to believe that a UK knowledge worker applying for a position in, say, Madrid or Athens could be successful.

FAMILY CONSIDERATIONS

Perhaps the most fundamental question an expatriate must resolve is whether they are going to take up a post on an unaccompanied status or whether they are looking for accompanied postings. Many people who apply for overseas jobs have not thought out the problems and have not reached a family agreement on the type of posting required. One of the major irritations affecting international recruiters is that some candidates apply for single-status jobs

Doree Bonner International

Doree Bonner International is one of the UK's leading International moving companies and has a wealth and breadth of experience as we have been helping people move overseas for over 90 years.

Doree Bonner is truly an International mover and from our network of branches throughout the UK we can deal with any destination in any country, however distant, using our global network of the most professional and reputable international removal agents in order to ensure the highest standard of service.

At Doree Bonner we understand that moving abroad is one of the most exciting decisions you'll ever make but can also be very stressful. All companies say they deliver a first class customer service, but what sets us at Doree Bonner apart is our uncomprising commitment to traditional values such as respect, courtesy and punctuality and that we actually deliver on our promises.

From your first call to Doree Bonner, our fully trained co-ordination and sales staff will guide you through the whole process with a member of our international staff visiting your home to ensure that your move is planned to your individual requirements . A comprehensive estimate and moving plan is then provided .

Come moving day, a specially selected trained team will commence wrapping and packing your goods using the highest quality packing materials. Our teams have been asssed by T.M.I (The Movers Institute) and have completed courses developed by B.A.R (British Association of Removers)

Doree Bonner can offer different methods of transport depending on the location by sea , air and overland and can also offer you a wide range of options for example a sole use container, shared use container on International moves and direct and shared loads on European moves.

Wherever your final destination, you will be advised as soon as your goods arrive in that country and after customs clearance your effects will be delivered directly to your new home.

For any items that aren't to be taken abroad, Doree Bonner can offer International Secure Storage either short or long term. These facilities are under 24 hour surveillance and are owned by the Doree Bonner Group. Storage can also be provided overseas by our agents should this be required.

Doree Bonner are proud to be accredited to the industry's leading bodies:

FIDI
FAIM
B.A.R Overseas Group

All our overseas agents are also FIDI / FAIM accredited to ensure the same levels of high service that you will receive from Doree Bonner.

Doree Bonner are also authorised and regulated by the Financial Services Authority so are able to offer comprehensive insurance coverage.

For your purrfect move across the globe why not call us right now on 0800 091 3517

Doree Bonner International LTD
19 Kennet Road
Dartford
Kent
DA1 4QN

Phone: 0800 091 3517
email: moving@dbonner.co.uk
www. emigratingoverseas.com

and then, at the final interview, state they are only prepared to accept an accompanied-status situation. This results in a complete waste of time and money for both parties and is guaranteed to reduce your chances of getting employment through that recruitment agent.

Before you even decide to apply for an overseas job you must discuss and agree with your family the status of posting that you are prepared to take, the countries you would want to work in, and the minimum remuneration and benefits package you will accept. Only when you have decided these points are you in a position to start making job applications. Furthermore, many dual-income couples will need to investigate in parallel the job opportunities for an accompanying partner in the new location, as many are no longer prepared to give up their own career for the sake of a foreign sojourn. The issues affecting the 'trailing spouse' are fully discussed in Chapters 4 and 8.

USING TECHNOLOGY

Advances in communications technology have certainly made the expatriate's life easier. Maintaining contact with colleagues, friends and family is easy. If you haven't already done so, become fully conversant with the internet. This has become an invaluable aid for the international community and provides quick and cheap global communication. Through search engines it also provides excellent information on any subject you care to think of, including country-specific information, job opportunities, government advice and so on. This book recognizes the impact of the internet on the expatriate community and, where possible, website addresses for relevant information are included. For this edition, where there are no websites available we have included the postal address and telephone number instead. However, website addresses change frequently, as does the content, and we are unable to take responsibility for the accuracy of these contact details. Once you are on the right track, using the links provided by many websites, it should prove a worthwhile and fruitful journey, arming you with the information required to settle into your foreign assignment. Where websites are not given, the ubiquitous Google search engine will probably provide information.

EMPLOYEE EXPECTATIONS

Chapter 3 focuses on the opportunities that employees may be offered to work overseas for various periods and the remuneration packages to look for when the market revives.

If you are not in the position of working for a company that may offer you overseas employment and do not expect to do so, you may prefer to omit this chapter from your reading. However, if you are considering company employment in an overseas operation the chapter may provide some understanding of the corporate perspective and the kinds of conditions and benefits that you may be offered.

You will note that multinationals today are looking hard at the high costs of their globally mobile staff and may be taking increasingly less generous attitudes towards benefits.

Chapter 4 offers specific advice to those who are considering engagement in short-term overseas assignments

CONCLUSION

The rewards of moving abroad to work can be high and usually offer the chance to make significant savings. The amount of your savings depends largely on the location chosen and your attitude to life abroad.

Perhaps the expatriate who finds life the most difficult is the married person with teenage children, since in many countries secondary education is either unavailable or extremely expensive. The alternative of a UK boarding school is also expensive, and tends to break up the family unit.

We strongly recommend that if you are seriously contemplating a job overseas you should research the job market very carefully. You should try to decide whether you have the ability to survive and succeed overseas and whether, where appropriate, your family can also adapt to the new lifestyle. Once you have made this decision honestly, you must first identify the countries that offer the rewards and conditions you require and then identify the companies that might offer you employment.

CONTRIBUTORS TO THE NEW EDITION

Previous professional contributors to this thirtieth edition of *Working Abroad* have revised their texts where necessary. These include Neill Ransom of Chelstoke International, Lloyds TSB International, Stephen Gill of Stephen Gill Associates and health insurance terms available to expatriates from AXA PPP healthcare and BUPA are updated.

There is also a new contribution this year from McKinley Plowman on emigration to, and finding work in, Australia.

On the website to which your password gives you access, the number of countries surveyed stands at 60 and current detailed information on the economies of each country is provided and is sourced from a combination of published KPMG, Deloitte International and BDO Stoy Hayward data.

Jonathan Reuvid

We can't afford a cheap health plan – so we pay less for a great one!

When you've got loved ones to care for, nothing but the best healthcare protection will do. And you can be sure our award-winning international cover won't let you down. You can rely on expert English-speaking medical help and advice; prompt access to treatment in a choice of hospitals; plus our plans are made to be portable – so you can be covered wherever you travel.

You'll also discover our prices˙ are less than our leading competitors. But don't just take our word for it, put us to the test...

To save on your international health cover call AXA PPP healthcare today on

+44 (0)1892 550817 quoting reference **WA2006** or visit
www.axappphealthcare.co.uk/wa

PPP HEALTHCARE

Part One

Job Opportunities and Employee Expectations

1

Independent Job Opportunities

It is difficult, if not impossible, to form any precise idea of the number of UK citizens currently working overseas. Despite the flood of human resource statistics which flows from Whitehall, there is no central register of expatriates. The broad trend can, however, be adduced by examining people's intentions, looking at the range of jobs on offer, and the numbers of applications for particular posts. The peak was probably reached about 30 years ago, before rising unemployment in many countries, political risks and terrorism in the Middle East and Africa and perhaps more optimism about prospects at home combined to make people more cautious. Moreover, reductions in UK income tax rates until recently tended to reduce financial incentives to work and live overseas. In the past two years, there have been signs that this trend has been reversed, with evidence of young and more mature families who find UK living conditions, taxation burdens and job prospects unattractive and decide to move abroad permanently.

However, expatriate employment, though continuing to be an attractive prospect to UK jobseekers, is no longer the Klondike it used to be. At present only the most intrepid and seasoned expatriates would consider taking up postings in most Middle East and some African countries. Economic and political problems have affected the expatriate job markets in Africa and Latin America, and opportunities for non-Chinese speakers in China or Hong Kong are increasingly limited. Multinational company appointments in China are now filled mainly by those with Chinese as a second (or first) language or by young, internationally educated Chinese people who have returned home. Compensating factors are a continuing demand in specific areas of employment, notably in the financial and retail service sectors in emerging markets, and the growth in short-term contracts.

Opportunities have diminished more markedly at technician and supervisory levels, because of competition from qualified personnel in developing countries who are prepared to accept much lower salaries, and also because of the gradual emergence of skilled workers among local nationals as the fruits of training schemes come on-stream. On the other hand, at more senior grades (bonus-buttressed bankers excepted) the relatively low level of British executive salaries by international standards continued to make UK managers an attractive proposition – at least up to mid-2008 – especially those who were prepared to be reasonably flexible about working and living conditions. The typical US expatriate employee will often expect to take with them the standard of living associated with an executive lifestyle in the United States. Consequently, many senior jobs go to British or European personnel.

FINDING A JOB ABROAD

So how do you set about trying to find a job abroad? Both new and old forms of media provide ample opportunities for jobseekers looking from their home country. And for the brave, there is always the choice of turning up on spec to search out job opportunities in the chosen destination, although this approach is not generally recommended.

Newspapers

Not only the nationals and the Sunday newspapers but also the trade press carry overseas job advertisements. Graduates can look in annual career directories for details of overseas employers. It stands to reason that any employer wishing to recruit UK personnel will advertise in the UK press, but there is another good reason why the 'overseas vacancies' pages are worth scanning: they give a very good indication of the going rates of salary and benefits in particular parts of the world. Indeed, even if you have been made an offer without having replied to an advertisement, it is worth looking closely at these pages over a few issues to make sure that the remuneration package being put to you is in line with market rates.

However, if you are actually looking for a job, do not just confine your reading to the ads. It is worth reading any news and features that relate to the countries you are interested in. Not only will news of general or specific economic developments – a new industry opening up, for instance – give you background information that might be very useful in an interview, but it might also in itself be a source of job leads. Indeed, if you can read the papers in the language of the country you would like to work in, so much the better. They will go into potential job-lead information in more depth and, of course, they contain job advertisements. How useful these are likely to be to the British jobseeker depends somewhat on the country in which the paper is published. In the Far East, for instance, employers would almost exclusively be looking for locals when advertising in a local paper. But in the EU, a response from a suitably qualified EU national might well produce a positive result. Quite a number of European countries are involved in projects in the Middle East and in other resource-rich countries where English is the dominant language. In those cases, some think in terms of putting UK nationals on location as well as their own people.

Apart from the major newspapers, there are useful websites that carry international recruitment advertising and news about working abroad. Perhaps the best of these is www.overseasjobs.com, which covers locations as far afield as Bangladesh, Ecuador, Egypt, Georgia and the UAE, as well as the United States and other less exotic places. Free membership is also offered to the Overseas Jobs e-mail newsletter.

The internet

One of the most effective ways of looking for a job abroad is to search the wide range of websites offering information for job-seekers. There are a number of ways in which the internet can help and *Online Job Hunting – Great Answers to Tough Questions* by Martin Yate and Terra Dourlain (published by Kogan Page) is a good source of help. Useful categories include:

- Careers libraries in schools, colleges and universities.
- Professional associations and journals.
- People doing the job you are interested in. You can 'talk' to people via the internet using a service such as Internet Relay Chat.
- Job advertisements, job descriptions and person specifications.
- Employers and employment agencies in the industries to which your skills and experience are relevant.
- Promotional organizations.

Many large employers have job advertisements and descriptions for every area of work and provide application forms online. Interesting sites are listed in the directory at the back of this book, but two good examples of employer websites can be found at Shell International on www.shell.com and Hewlett-Packard on www. jobs.hp.com. Another invaluable resource is The Monster Board, which has information and sites in Canada, Australia, Belgium and the Netherlands on www.monster.com. Most large employers have sites and they are well worth a visit to assess what kinds of international opportunities are available. The advantages of carrying out a job search on the internet are listed on the next page.

FINDING A JOB ON SPEC

Possible sources of job information are, of course, legion and they change constantly. Apart from keeping a close watch on the papers, another good move is to get in touch with trade associations connected to the country in which you are interested or local chambers of commerce there. They will not be able to give you any job leads as such, unless you are very lucky, but they can usually give you lists of firms or other organizations that have a particularly close connection with the UK. Preliminary leads of this nature are essential if you are going to a country to look for a job on spec, and, except in the EU, you should never state this as your intention when entering a country. In most places now you need to have a job offer from a local employer in order to get a work permit, so you should always state that you are entering as a visitor, whatever your subsequent intention might be. It must be said, however, that

Advantages of internet web searches

- The main sources of information on vacancies are unchanged. However, they are made more accessible to all by means of the web.
- Searching for vacancies on the web should be quicker and more effective than by other means. Dedicated search tools make finding appropriate jobs in newspapers and with agencies quick and straightforward.
- There are simple ways of arranging to be notified of suitable vacancies by e-mail.
- Some employers encourage and facilitate speculative applications via their websites.
- CV databases enable you to make your skills and abilities known to a large audience of potential employers.
- Web-based vacancy searches should enhance, not replace, other means of job hunting.

Source: *Net That Job!* **Irene Krechowiecka**

some countries do not permit turning a visitor's visa into a work permit – that is something you will have to check on, discreetly, before you go.

In general, however, going abroad on spec to find a job is not a good idea. Even in the EU, where it is permitted, some jobseekers have had unhappy experiences even if they are in a 'hot' area such as electronics. By far the best plan is to get interviews lined up before you go or at least get some expressions of interest from potential employers – they will probably not commit themselves to more than that from a distance, even if there is a job possibility. To do more might put them under an embarrassing moral obligation when you turn up on their doorstep, having spent a lot of time and money to get there.

British jobseekers now have greater access to vacancies in Europe with the introduction of the EURES (European Employment Services) computer network, which provides jobseekers with free information and guidance on current opportunities throughout the EU. The database includes up-to-date information on living and working conditions in other member states. In Britain, anyone interested in working abroad can access the EURES database, and obtain advice from a Euroadviser, via their local Jobcentre. The International Job Search Advice unit of the Employment Service produces a useful information booklet *Working Abroad*, as well as a series of guides entitled *Working in...*, concerning specific countries. These deal with entry requirements, information sources, benefits, liabilities, taxation, state of the market and cultural notes. The unit also holds information on work overseas in specific professions. Write with your details to International Job Search Advice, 6th Floor, Whitehall II, Whitehall Quay, Leeds LS1 4HR (tel: 0113 309 8090) or visit www.jobcentreplus.gov.uk. Alternatively, consult the linked website www.eures-jobs.com on which job vacancies across the EU are advertised and you can post your CV and details.

Further useful information on the EU and its members can be accessed via Public Information Relays (PIR), European Documentation Centres (EDC) and Euro Info Centres (EIC) set up in libraries or at regional government offices or Business Links. Contact your local library for details of your nearest source of EU information.

Writing on-spec letters to potential employers is a subject that is well covered elsewhere. In essence what you have to do is address yourself to something that you have identified as being the employer's need or possible need – this is where researching the background on the internet and elsewhere and looking for job leads comes into play. For instance, if you have read in *Der Spiegel* or in *Frankfurter Allgemeine Zeitung* of a German firm being awarded a large contract in the Middle East, it is likely that they will respond in some way, provided your letter demonstrates that you have relevant skills and experience. Even if they intend advertising the job, the fact that you have taken an intelligent interest in their activities will count in your favour.

It is seldom worthwhile advertising in the situations wanted column, though writing to headhunters is a good move, especially if you are qualified to work in one of the fields in current demand. Letters should be kept short and your CV should not exceed two pages – highlighting and quantifying achievements, rather than just listing posts you have held. With technical jobs you may have to show that your knowledge of the field is up to date with current developments, especially in areas where things are changing rapidly.

When a job is actually advertised, the interview will probably be in London, or your fare will be paid if you are called upon to travel abroad. Here again, the rules for replying to an advertisement are no different from those relating to UK employers: read the text carefully and frame your reply and organize your CV in such a way as to show that you meet the essential requirements of the job. As one Canadian employer put it recently, paraphrasing, no doubt, John F Kennedy's much quoted presidential address, 'The question to ask is not what I can gain from moving to your company, but what your company (or organization or school) can gain from me.'

If you need to arrange your own travel, companies such as CIBT®, the global visa and passport service at www.uk.cibt.com, specialize in processing applications for business, working-holiday and tourism visas and passports on your behalf, which is particularly useful for those living outside London, where most embassies and consulates are located. Most professions have specialist agencies to help find work both nationally and internationally, and these could be a first port of call. Non-professional jobs such as au-pairing or voluntary work are also well served and details are given further on in this chapter.

SPECIALIST AREAS

Engineers and technicians

These terms cover many grades of expatriate worker, from truck drivers and road builders to site supervisors and project directors. Many overseas companies, especially airlines and construction companies, recruit directly in the UK by advertising in UK newspapers. Examine all such offers carefully. Many companies will arrange for technicians going abroad to meet compatriots on leave, who can answer their questions.

However, this is one field where opportunities are now very limited indeed. Workers from countries such as Korea, the Philippines, India and Pakistan, China and, of course, the new member states of the EU now predominate at this end of the labour market.

At the top end of the scale, the Malla Technical Recruitment Consultancy, a part of the Synergy Group, at 77 Cornhill, London EC3V 3QQ (tel: 0800 0725 900, e-mail: recruit@malla.com, website: www.synergygroup.co.uk) has a register of international engineering experts on all subjects who are leased out on contract worldwide. A visit to www.eurotech.org may be worthwhile.

The professionally qualified

The professions and qualifications most in demand overseas are medicine, agriculture and food, process engineering, financial services, civil engineering and construction. In general, positions in these areas can best be found through the companies themselves or through management consultants and headhunters (executive search consultants). Many consultants specialize in particular professions such as accountancy.

Some are on a small, specialist scale. An example of an international, multi-purpose agency is Eurotech Associates Limited (The Old Coach House, 56 High Street, Harston, Cambridge CB2 5PZ; tel: 01223 875100, fax: 01223 875150, website: www.eurotech.org). Eurotech recruit only for the Middle East, the Far East and North Africa. They are a major international training and recruitment agency specializing in executive, managerial, technical and scientific fields. They are particularly involved with the oil industry, and their activities range from construction, maintenance and operations, engineering, oil and petrochemicals to health care, hospitals, and general financial and commercial management.

People with professional qualifications will obviously consult their appropriate professional association or trade union. In the medical profession, jobs are usually found through advertisements in the medical press. BMA members are advised to contact the International Department at the British Medical Association (BMA House, Tavistock Square, London WC1H 9JP; tel: 020 7387 4499, fax: 020 7383 6400, website: www.bma.org.uk) for information and advice on working abroad. Many intending emigrants would prefer to work in North America and Australasia, but opportunities are limited. Within the EU there is recognition of medical qualifications. Remuneration is highest in Germany and Denmark, followed by France, Belgium and Luxembourg, with the UK towards the bottom of the scale. But there is unlikely to be much of a 'brain drain' to Europe since there is already a surplus of doctors in training there and the profession is becoming particularly overcrowded in Italy and Scandinavia. Indeed the reverse is true with the National Health Service actively recruiting doctors and dentists from the Central and Eastern European countries that are now EU members.

The developing countries, by contrast, are in urgent need of doctors and nurses. The average doctor/patient ratio in these countries is about 1:10,000 compared with 1:750 in the UK; in some areas it is as high as 1:80,000, with rural areas being almost completely neglected. The International Health Exchange (1 Great George Street, London SW1P 3AA; tel: 020 7233 1100, fax: 020 7233 3590, e-mail: info@ihe.org.uk, website: www.ihe.org.uk) helps provide appropriately trained health personnel for programmes in countries in Africa, Asia, the Pacific, Eastern Europe, Latin America and other areas seeking assistance. It maintains a register of health workers for those actively seeking work in developing countries and areas requiring humanitarian aid.

International demand for UK nurses has been reduced by radical health service reforms in many countries, but opportunities still exist, particularly in the United States and the Middle East, for those with sound, post-registration experience and qualifications. The International Office of the Royal College of Nursing, 20 Cavendish Square, London W1G 0RN; tel: 020 7409 3333, website: www.rcn.org.uk, provides overseas employment advice to its members, and overseas vacancies appear in weekly nursing journals such as *Nursing Standard*, on sale at newsagents.

In the UK, the Department for Business, Industry and Skills (BIS) provides information on the mutual recognition of professional qualifications at degree level and above and has overall responsibility for the operation of the UK Certificate of Experience Scheme, which is run by the British Chambers of Commerce on behalf of BIS. The Department for Children, Schools and Families (DCSF) provides advice on qualifications below degree level.

Further information can be obtained from BIS at Bay 212, Kingsgate House, 66–74 Victoria Street, London SW1E 6SW; tel: 020 7215 5000, website: www.bis.gov.uk, and from DCSF at Room E4b, Moorfoot, Sheffield S1 4PQ; tel: 0870 000 2288, e-mail info@dfes.gsi. gov.uk for advice on international recognition of qualifications.

Information on the Certificate of Experience Scheme is available from the Certification Unit, British Chambers of Commerce, Westwood House, Westwood Business Park, Coventry CV4 8HS; tel: 024 7669 5688, website: www.britishchambers.org.uk.

Finally, one can get a direct comparison between any UK qualifications and those recognized in any EU country via the National Academic Recognition Information Centre (NARIC). However, you can only do this from abroad to the local jobcentre equivalent by asking to contact the local NARIC representative.

Business schools

For high-flyers, a possible route into the overseas job market is a course at one of the European business schools – either a short executive programme or a full-scale MBA. The latter course is in huge demand and is offered by a very large and ever-increasing number of schools worldwide, whether on a full-, part-time or distance-learning basis. The internet has also been adopted as a learning medium. However, one should weigh up its worth with care, given the effort, time and considerable expense involved. A book and directory of business schools approved by the Association of MBAs is the annual *AMBA Guide to Business Schools* (FT/Pitman).

Another possibility lies with the Open University Business School, which offers a range of six-month courses on a distance-learning basis: OUBS Customer Relations Centre, PO Box 625, Milton Keynes MK1 1TY; tel: 0845 366 6035, website: www.open.ac. uk/oubs.

The longest-established European business school is INSEAD. Founded in 1959, today the school is widely recognized as one of the most influential business schools in the world. Its global scope and multicultural diversity make it the model for international management education. Located in Fontainebleau, France, INSEAD runs a 10-month MBA programme, a PhD programme and shorter executive development courses with a focus on general management in an international environment. Holders of the MBA can find jobs through the INSEAD Career Management Service. The emphasis is on international business management. Each year several hundred companies find that INSEAD is an excellent source for recruiting talented, multilingual and geographically mobile managers with high potential. Over one-third of graduates go on to start their own business sometime in their career. Students come from more than 50 countries with no single nationality dominating.

The majority of MBA students come as non-sponsored individuals. Various scholarships and loans are available. INSEAD is clearly a good investment for your future if you have the right background. Courses are taught in English but a fair knowledge of French is required. A third language is required in order to graduate and courses in German and Spanish are available. For further information contact INSEAD, MBA Admissions, Boulevard de Constance, F-77305 Fontainebleau Cedex; tel: +33 1 60 72 40 00, fax: +33 1 60 74 55 00, website: www.insead.edu.

Department for International Development

The Department for International Development (DfID) manages Britain's programme of aid to developing countries. The range of skills required under the programme is vast and constantly changing. Workers are drawn from a large number of backgrounds and professions such as agriculture, education and engineering.

The minimum requirement for most vacancies is usually a professional qualification and at least two to three years' relevant experience, including some in a developing country. A limited number of postgraduate study awards are also offered. Successful applicants are usually given assignments of up to two to three years as either a cooperation officer, employed by the DfID and 'on loan' to the overseas client government, or as a supplemented officer, under contract to the relevant government on local salary, with a supplement provided by the DfID to equal UK pay level.

Where the DfID needs immediate expert advice, consultants are used on appointments lasting from a few days to several months. Such assignments are open to both employed and self-employed specialists. The DfID also provides assistance to the United Nations and its specialist agencies (eg International Labour Office) in recruitment to field programmes, as well as the Junior Professional Officers Scheme.

For further information please write, enclosing a CV, to the Service and Resource Development Group, Room AH304, Department for International Development, Abercrombie House, Eaglesham Road, East Kilbride, Glasgow G75 8EA (tel: 01355 844000, fax: 01355 844099; website: www.dfid.gov.uk).

The British Council

The British Council (10 Spring Gardens, London SW1A 2BN; tel: 020 7930 8466, website: www.britishcouncil.org) promotes Britain abroad. It provides access to British ideas, talents and experience through education and training, books and periodicals, the English language, the arts, science and technology.

It is represented in 109 countries, 209 libraries and information centres and over 118 English language schools and has offices in 228 towns and cities. The Council provides an unrivalled network of contacts with government departments, universities, embassies, professional bodies and business and industry in Britain and overseas.

The British Council is an independent and non-political organization. In developing countries it has considerable responsibilities for the DfID in the field of educational aid, and in recent years it has become involved in the design and implementation of education projects funded by international lending agencies such as the World Bank.

The Council also acts as an agent for governments and other employers overseas in recruiting for contract teaching and educational advisory posts in ministries, universities, training colleges and secondary and primary schools. The Council usually guarantees the terms of such posts and sometimes subsidizes them. In these appointments it works closely with the DfID. Teachers are also recruited on contract for the Council's network of English language schools.

Vacancies include teacher trainers, curriculum designers and British studies specialists for posts in projects or for direct placement with overseas institutions. Candidates must be professionally qualified and have appropriate experience.

Appointments are usually for one or two years initially and often renewable by agreement. Vacancies are advertised in *The Times Educational Supplement*, the *Guardian* and other journals as appropriate.

Teaching English as a Foreign Language

EFL teachers are in demand in both the private and public education sectors abroad. Public sector recruiting is usually done by the government concerned through the British Council; private recruitment varies from the highly reputable organization (such as International House) to the distinctly dubious. Most EFL teachers have a degree and/or teaching qualification. A Cambridge CELTA qualification will also be required. Most employers will accept the Trinity College London Certificate (TESOL) and their Diploma as equivalents of CELTA and DELTA (website: www.tesolcourse. com). A four-week Cambridge Certificate in CELTA (Certificate in English Language Teaching to Adults) or the associated Diploma (DELTA) are available at International House in London and Hastings (website: www.ihlondon.com), and at a number of other centres. The University of Cambridge Local Examinations Syndicate (tel: 01223 553311) can provide comprehensive lists of the centres running courses leading to these awards, worldwide. Alternatively, the website www.cambridgeesol.org/centres/ teach.htm has information on all training providers.

Bear the following points in mind when applying for an EFL post abroad:

- Will your travel expenses be paid? Some schools refund them on arrival or at the end of the contract.
- Is accommodation provided? If so, is it free or is the rent deducted from your salary? Is your salary sufficient to meet the deduction? If you find your own accommodation, are you helped to find it, especially if your knowledge of the local language is modest? Does the school lend you money to help pay the accommodation agency's fee and deposit? If the accommodation is provided, does it include hard or soft furnishing, and what should you bring with you?
- Contracts and work permits. Will you have a contract, how long for, and will the school obtain the permits to legalize your position in the country?
- Salary. Are you paid by the hour, week or month? If you are paid by the hour, is there a guaranteed minimum amount of teaching available for you? Do ensure that you can survive financially in the face of cancelled classes, bank strikes and numerous public holidays. Are there cost-of-living adjustments in countries with alarming inflation rates? Salaries are generally geared to local rates, but do make sure they are adequate. In sterling terms, one may earn a very low salary (in Rabat, for instance) yet enjoy a higher standard of living than a teacher earning double in Italy, or three times as much in Singapore.
- How many hours are you expected to teach? Be wary of employers who expect you to teach more than about 25 hours a week (remember you need additional time to prepare lessons). What paid leisure time do you expect? This is variable, but two weeks at both Easter and Christmas is fairly common.
- What type of student will you be teaching? Children or adults, those learning general English or English for special purposes (ESP)?
- What levels will you be teaching and what course books will be used? Will there be a director of studies to help you over any initial difficulties and provide some form of in-service training?

A knowledge of the local language is an asset; in some situations, it is absolutely essential. Without it, one's social contacts are restricted to the English-speaking community which, in some areas, is virtually non-existent.

Locating the vacancies

1. International House recruits teachers only for its own affiliated schools, of which there are 100 in 26 countries. Vacancies elsewhere can be seen on the IH noticeboard in the Staffing Unit, 106 Piccadilly, London W1V 9FL (tel: 020 7518 6999, fax: 020 7518 6998, e-mail: info@ihlondon.co.uk, website: www.ihlondon.com). Other major reputable EFL institutes that anyone looking for a job would do well to try are:
    - Bell (www.bell-centres.com)
    - English First (www.englishfirst.com)
    - InLingua (www.inLingua.com)
    - Linguarama (www.linguarama.com)
    - Regent (www.regent.org.uk)
    - Saxon Court (www.saxoncourt.com)

2. Advertisements appear in publications such as *The Times Educational Supplement* (Fridays) and *The Guardian* (Tuesdays). Of course, many teachers are already overseas and can't get these newspapers. The international edition of *The Guardian* carries some advertisements, but many people look online: www.jobs.guardian.co.uk.

3. The British Council Teacher Recruitment Unit recruits EFL teachers for the British Council's Language Centres around the world. It can be contacted at 10 Spring Gardens, London SW1A 2BN (tel: 020 7389 4931, website: www.britishcouncil.org or via e-mail at teacher.vacancies@britishcouncil.org). British Council vacancies are also advertised in the press. The British Council Overseas Appointments Services recruits for posts funded directly by overseas employers. It can be contacted at Bridgewater House, 58 Whitworth Street, Manchester M1 6BB; tel: 0161 957 7383.

4. The Centre for British Teachers, CfBT Education Trust, 80 Queens Road, Reading, Berkshire RG1 4BS (tel: 0118 902 1000, fax: 0118 902 1434, e-mail: international@cfbt.com, website: www.cfbt.com) recruits teachers for English language teaching projects in Brunei, Oman and Turkey and educational specialists

for consultancies on donor-funded projects in Eastern Europe, Africa, Asia and India.

5. If you want to learn more about English language teaching qualifications, Cactus Teachers are a helpful source of information (www.cactusteachers.com). They specialize in advice on CELTA and the Trinity College Certificate.

Voluntary work

Those who are technically skilled or professionally qualified and who would like to share their skills with developing countries could apply to VSO (Voluntary Service Overseas). VSO has over 1,750 skilled people working in 58 countries: in Africa, Asia, the Caribbean, Eastern Europe and the Pacific. Placements are in education, health, natural resources, technical trades, engineering, business, communications and social development. Volunteers are aged from 20 to 70, usually 23–60, with no dependent children.

Accommodation and a modest living allowance are provided by the local employer. Flights, insurance and other allowances are provided by VSO. Posts are generally for two years, but many volunteers stay longer.

Working as a VSO volunteer is very much a two-way process; volunteers often feel that they learn more from the society and culture they are involved with than they can possibly contribute. For further information contact The Enquiries Unit, VSO, 317 Putney Bridge Road, London SW15 2PN; tel: 020 8780 7200, website: www.vso.org.uk.

Checklist: Independent job opportunities

1. Research professional and national media for overseas jobs.
2. Investigate opportunities on the internet and place your CV with databanks on the web.
3. Check out the possibilities of turning a visitor's visa into a work permit before you look for a job on spec.
4. Contact your trade or professional associations for overseas vacancies and guidance on employment conditions and what to expect.
5. Consider taking a qualification, such as an MBA, in a foreign business school as a way to open doors overseas.
6. Examine the pay and conditions of language schools.
7. For teaching assignments, research opportunities through the British Council.
8. Have realistic expectations of short-term work such as au-pairing or working on a kibbutz, and ensure that all details are given in writing before departure.

2

Where the Grass Is Greener – the Emigration Option

Permanent emigration from the UK with the aim of improving quality of life and of securing a better livelihood has always been an option for the more adventurous. Normally, there are alternative scenarios: permanent emigration as a result of taking up a job overseas on a short- or medium-term basis and then taking a family decision to stay; or emigration on speculation, with no firm job opportunity but with the confidence to take the plunge. In the latter case, there is an implication of dissatisfaction with life in the UK or a conviction that there is a better future waiting for the family or individual in another country. There are probably more families in this category than at any time in the past 30 years.

Plainly, there is risk in moving out permanently with no certainty of employment, however well-qualified you may be, even if your research into the conditions of your industry, profession or occupation where you are going has been meticulous and the conclusions positive. In good times, when the economy of the country that you have chosen is thriving, the risks in entering the job market there are mitigated; you may even be able to identify that there is a shortage of the skills or qualified people in your occupation so that the employment outlook for newcomers is positive. However, there are only a few economies in 2010 which are not in recession or have suffered severe downturns, so that employment markets are depressed and the downside risks of leaving the UK now for greener pastures and expecting to find work easily are greatly increased.

THE OUTLOOK FOR LIFE IN THE UK

On the other hand, living conditions in the UK are deteriorating and many of us have already experienced a noticeable downturn in our standard of living and quality of life which was unimaginable three years ago. Of course, we've suffered recessions before in most of our living memories and were able to soldier on for a year or two in the firm expectation that the economy would revive, high unemployment would fade away, positive equity in house values would be restored and, in short, the good times would return. This time, however, the recession was deeper and more prolonged for the reason that the banking system has stalled and the credit facilities that are normally available to help the private individual and aid business recovery are greatly restricted.

The massive level of debt with which the government has burdened the taxpayer in order to rescue and support the failing banks will overshadow the economy for more than a decade and make it certain that higher levels of personal taxation will be levied from 2011 by whatever government is in power, and will be with us for years to come. Against this gloomy scenario that is now overshadowing the British citizen, it is hardly surprising that more and more of us are considering emigration.

ASSESSING THE EMIGRATION ALTERNATIVES

The first step in your research is to identify the countries in which the grass is likely to be greener now and, even more so, as recession has receded. As an active member of the working population, there will be two primary sets of criteria to apply in evaluating each country:

- Are there job opportunities that match your skills and qualifications and will that job market continue to flourish?
- Are the quality of life and standard of living you could achieve compatible with the aims and requirements of your family?

On the Kogan Page website, to which your password gives you access (www.koganpage.com/workingabroad), looking at the country surveys will help you to evaluate the economic outlook and living conditions of 60 countries, and the research activities described in Chapter 1 should give you a reasonable insight into the current job market. Travel literature, the internet generally and TV documentaries provide background information on living conditions and the environment and may fire the imagination. Best of all, a holiday visit to preferred locations if you can afford one will help the family to reach a decision.

However, satisfying both sets of criteria may not be easy. Countries that provide the best job opportunities may not be those that offer the most attractive living conditions and quality of life for the family. Locations that may be tolerable, if not wholly compatible, for a medium-term assignment of three years may be wholly unacceptable to you and your partner for permanent residence. While it is possible to live comfortably in some distant location where there is a strong expatriate community for a limited period without integrating with the local community, that is not a model for success as a long-term resident. And social integration may be difficult where linguistic and cultural differences are wide. All of the considerations discussed in this book, such as education facilities and opportunities for partners to pursue their careers, take on a further dimension in the context of living permanently in a new country.

Given the scale of economic problems in Europe it is unlikely that any Western European country or other EU member will provide promising job opportunities for several years, except for those Britons who transferred there on secondments. In any case, some of those countries may not satisfy the second set of criteria for permanent family residence, and given the difficulty of satisfying 'green card' requirements for acceptance as a permanent immigrant to the USA, nor will there be a flood of UK families transferring residence to America even when the US economy is further down the road to recovery.

Not surprisingly, there is always a high level of interest in the countries with longstanding membership of the British Commonwealth, where the commonality of language, cultural heritage and shared values ease the transition for British families as immigrants. Australia and New Zealand, in particular, are natural magnets for potential British immigrants. The section that follows provides an Australian perspective of how you are likely to be received.

With over 42 years of publishing, more than 80 million people have succeeded in business with thanks to **Kogan Page**

www.koganpage.com

A NEW REALITY DOWN UNDER

Evelyn Duffy

Mention prospects for jobs galore, abundant business, career and investment opportunities and appreciating property values and the average Brit may tell you to take a reality check.

For Britons emerging from the grip of another cold winter and a relatively depressed economy, such optimistic forecasts, which are thrown in with promises for endless sunshine, read more like fantasy than apt description. However, this positive scenario is shaping up to be very much a part of the Australian landscape.

While many developed nations continue to focus on recovering from the global financial crisis (GFC) Australia's collective mindset now looks towards the next economic boom. This is especially evident in Western Australia (WA) where billions of dollars of resource projects, including the $30 billion Gorgon liquefied natural gas project, are either under way or about to go ahead.

The economic outlook is upbeat and demand for skilled local, foreign and interstate workers is on the rise. Commentators say the resultant population boom will underpin strong growth in property prices as well as generate business opportunities in areas as broad as retail, liquor stores and pubs, wholesaling, fast food outlets and caravan parks.

'This all stacks up to an ideal environment for new immigrants,' says Murray McKinley, a certified practising accountant who has specialized in assisting United Kingdom expatriates for over a decade.

Mr McKinley says that, with economists forecasting the WA economy will grow by 1.5 per cent this year and 6 per cent by 2012–13, there are signs that the labour shortages that troubled the state during the recent boom will return.

'Many of our business clients tell us the labour market is once again tightening up and it's becoming a challenge to find suitable employees,' Mr McKinley says. 'This, of course, is great news for people looking to emigrate and find work here.'

Mr McKinley is a partner in McKinley Plowman, a thriving accounting, financial planning and finance practice located in the Perth suburb of Joondalup, where over 20 per cent of the population hails from the United Kingdom. Located 25 minutes north of Perth city, Joondalup is close to pristine beaches, and is well serviced by public transport, retail, education and recreational facilities.

McKinley Plowman provides advice on financial issues including UK pension transfers, tax minimization, personal investment and mortgages, as well as business set up and assistance with the purchase of businesses for migrants. The firm also specializes in assisting immigrants – with no prior borrowing history in Australia – to obtain finance for property, business or investment purposes.

Mr McKinley, who travels to the United Kingdom several times a year, says he speaks to many Britons who are keen to emigrate, yet worry about selling UK property into a depressed market and transferring cash assets. He says these people will fare better by emigrating now instead of waiting for economic recovery in Britain.

He also says that while Australia's high-valued dollar will result in a lower exchange rate, immigrants will soon regain ground. Any loss on the exchange rate will be made up by getting a foothold in the fast-moving property market. It is also likely, given the nation's Reserve Bank's bias for increasing interest rates and a strengthening economy, that the Australian dollar will remain strong.

Unlike Australia, many developed countries will suffer ongoing economic weakness as high debt compounds underlying woes for the United Kingdom, the United States and European Union countries.

The key to a successful relocation lies in the quality of professional advice a person takes prior to moving and immediately after arriving. Unlike most British, many Australians use accountants and financial advisers. A financial adviser will show newcomers how major differences between the two countries in issues such as insurance, taxation and pension issues will affect them.

For example, expatriates are used to having endowment policies on their home mortgages to protect the family against the risk of death or disability whereas Australians use term life insurance and mortgage insurance.

Australia's market-based superannuation system is also a concern to expatriates – used to a defined benefit pension system – who fear being subjected to the volatility of the market.

However, Murray McKinley points out that moving pension funds to tax-effective qualifying Australian superannuation funds offers a tax-free retirement income, flexible investment opportunities, potentially higher returns and long-term asset protection.

'Unlike UK pensions where the spouse loses half the asset value when a member dies, Australian superannuation assets are passed on to a partner or beneficiaries in full,' he says. 'Also, Australians can take 100 per cent of their super at age 60, whereas UK laws only allow for 25 per cent to be taken as a lump sum.'

Mr McKinley says that newcomers must be aware of the importance of transferring British pensions to Australian Qualifying Regulated Overseas Pension Scheme (QROPS). He says those transferred to a non-QROPS fund face a UK tax rate of 55 per cent on the pension by Britain's Inland Revenue.

The transfer process, which can take up to four months, should be commenced as soon as Australian residency is obtained to avoid additional tax. Pension transfers made after six months of gaining residency are subject to an Australian tax of 15 per cent, which applies to any capital gain made by the UK pension between the time someone moves to Australia and the time pension funds arrive here.

Mr McKinley says that although many Britons worry about subjecting their pension assets to the market, the right portfolio balance will minimize losses in a falling market and maximize gains in a rising market. Investors with diversified portfolios in blue-chip shares and good listed property trusts do not have much to worry about over the long term.

While news of the GFC dominated the local press, McKinley Plowman's expatriate clients appreciate that living in Western Australia has insulated them from the full brunt of the financial crisis.

Despite the economic turmoil of the last year, the unemployment rate for Western Australia reached 5.1 per cent compared to 7.8 per cent in the United Kingdom. Moreover, according to major employer group, the Western Australian Chamber of Commerce and Industry, the average weekly wage is now $1,306 – which is 6.9 per cent higher that a year ago.

Predictions are that wages will rise by between 4 per cent and 4.75 per cent annually until 2012–13. However, amidst all the positivity, Mr McKinley advises newcomers to hold realistic expectations, particularly during the early months of settling in Australia.

Just as it is with settling in to any new place, it takes time to build social and professional networks, he says. 'Our advice', says Murray McKinley is 'don't set your expectations too high to start with, get going, build up your network of friends and associates and progress up the human resources ladder.'

This sentiment is echoed by British migrant and client of McKinley Plowman, Debra Rogers.

CASE STUDY:

Ms Rogers, a teacher's aid who emigrated with husband Gareth Thomas and son Ryan in 2004, says that while Australia has been very kind to her family it is naïve to think there won't be challenges when moving here. She urges expatriates to do plenty of research before deciding on professional services, housing, schooling or investing.

Ms Rogers says that, just as it is back home, there is a ladder process to establishing oneself in a new country.

'For example, you may not walk into that dream job straightaway because you don't have local references,' Ms Rogers says. 'But keep at it and you will get that dream job eventually.'

Mr McKinley says that the advice about managing expectations also applies to business migrants. McKinley Plowman, which assists migrants with purchasing a business as well as business set up, tells clients to bear in mind that Britons are surrounded by a market of 60 million people compared to an Australian market of 20 million and just 2.2 million in the more sparsely populated Western Australia.

Murray McKinley advises those in search of a business opportunity to begin their research by seeking advice from a reputable accountant, a business broker, migrant agent, and small business advisory bodies such as Western Australia's Small Business Development Corporation.

Just as it is important in the United Kingdom, exercising detailed due diligence before buying a business in Australia, or any new country, is paramount. One of the biggest mistakes British people make when moving to Australia is not to seek enough advice from accountants and solicitors before entering into the broad range of agreements relating to their business activities.

Mr McKinley adds that, along with providing professional accounting services, his firm acts as a business network for immigrants. 'We put them in touch with reliable professionals in the areas of real estate, legal services and insurance and importantly give them access to local business links.'

Although the conditions for moving to Australia are favourable and the outlook for living and working there is positive, the same cannot be said for removals to the United States, as the following analysis makes plain.

TRANSATLANTIC MOBILITY

Stephen Asher and Cherysse Sampson-Bennett, Frank Hirth

Although the great Atlantic Ocean divides the USA and Europe geographically, they are bound closely together by a deeply integrated transatlantic economy. Now felt by us all, business confidence on both sides of the Atlantic is significantly low as a result of the global economic crises. There has been an increase in domestic unemployment rates on both sides of the Atlantic and a drop in inward investment in both directions. Add to that, a growing risk of regulation that may make it harder to identify transatlantic employment opportunities.

However, those transatlantic working opportunities are represented by a number of significant statistics; according to some estimates, the transatlantic economy generates more than $3 trillion in sales and employs nearly 14 million workers on both sides of the Atlantic. These workers enjoy high wages and good-quality working environments.

Traditionally, these employees have been employed predominantly in financial services, oil and gas, media and entertainment sectors. However, it may be time to start looking further afield for working opportunities in the energy security sectors, sustainable economic development, global climate change and existing services that have been subject to wide ranging reforms; such as aviation, health care or telecoms.

Currently, Europe is a significant foreign employer in the USA, with European-owned firms employing more than 5.5 million Americans in the USA. Each year, 85,000 employment visas are granted for foreigners with advanced skills and education. At any one time, more than 50,000 people living abroad are waiting for working visas. Foreign nationals living in the USA also account for over a quarter of all national patent applications and nearly 250,000 foreigners are enrolled in USA graduate programmes, more than half of which are in engineering, biological and physical science occupations.

Despite the obvious cultural interconnectivity and continued economic kinship, people are put off transatlantic working by the difficulties in determining tax residency, understanding taxation costs and health care costs, and the exchange rate between the dollar and sterling.

Breaking UK tax residency

Becoming non-resident for UK tax purposes where employment and other ties remain here is more difficult than ever, but not impossible with the right fact pattern and careful planning.

At the heart of this planning is the question of in what circumstances (when a long-standing UK tax resident moves abroad) can they be certain they have, in effect, achieved a clean break from being resident for UK tax purpose.

Typically, tax residency planning involves trying to find specific pointers such as the right fact pattern. There is a need to take into account, weigh-up, and balance all relevant factors in each case.

Typically, you would need to consider the nature of the visits to this country, including:

- the duration of their presence in the UK;
- the regularity and frequency of visits.

You would also need to take into account continuing links to this country and any connection with the US, including ownership and use of a house, and activities, ties and other connections there. Ownership and use of a house in the US may not be considered conclusive that you do not reside in the UK, but it might be a relevant factor to be taken into account along with the following list of factors about your UK ties:

- retaining a house in the UK;
- on the electoral roll in the UK as a resident;
- post was sent to you at a UK address;
- keeping a car in the UK;
- retaining a bank account in the UK into which your salary is paid;
- registering with a dentist in the UK;
- relatives in the UK;
- spouse and children continue to live in the UK;
- membership of a UK professional body.

A UK tax resident is unlikely to have left the UK unless there has been a definite break in their pattern of life. In the absence of a statutory residence test (along the lines of the USA) planning to make a definite break requires careful consideration of non-statutory residence factors as outlined above.

In recent years, the rules have changed and we have new practice which impacts, if nothing else, on the way that the count of days is made – now including all days where you are here at midnight – for helping determine residence. HM Revenue & Customs (HMRC) have said their replacement guidance, issued following changes to the rules on non-domiciled individuals from 6 April 2008, is not a direct replacement for the old guidance, but represents a guide to the unrepresented taxpayer. There is further guidance for the advisor scheduled, but this has not been forthcoming to date. What has clearly been reliable guidance for the last 25 years has now been swept away by uncertainty.

There is no such lack of focus in the UK tax authority's attempts to systematically raise enquiries and coordinate their approach in relation to dealing with High Net Worth and internationally mobile individuals. HMRC are pooling resources and experiences, and entering into exchanges of information with various tax havens; a real sign of greater cooperation on sharing information with other foreign revenue jurisdictions.

In the case of an individual who has been resident in the UK, the making of a 'distinct break' in their pattern of life, including establishing a residence elsewhere, may mean that even lengthy or regular visits to this country may amount to continued or resumed residence. What is unmistakable is that established practice is no longer as clear and distinct as it may have appeared for many years. The lack of a statutory residence test makes planning for non-residency status more challenging.

Once a UK national moves to live in America permanently, they become a tax resident in the US, and are subject to the relevant state taxes. There is an initial period of 183 days, following which the UK national's entire worldwide income and assets will become liable to US income and capital gains tax. Those moving to the US need to ensure they get their financial affairs in order before they leave so that they do not expose themselves to unnecessary taxation.

For example, while income tax in the US is lower than income tax in the UK, the additional federal, state and local city taxes can push effective income tax rates above the UK's rates.

Those who have a house to sell in the UK might be best advised to sell it before their initial 183 days in the US are up so they will be able to sell it free of capital gains tax (CGT) in the UK. After 183 days of residence in the US, they will have to pay a certain amount of CGT on the sale of even a primary residence.

Another example is inheritance tax (IHT). The UK tax system tries to ensure you remain within its net even if you do take up residence overseas. For the first seven years that a UK national resides in the US, they will still be deemed domiciled in the UK and their estate will be subject to UK inheritance tax laws.

Many people are aware that health insurance costs are exceptionally high in the US. This is why travel, and even expatriate medical insurers, charge a huge premium if the policy holder is planning to spend time in the US. Getting health insurance in the US is exceptionally expensive and often complex. Many US-based insurers refuse to take those over a certain age or those who have not been fully resident in the US for a few years. This means that it is essential to get a good, basic level of expatriate coverage until it is possible to take out US health care cover.

Ways to keep premiums low include building up a large excess. Of course this can back fire if you do fall ill and need to claim, as you will have to be able to afford to pay the excess. Those who can prove a history of good health, either personal or family, who do not smoke, drink or participate in extreme sports, will get the lowest premiums. While health insurance in the US is expensive, not having it may prove even more costly!

And finally, exchange rates can play havoc with your planning. UK nationals working in the US may find a devalued dollar attractive. Currency fluctuations are a very real phenomenon and you need to consider how to protect yourself against adverse fluctuations in advance. Methods might include developing a variety of investments across currencies, cashing in certain policies that are not recognized as tax free in the US or switching funds or policies. UK nationals could even secure the conversion rate for a large lump sum that could be derived from a house sale in the UK, to be used on housing in US.

The days when the UK was considered an attractive nation for internationally mobile professionals have long gone. The high taxes and charges on non-domiciliaries are sending foreign workers from the likes of the US back home, or elsewhere overseas. They feel increasingly that the UK is not an attractive location in which to work.

The City of London may no longer be seen as a draw for high earning executives, and the UK no longer a good place for international families to bring up their children.

A number of US nationals currently working in the UK are either returning to the US or are considering moving to live and work in more fiscally attractive locations.

3

Internationally Mobile Employees' Expectations

Employees of companies who are asked to transfer abroad by their employers are in a different category from overseas jobseekers. This chapter is intended to provide guidance to those in this situation before they make a decision, both on the terms of the remuneration package that they might look for and on the likely reasoning behind their employer's offer in the first place. Readers who are not working for a company now and do not intend to work in a corporate environment in the near future may prefer to omit this chapter and go forward to Chapter 4.

CATEGORIES OF OVERSEAS EMPLOYMENT

There are three situations in which your corporate employer might invite you to work abroad:

- on a short- or medium-term assignment, either as a commuter or as a temporary resident to provide management expertise or training (eg in the case of an acquisition) or support skills (eg for a technology transfer project);
- as a more permanent relocation to perform a particular local role, usually in a senior management position;
- as a part of a globally mobile executive cadre who move frequently from country to country in line with corporate strategy.

The third category of globe-trotting 'suits' is normally an organizational feature of multinational corporations or government foreign services. Their terms of overseas employment have evolved from experience of managing internationally mobile employees, often over decades, and are codified into HR policies and practices. If you are in this category, there will be very little or no scope for bargaining and you need to be sure that you are comfortable with company policies before you sign up for the long haul. The detail of this chapter may therefore be of interest only as an indicator of what other companies offer.

Before focusing on the remaining two categories of short- or medium-term assignments, let's take a look at the circumstances in which your company may want you to make a move.

WHEN AN OVERSEAS APPOINTMENT IS REQUIRED

The need to fill an appointment overseas with a manager or skilled employee, instead of appointing a local national, can apply equally to large multinational companies or smaller companies whose activities have extended from their home base into as little as one export market or one manufacturing unit abroad.

The circumstances of the organization may extend from:

- companies engaged only in the export of goods and/or services abroad; to
- international companies with either overseas subsidiaries or loosely associated, autonomous operations in a few locations; to
- multinationals with operations in a number of countries in one or more regions, having common systems (in particular, IT and financial controls) and processes; to
- global corporations covering most developed and significant emerging economies, with universal branding, integrated marketing and manufacturing strategies and centrally controlled financial, corporate planning and human resources (HR) functions.

The continuing trend towards multinationalism reflects the ever-increasing economic interdependence of countries and the growing volume and diversity of transactions between them.

THE EMPLOYER'S PERSPECTIVE

HR strategy issues

For both the home company sending employees abroad and the host countries receiving them the key issues are clear: the transfer of skilled and experienced management or staff will inevitably disrupt the smooth running of their local businesses and almost certainly give rise to other staff deployments locally.

In the case of multinational and global corporations the issues are more complex. They will need to balance the interests of the home and host operations with the overriding group interests, which will include building and maintaining a cadre of well-motivated, experienced and effective internationally mobile employees. The development of a comprehensive HR policy for employees on international assignment is an essential element of their strategy without which the company is exposed to creating precedents and anomalies in terms of employment and remuneration packages that are likely to come back to haunt them when making fresh appointments or addressing employee grievances.

Even in smaller international or export-orientated companies there are some functions that are usually performed by expatriates from the headquarters country, such as start-ups in a new territory or training to deliver skills or transfer technology in local markets. In post-acquisition situations it is normal to import an expatriate general manager and financial controller for a time unless there are experienced, successful and adaptable local managers in post.

Whatever the size and scope of organization, there are common areas for which each company individually defines its overseas assignment strategy:

- the business need;
- the extent to which local managers can be used;
- at what levels and in which functions expatriate managers will perform.

Profiling the candidate requirements for expatriate appointments

Inevitably, the different categories of assignment will demand different characteristics and qualities in the candidates from whom an appointee is selected.

Appointments of six months or less are commonest in the case of training local staff for skills or technology transfers, and appointees are usually drawn from mid-career managers or case-hardened older managers who are nearing the end of their careers. Aside from their technical prowess, successful appointees will need communication skills, patience and the willingness to tolerate unfamiliar living conditions for a limited period. Family considerations are unlikely to affect the decision to accept the appointment except in the case of single parents or those with dependants who cannot be left in the care of others.

Longer-term assignments of two to five years (some of which could result in localization at the end of the appointment) are usually allotted to the same categories of manager, but the personal considerations are much more complex, involving the uprooting and relocation of families, with all the attendant considerations that are the subject of this book. However, there may be significant long-term career issues that those who are offered expatriate employment will also need to address.

The trend towards so-called 'commuter' appointments where the internationally mobile employee travels from their base every week, usually within the same geographic region, has been growing. This is unlikely to be the employer's first choice for assignments to one location of more than six months, but may result from the unwillingness of the appointee's family to move. Generally, this is a bad solution. Although the considerable cost of moving a partner or family may be avoided, commuting imposes many strains on the employee, both socially and in work performance. It may also have a negative impact on peer relationships with local managers who resent the apparent privilege and dilution of involvement.

Career considerations for expatriate employees

In larger companies HR strategy may be focused on offering expatriate assignments to the most promising mid-career managers who are potential candidates in the future for top-level executive positions and for whom successful management experience abroad is a prerequisite. Turning down such an appointment for perfectly reasonable family considerations in such circumstances may mean accepting a ceiling to career advancement within the organization. It is important for you to recognize the implications if you are in that position and for you and your partner to talk through the consequences before taking a decision.

Senior managers nearing the end of their careers for whom an expatriate appointment may be the final assignment before retirement should focus on their position when the assignment comes to its end or is terminated prematurely. Pension benefits will be a prime consideration.

Many years ago, a friend of mine worked for a foreign multinational corporation in its London office. A British colleague in his late fifties who had worked for the company in South Africa in a senior position with a generous salary and benefits, he had returned to the UK subsidiary for his final five years' employment. Without the overseas benefits, his salary and prospective pension were no longer attractive against the higher cost of living in Britain. Realizing that this was the HR policy for nationals of countries other than that of the parent company, my friend wisely chose to change his employer when offered a marketing appointment in the South African subsidiary.

Selection criteria

The most common competencies required for international managers are listed by Towers Perrin, the international executive employment consultants, as:

- cultural sensitivity;
- interpersonal skills;
- listening;
- flexibility/adaptability;
- ability to learn;
- personal ambiguity tolerance;
- emotional stability;
- technical competencies.

These qualities are perceived as of greater importance for longer-term assignments than technical skills and abilities by many employers.

In a survey several years ago, Towers Perrin also found that there was a close correlation, in descending order, of the perceived relative importance of the following characteristics between employers and employees:

- family flexibility;
- personal resilience;
- personality;
- cultural sensitivity;
- interpersonal skills;
- international experience;
- employability;
- language skills.

Except for language skills, rather higher percentages of employers than employees mentioned each factor.

TERMS OF EMPLOYMENT AND REMUNERATION

From the employee's perspective, the most important issues to be resolved with the employer are the contract and the remuneration package. The latter is, of course, a key element of the contract terms.

The employment contract: basic terms

Given that there is no job security in today's business world, it is normal for a contract of expatriate employment to specify:

- the length of the appointment;
- salary and benefits administration;
- a procedure for discussing repatriation in the final 6 to 12 months of the appointment;
- an extended period of notice in the event that a further appointment is not on offer.

Bearing in mind that some 40 per cent of international assignees are said to return early, it is important that your contract should include provision for the costs of repatriation in whatever circumstances are reasonably foreseeable and certainly in the event of dismissal.

You should also ensure that your expatriate employment contract includes provision for an annual appraisal, even if your compensation is not performance-related. The appraisal should include a review of personal performance against responsibilities and tasks defined in a job description attached to the contract and the joint setting of objectives for the next year. As well as being best practice among international employers, annual appraisals may be the only way of confirming your employer's view of your progress, successes and failures in the appointment when regular communication with home-country management colleagues and superiors throughout the year may be limited. Appraisals will also contribute to your peace of mind and effectiveness.

The compensation package

As already discussed, most international companies and all multi-national or global corporations will have a detailed HR policy, which will include defined compensation packages for each grade of expatriate employee. These terms are unlikely to be negotiable, but you should be sure that you are comfortable with them.

If possible, you should ensure that, in addition to annual salary and cost of living reviews, your compensation package includes an equitable and fair element of reward incentive. You will find that there is a trend towards the inclusion of incentive rewards by many international companies.

If you are working for a smaller organization, whose overseas appointments are occasional or sporadic, you may find that there is no established HR policy in place and that expatriate assignments are managed on an ad hoc basis. Therefore, there may be more scope for negotiation.

For example, in the case of an international company that has decided to develop a new manufacturing operation involving a transfer of technology from the home plant, the only practical course of action may be to send a senior factory manager for a period of two to three years to handle the start-up and to develop a local management capability. If an external appointment is not feasible because of the technology transfer and there are no more than one or two internal candidates, the company may find that its opportunistic decision to invest is matched by the preferred candidate's equally opportunistic demands for the most favourable reward package achievable. If you are the preferred candidate in such a situation, you may be wise not to push your demands to the limit. An exorbitant package, granted reluctantly, is likely to generate lingering resentment and you may find that there will be no commitment to a further appointment on your return.

CONCLUSION

Offers of an overseas appointment from an existing employer or resulting from recruitment always present an exciting challenge for you and your family. However favourable the terms may appear to be initially, be sure to work through the detailed checklist that follows before making an irrevocable decision.

Checklist: Employment conditions

If you have been offered employment abroad, bear in mind that you will incur a whole range of expenses which would not arise if you were employed here. It is vital to consider these expenses and to check whether your remuneration package covers them, either directly or in the form of fringe benefits.

If you are going to work for a reputable international company, it will probably have a standard reward package that includes the fringe benefits that it is prepared to offer. But if your employer is new to, or inexperienced in, the game of sending people to work abroad (especially if they are a native of the country to which you are going and therefore possibly not aware of expatriates' standards in such matters as housing) here are some of the factors you should look at in assessing how good the offer really is.

To help you arrive at realistic, up-to-date answers to the following questions, it is worth trying to talk to someone who has recently worked in the country to which you are thinking of going, as well as reading the relevant sections in this book.

1. **Family**
   (a) Is your employer going to help your partner find a job or to identify other opportunities such as further education or voluntary work?
   (b) If your employer is not able to help your partner find work, do they have a policy of reimbursing for loss of income?
   (c) Is your partner involved in the briefing sessions provided by your employer before departure?
   (d) Does your employer provide a support network for your partner?

(e) Will your employer provide details of schools?

(f) Do you have contacts provided by your employer to talk to before you move?

(g) Is your employer going to meet the cost of travel out from the UK for your family as well as yourself?

2. **Accommodation**

(a) Is your employer going to provide accommodation? If so:
   - Of what standard?
   - How soon will it be available after you arrive?
   - Is it furnished or unfurnished? If furnished, what will be provided in the way of furniture?

(b) If accommodation is not free, but there is a subsidy, is this assessed:
   - As an absolute sum? In this case, is it realistic in the light of current prices? If not, is there any provision to adjust it?
   - As a proportion of what you will actually have to pay?

(c) Who is going to pay for utilities (gas, water, electricity, telephone)?

(d) If there is no subsidy and accommodation is not free, are you sure your salary, however grand it sounds, is adequate? Do not accept the job unless you are sure about this.

(e) Will the employer subsidize or pay for you and your family's hotel bills for a reasonable period until you find somewhere to live? Is the figure realistic in the light of local hotel prices?

3. **Removal assistance**

(a) Will you be paid a disturbance allowance? Is it adequate to cover the cost of shipping (and, possibly, duty at the other end) for as many household and personal effects as you need? Will your eventual return to the UK as well as your departure be taken care of?

(b) What arrangements will be made:
   - To cover legal and other fees if you have to sell your UK home?

     – To cover the difference, if you have to let your
UK home while you are away, between the rental
income and such outgoings as insurance,
mortgage interest and agent's management? Will
you be compensated for any legal expenses you
incur, eg to get rid of an unsatisfactory tenant?

     – To cover the cost of storing household effects?

4. Personal effects and domestic help

(a) Will you be paid a clothing allowance, bearing in
mind that you will need a whole new wardrobe if you
are going to a hot country? Will it cover just your
clothes, or those of your family as well?

(b) Will your employer pay for or subsidize household
items (eg air conditioning) that you will need in a hot
climate and that are not included in an accommodation
package?

(c) Will your employer provide/subsidize the cost of
domestic staff? If not, is your salary adequate to pay
for them yourself, if they are necessary and customary
in the country and at the level at which you are being
employed?

(d) Is a car going to be provided with the job – with or
without driver?

(e) Will the employer pay for or subsidize club
membership and/or entrance fees?

(f) Will you be paid an allowance for entertaining?

5. Leave entitlement

(a) If your children attend UK boarding schools, what
arrangements are there for them to join you in the
holidays? Will the employer pay for their air fares and
if so will this be for every holiday or only some of
them? If the latter, can you arrange for them to be
looked after at Christmas or Easter?

(b) What arrangements are there for your own leaves?
Does the employer provide return air fares to the UK
or another country of your choice? Will these cover
your family? And for how many holidays?

6. **Personal finance**
   (a) Will the employer pay for/subsidize all or any additional insurance premiums you may incur? In some countries (eg Saudi Arabia) it is advisable to insure your domestic staff. The cost of motor vehicle insurance may be inordinately high because of poor roads and low driving standards.
   (b) If social security payments are higher than in the UK (eg in some EU countries), will your employer make up the difference?
   (c) Will the employer contribute to your medical expenses if free medical attention is not available or is inadequate?

7. **Salary**
   (a) If your salary is expressed in sterling, would you be protected against loss of local buying power in case of devaluation? Equally, if your salary is in local currency, would it be adjusted for a rise in sterling against that currency?
   (b) Is your salary in any way index-linked to the cost of living? How often are the effects of inflation taken into account in assessing and adjusting your current level of remuneration?
   (c) If there are any restrictions on remittances, is your employer prepared to pay a proportion of your salary into a UK bank or that of some other country with a freely negotiable currency?

8. **Language**
   (a) Will your employer contribute towards language teaching for you and/or your partner?

9. **Legal status**
   (a) Is the legal status of your appointment clear? If you are held to be your employer's sole or principal representative, you may be personally liable in some countries for any obligations incurred, eg the payment of corporate taxes or social security contributions.

(b) Have all the terms of the job and the provisions of the remuneration package been confirmed in writing concerning the contract and conditions of employment subject to English law and, if not, do you or your advisers clearly understand how they should be interpreted should a dispute arise?

10. **Working for a foreign company**

(a) If the job is with a foreign company, particularly a locally based one rather than a multinational, there are a number of points that need special attention:

- Are the duties of the job clearly spelt out in writing in a contract of employment?
- Are the normal working hours laid down? How long will your journey to work be?
- Are all matters affecting pay, including when it is due and whether you will be paid for overtime, clear and in writing?
- If there is a bonus, are the conditions under which it is due unambiguous?
- Are there satisfactory arrangements for sick pay?
- Would there be any restriction on your changing jobs if you got a better offer from another employer or decided to leave? (This one obviously has to be handled with particular tact!)
- Do leave conditions clearly specify whether the leave is home or local? For the former, has the employer unambiguously declared the intention of paying your return air fare and that of your partner/family?
- Will legitimate expenses be paid in addition to salary?

(b) Have you taken any steps to check the bona fides of the prospective employer, eg through a Chamber of Commerce (the local/British Chambers of Commerce to be found in many main centres are often more obliging and better informed than commercial sections of British embassies), bank, trade association, or Dun & Bradstreet's Business Information Services?

11. **Personal protection**
    (a) Is there a legal obligation on the employer in a high-risk country to continue to pay your salary if you are taken hostage?
    (b) Will the employer offer you a special training course to cope with the risks involved in living in a very high-risk country?

(Much of the background information for this chapter was provided by Valerie Vardy and Mike Langley of Towers Perrin whose collaboration in previous editions the author gratefully acknowledges.)

Expatriate Employees' Expectations

Stephen Gill, Stephen Gill Associates

THALES'S WELL

An amusing story relates how Thales of Miletus, the sixth-century BC Greek philosopher, fell into a well one night while observing the night sky. He had been so intent in observing the heavens that he failed to watch where he was walking. The attractive servant girl who answered his cries for help mockingly asked him how he expected to know anything about the stars when he didn't even know what was on earth under his own feet.

BACK TO THE FUTURE

I am often reminded of Thales's tumble when I hear of certain expatriate mishaps that occur. It is all too easy to focus on distant places and miss the obvious that is near at hand. Expatriates and their families have high expectations that often cause them to take their eye off the road ahead. Using Thales's fall as a metaphor, there are many potential pitfalls lying in wait for the expatriate, and the phrase 'overseas business trip' can take on a whole new meaning for the unwary. It is not possible to cover all the pitfalls here, but with Thales's fall firmly in mind we will start by looking at the area that for many is the expatriates' own bump back down to earth: repatriation.

Repatriation is the process of expatriates returning home from the international assignment, and it completes the cycle of the expatriation process. It is a commonly held belief that it will be a 'return to normal'. Unfortunately, repatriation is rarely an event that feels either easy or natural. On the contrary, it can also be made all the more difficult as repatriates themselves do not expect this 'reverse culture shock' to occur, as they are returning 'home' and are not prepared for it.

'Reverse culture shock' can be caused by the mismatching between the expatriates' high expectations prior to their return and the reality that they actually encounter after the return. Expatriates always expect they will hold similar, if not higher, hierarchical positions upon their return where there will be good opportunities to use the skills and knowledge that they acquired abroad.

In practice, it is often unrealistic and sometimes impossible to guarantee to expatriates the specific position they are expecting upon their return. Consequently, it is crucial for companies to be honest to expatriates in an attempt to try to minimize any readjustment difficulties when they return. Unfortunately, this seldom happens, as companies do not want to unsettle employees before the end of the assignment, and it is easy for companies to put it off until expatriates eventually arrive back.

A key ingredient for effective repatriation is to start early to make expatriates aware of all the possible outcomes from this career decision. Poor handling of repatriation may cause a high staff turnover problem or lower the expatriates' morale, thereby shrinking the potential expatriate pool if it is not handled properly.

One problem of repatriation is that many companies may not cherish the competencies and wisdom that their repatriates gained from their international assignments and may not take full advantage of the skills and knowledge that they acquired from working abroad. Expatriates' tolerance for ambiguity, magnified intercultural understanding and ability to relate effectively with people of different cultures are commonly not used by the expatriates' home organizations.

Disregarding the knowledge gained by expatriates could be counterproductive and expensive for the parent company, as considerable investment has been devoted to these members of staff. Therefore, for companies to ignore expatriates' gained knowledge could be viewed as poor management. It would be far better to provide chances for repatriates to use their skills, and that would encourage them to work more enthusiastically for the parent company.

However, companies that do not take advantage of the knowledge gained by their expatriates may unwittingly force repatriates to seek employment elsewhere, possibly with their competitors. As companies invest significant sums of money training expatriates, it would also be sensible to try to retain this knowledge and experience in the organization. Therefore, potentially, the inability and failure to exploit the intellectual capital gained by expatriates could also be considered as another form of management failure, as the company cannot realize the full benefit from the expatriates' assignment.

For expatriates themselves, it can be naïve to think that your high expectations will be truly fulfilled upon returning or that the company will be able to satisfy your new-found needs. If you are like most people, you will not be unaffected by the experience of working abroad, and you are probably not exactly the same person that you were when you left. It is difficult, when in the midst of change, to take stock and be aware of your own expectations, but if you really want to avoid some form of disappointment, looking ahead to repatriation and considering the options as early as possible are advisable.

FAMILY CONSIDERATIONS

Of course, looking so far ahead, right through to the conclusion of an assignment, is not so easy when expatriates are first faced with the prospect of an assignment. It is usual at this early stage to discuss the opportunity with a spouse to gain their support. The focus of the attention is usually the job itself and the working conditions for the expatriate. If it is an extended assignment it is possible that the spouse and family will have the opportunity to travel with the expatriate. Whether the family accompanies the expatriate or is left behind, the importance of the role that it plays in international assignments should be recognized.

Family-related issues often have important influences upon expatriates' own adjustment processes and their ability to perform effectively on the assignment. Challenges regarding the children, language and the adjustment of spouses are likely to heighten the expatriates' levels of stress and uncertainty. Those expatriates whose family members are having difficulties adjusting are likely to feel responsible for their unhappiness, whereas contented families are obviously more likely to provide support.

The family generally experiences a more difficult adjustment process than the expatriates, as expatriates still feel the familiarity of the work. Families actually experience 'excessive culture shock' in many circumstances. This may lead to families facing challenges such as loss of self-esteem, lack of contact with friends and family, and social and cultural ostracism; disruption of children's education is also a contributing factor.

Therefore, a vital factor in successful expatriation is the ability of the expatriate and the trailing spouse and family to adjust to an unfamiliar foreign culture. It is a realistic claim that one of the main reasons for the premature return of expatriates is the inability of their spouses to adapt to the foreign environment and culture. Unfortunately, family circumstances are still the least likely to be considered before going on an assignment, which is a shame, as no organizations should underestimate the role that the expatriates' families play.

It seems that, while organizations acknowledge that it could be vital to the success of expatriate assignments that they formulate strategies to include families as much as the expatriates, perhaps they feel that they would be interfering in expatriates' personal lives to go so far as to include the families in preparation and adjustment programmes. This reluctance to involve partners earlier may in fact prevent organizations from choosing the most suitable couples, which would reduce the risk of expatriate failure.

Fortunately, not all companies are the same, and organizational concern about expatriate performance is increasing. It is now more widely understood that the parent company constitutes the initial source of support and provides benefits and services prior to arrival and that, once the expatriates are in the foreign country, these will affect expatriates' quality of life and work there.

Such support and services include financial benefits to maintain the standard of living to which expatriates are accustomed in the home country, cross-cultural training, assistance in housing relocation, membership of clubs in the foreign country, rest and relaxation, vacation leave, and assistance with schooling for children, as well as maintaining communication with the expatriates to ease anxieties.

Social support from a host-country national can help family members' adjustment by providing feedback on the appropriate behaviour, and this can serve to lessen uncertainty regarding the local culture and thus facilitate a spouse's adjustment. To assist in this, a number of employers may help to provide spouses with a host-country mentor to carry out these functions and help trailing spouses to establish networks with host-country nationals.

Some companies are now providing expatriates with pre-departure and post-arrival training to help them and their families to adapt more successfully to the foreign culture. Thus the purpose of the training is to reduce the amount of culture shock that the expatriates or their families encounter by familiarizing them with the host country. Training also helps to increase the expatriates' commitment to the parent organization, perhaps also leading to higher performance.

In addition, training can make the change easier for people to accept because it reduces the fear and uncertainty that accompany many changes. Once employees have been selected for expatriate positions, pre-departure training is considered to be the next necessary step in attempting to ensure they can work effectively and successfully abroad.

Some companies go further and help expatriate family members adjust to the foreign environment by either providing job opportunities to the spouses or encouraging them to participate directly in the expatriation process to enhance the likelihood of success. Such support also extends to children, where it is recognized that it should focus more on language skills prior to expatriation and on continuing learning in the host country to help increase the children's cultural sensitivity and teach them to avoid premature judgement of the culture.

Everyone involved in an expatriate assignment wants it to be a success, but unfortunately it is often the task that receives all the focus while many elements that contribute to the success or failure are overlooked until they become a problem. Working abroad is an important step for anyone. If you are to avoid losing your footing as Thales did, beware the pitfalls that lie ahead.

Part Two

Managing Personal Finance

5

Domicile and Residence

When leaving the UK on secondment you must consider the impact on your residence and domicile status, as this will dictate how you are treated for taxation purposes during your assignment. With effect from 5 April 2008, non-UK-domiciled persons working in the UK have been severely penalized. If you are thinking of staying abroad at the end of an assignment and commuting to the UK to work, you should review the consequences carefully.

THE CONCEPTS

Domicile is a complex legal issue, but normally you are domiciled in the country in which you have your permanent home. The place of domicile is where you intend to reside indefinitely and the country to which you ultimately intend to return.

A domicile of origin is usually inherited from your father at birth (or from your mother, if either your parents did not marry or your father died before you were of legal age). Establishing a new domicile of choice is extremely difficult, and in the case of someone with a domicile in the UK is only achieved by emigrating permanently to another country with no intention of returning to the UK and by severing all ties with the UK.

Your residence status for tax purposes is determined by the facts and your intentions and is therefore likely to be affected by an overseas assignment. UK tax law distinguishes between 'residence' and 'ordinary residence'. Whereas residence is based on UK physical presence in each tax year, ordinary residence equates broadly to habitual residence and takes into account the individual's intentions and UK presence over the short and medium term.

UK nationals leaving the UK for an assignment abroad will remain UK resident for tax purposes unless the overseas employment contract and the absence abroad cover at least one complete UK tax year (6 April to 5 April). In addition, the individual's visits to the UK must not exceed 183 days in total in any one tax year or an average of 91 or more days per tax year averaged over a maximum of four years.

When working abroad you should always consider the host country's definition of residence and domicile. Most countries without a legal system inherited from the UK do not have the concept of 'domicile' as understood in the UK and may base domicile on factors such as the intention to reside long term. Other countries may use the word 'domicile' or its equivalent in their language to mean no more than a place of abode.

Having a UK domicile and UK-resident status does not preclude you from becoming a resident or domiciliary of the host country under its domestic tax law. In these circumstances, double taxation may arise and complicate the situation.

THE IMPACT ON UK TAXATION

The expatriate who does not break UK residence

If you are domiciled in the UK and remain resident and ordinarily resident during your assignment, your liability to UK tax on your worldwide employment and investment income, capital gains and assets will continue. Capital gains tax and inheritance tax will be chargeable irrespective of the location of the relevant assets. Explained below is the way that the correct use of foreign tax credits, double tax treaties and effective planning can prevent double taxation and mitigate your overall exposure to taxation.

One advantage of remaining UK resident is that you remain eligible to contribute to tax-efficient investments like ISAs. However, being non-resident does not always result in losing your right to make tax-deductible pension contributions (see below).

The non-UK resident expatriate

A non-UK resident is taxable in the UK only on employment income relating to duties performed in the UK. If these UK duties are, however, merely incidental to the overseas duties (eg receiving instructions, reporting on progress, or up to 91 days each year of training during which no productive work is done), the earnings should not be liable to UK income tax.

Nevertheless, you may still be liable to UK income tax on employment income received while non-resident. This arises in the case of bonuses, termination payments and the exercise of unapproved stock options (if you were UK resident when the option was granted or the grant relates to UK duties). As these items are earned over a period of time, HM Revenue & Customs (HMRC) in the UK may tax the proportion of the income that relates to the period of UK residence and to any non-incidental duties performed in the UK when non-resident.

If you are not UK resident, income from your foreign investments is outside the scope of UK income tax. Even if you are UK resident, it will not be chargeable to UK tax if you are not UK domiciled and you do not bring any of the income into the UK. Income from UK investments such as rental income from UK property, dividends on UK shareholdings and interest on UK accounts will continue to be liable to UK income tax.

Subject to any legislative changes that may be introduced in a post-election 2010 Finance Act, capital gains tax cannot normally be avoided by being non-UK resident at the time the gain arises. Individuals who have been resident or ordinarily resident in the UK during any part of four out of the previous seven tax years and leave the UK may be liable to capital gains tax in the year of their return on any gains made during their absence. A UK absence of five complete tax years or more, however, negates this rule. The rule also usually only applies to assets already held by the individual when they leave the UK (so that gains on assets that are both acquired and disposed of during a shorter non-resident period can be tax-free). Note that the terms of a double tax treaty between the UK and the new country of residence may also override the UK charge. Specific professional advice should be sought if you might dispose of assets during your UK absence.

You should note that, subject to certain conditions, capital gains tax is not usually chargeable on the sale of your UK property if it has been your only or main residence. Advice should be obtained to ensure that maximum advantage is taken of this generous relief.

The assets of a UK domiciliary may be charged to UK inheritance tax on death or earlier transfer, irrespective of their location and the residence status of the individual. Individuals who are not UK domiciled should note the 'deemed domicile' provisions, which impose UK inheritance tax on their worldwide assets if they have been UK resident for 17 out of the last 20 tax years. Specialist advice should always be obtained before making any gifts, and an appropriate will is essential for all expatriates.

If you remain employed by the UK company or a group company while working abroad, you can continue to contribute, and to have employer contributions made, to your UK occupational pension scheme. This can normally continue for 20 years or longer with HMRC approval and provided that you intend to return to work in the UK. The non-UK consequences of maintaining a UK pension scheme should always be considered, as the employer contributions may be taxable in your host country.

It is also possible to continue making contributions to a personal pension plan (including one that is funded by your employer) for up to five UK tax years of non-residence, provided that certain conditions are met. Income tax relief will be given at source on your personal contributions at the basic rate (reduced from 22 per cent to 20 per cent from April 2008) even if you do not have any UK-taxable income.

When you are non-resident in the UK, you will no longer be eligible to take out new tax-efficient investment schemes (such as ISAs) or to contribute to them, although you can continue to retain existing schemes. Tax relief on life assurance premiums on pre-March 1983 policies is also forfeited for your period of non-residence.

YOUR EMPLOYMENT PACKAGE

Employers have many options when considering how to structure an expatriate remuneration package. The decision is based on many factors, of which tax is just one. Set out below are the three main categories of expatriate package, and the type of expatriate to whom they are usually offered.

Tax equalization

The basic principle of equalization is that the expatriate continues to pay the same amount of tax as would have been paid if they had continued working in the home country (on the home country package). Social security contributions may also be included in this calculation. The employer deducts an amount equal to the normal home country tax (hypothetical tax) from the employee's salary and then assumes responsibility for paying the individual's actual tax liability, wherever it arises.

The actual tax paid on behalf of the employee by the employer is, in itself, a taxable payment and must be grossed up. The employer meets any additional liability to tax in excess of the hypothetical tax, but equally will retain any tax savings that arise during the assignment. For example, an employer settling tax on behalf of an employee liable at 40 per cent actually has to pay UK tax at 100/40 (a 67 per cent effective rate), but is able to use the hypothetical tax withheld from the individual to fund this. There may also be tax savings from tax breaks in the home and host countries as a result of the assignment. Companies with large expatriate populations tend to use this method because it encourages mobility, since it provides expatriates with more certainty about their take-home pay.

Tax protection

This method can be less expensive for the employer, but can be more difficult to administer. The principle is that expatriates will pay no more tax than they would have done had they remained working in the home country. No hypothetical tax is withheld by the employer. Instead the individual pays the actual home and host country tax up to the amount of the normal home country tax liability. If the actual overall tax liability is higher, the employer will pay the excess. If there is a saving by comparison to the normal home country liability, the expatriate keeps it. Sometimes only part of the expatriate's earnings is tax protected, for example foreign accommodation costs paid by the company.

This method is often used by companies sending expatriates to countries with lower tax rates than the home country. It can discourage mobility, as it provides a financial incentive for assignees to move to low-tax countries from high-tax countries and to stay there.

Laissez-faire

This method does not involve the employer at all (apart from any responsibilities like employer's social security contributions). The individual is simply responsible for their own tax liability in the home and host countries. This may be beneficial if the overall tax rates on assignment are lower than the normal home country rates.

This method is often applied where the expatriate has requested the assignment, to career development assignments by companies with little experience of international assignments, and by companies continually sending expatriates to countries that have no income tax or very low tax rates.

PLANNING POINTS

Timing

As explained above, UK non-residence is normally only achieved where a full-time overseas employment and the employee's UK absence cover a complete UK tax year. Thus, if the assignment was planned to begin on 20 April, you should consider bringing forward the date that the overseas employment commences and the UK departure date, so that they fall before 6 April.

There are tax reliefs for certain overseas assignments of two years or less, the details of which are set out below. HMRC will reject claims to relief from the date when there is a clear intention for the assignment to last more than two years or where the employee is under an employment contract with the company in the host location. Indicators such as work permits, social security certificates and assignment letters will be taken into account.

An overseas assignment that results in the individual being present in the host country for less than 184 days and during which they remain resident in the home country may provide the opportunity to avoid an income tax liability in the host country under the terms of a double taxation treaty. Remember that in most countries the tax year is the calendar year, so there may be scope for some planning on this point, although some tax treaties count the individual's days on a different basis to the tax year (see below).

If you are about to be granted share options, you should consider carefully whether it is preferable for you to be granted them before or after your UK departure. The option gains are likely to be taxable in either the home or host country (if not both) and your marginal tax rates in each country should be considered.

Non-contractual payments on termination of employment may be wholly or partly exempt from UK tax, if the employment involved periods of foreign service. You should seek advice if you receive such a payment, as the UK tax savings can be considerable but there may also be a foreign tax charge.

Avoiding double taxation

The UK has double tax treaties with numerous countries, which try to prevent double taxation of individual income and gains. There are also a few treaties that cover potential double taxation of capital assets. Although treaties vary and they should be examined in detail in every case, the rules for exemption of earnings from tax in the host country are normally:

- You must be UK resident under the definition in the treaty.
- You should not be present in the host country for more than 183 days (in the fiscal year, the calendar year or any 12-month period, depending on the treaty).
- You must remain employed by a business that is resident in the UK and that is not resident in the host country.
- The costs of your assignment must not be borne by a branch or permanent establishment of your employer in the host country (or, in some countries, by a subsidiary or parent company).

In some circumstances, double taxation is unavoidable. In these cases, the UK HMRC will normally reduce the UK tax by the foreign taxes paid on the double-taxed earnings, up to the amount of the UK tax otherwise payable.

Expatriate reliefs and allowances

Where an expatriate does not break UK residence, there are a number of tax reliefs that should not be overlooked. These include the following:

- For assignments that are not expected to exceed two years, a tax deduction can normally be claimed in respect of your additional living costs on the basis that you are working away from your normal workplace. The deduction can include the cost of the overseas accommodation and related costs, meals, travel and subsistence (but you must be prepared to produce receipts or other documentation to support your claim). Equally, if the employer reimburses these costs, HMRC will not normally tax them if they meet the conditions for the deduction. Alternatively, a tax-free, flat-rate allowance of £10 per night is available to cover incidental expenses when working abroad.

- For longer-term assignments, the following reimbursed expenses are normally not taxable in the UK:
  - qualifying relocation costs of up to £8,000, when leaving the UK and on returning from the assignment;
  - outbound and return travel costs for you and your family (including children under 18 at the start of the outward journey);
  - home leave travel for certain family members.
- All individuals who are Commonwealth or EEA nationals are entitled to a personal allowance that is deductible from their income taxable in the UK, as are nationals of certain other countries with which the UK has a double tax treaty regardless of whether they are resident or non-resident in the UK. This allowance was £5,435 for the 2008/09 UK tax year.

Tax on investments

If you are going to become non-UK resident, you may consider moving your UK investments offshore prior to your departure. This can potentially avoid UK tax on income arising from those investments while you are on assignment (but note that there may be a tax charge in the host country).

Before you return to the UK, you should close down all interest-bearing overseas bank accounts before the date on which you resume UK residence, in order to avoid UK income tax on the interest credited while you are non-resident. If you close the accounts after you have resumed UK residence, the interest credited from the date UK residence resumed will be taxable in the UK.

Finally, you should be aware that the host country may tax your investment income during your assignment, in particular where the local rules tax residents on their worldwide income and gains.

CONCLUSION

The key issue in expatriate taxation is to plan in advance. You might be able to save yourself a substantial amount of tax by merely adjusting the terms of your assignment package, but this must be weighed up against the personal and commercial needs of your secondment.

Checklist: Tax aspects of leaving the UK

1. Plan ahead. Consult a tax professional to ensure that your remuneration package and investment portfolio have been structured tax-efficiently, from both a UK and host country perspective. Ideally, you should try to meet a UK adviser before you leave the UK, and a host country adviser on arrival in the new location.

2. Inform HMRC. File a UK HMRC departure form P85. Take care with the wording of your answers on this document, as it will form the basis of the HMRC's evaluation of your residence status during your assignment (and may therefore affect the amount of tax you will pay). If you intend to let your UK property while you are non-UK resident, you should complete a non-resident landlord form NRL1 so that your rent can be received without the requirement for the tenant or agent to withhold tax from the rent. Remember, you may be required to file arrival forms and annual documentation in the host country.

3. Inform your bank, building society and insurer. Even if you do not expect your UK bank interest to exceed your tax-free personal allowance, if you will not be ordinarily resident in the UK you can receive bank interest gross while overseas (ask for the form at the bank or building society). This will save you from having to file a tax return to obtain any refund of withholding tax. If you believe your UK-source income will exceed your tax-free personal allowance, you may wish to set up an offshore bank account so that your bank interest is not liable to UK tax. You should advise your insurer that you will be living and working abroad, as this may affect the cover under your life and household policies.

4. Notify your payroll department. In many cases, you will need to stay on the UK payroll in order to continue making UK pension and UK National Insurance (social security) contributions. If you expect to become non-UK resident, apply to HMRC for an NT (no tax) code to prevent withholding of tax (PAYE) from your salary. If you are going to remain UK resident and expect to pay foreign tax on your earnings, you should apply for the foreign tax to be included in your PAYE code number or set against your UK PAYE by your payroll department, to avoid double tax during the year.

5. Inform your pension provider. Check whether you remain eligible to make tax-deductible contributions to your pension scheme.

6. File a UK tax return. The tax reliefs and allowances available to expatriate assignees must be claimed on your UK tax return. A repayment of UK tax may be due, as personal allowances are given in full for each tax year, even if you are only UK resident for part of the year.

7. Register in your host country. Do this on arrival and take appropriate professional advice to avoid the risk of large and unexpected tax bills at the end of the tax year.

Checklist: Tax aspects of returning to the UK

1. Plan ahead. Seek advice if you have made capital gains, received large payments such as termination payments, or have a complex investment portfolio. If you are considering exercising stock options you should seek advice on timing issues.
2. Close offshore accounts. To prevent the UK from taxing the accrued interest, ideally you should close the accounts in the tax year before the year in which you return to the UK.
3. Deregister with the host country. Ensure you have informed the appropriate authorities of your departure, to prevent any attempt to dispute your actual date of departure.
4. Register with HMRC. File an arrival form P86. This form will not only dictate your tax treatment from the date of your UK return date, but also validate your tax treatment during your absence.

6

Banking, Financial Planning and Asset Management

For most people, working abroad means a rise in income. For those in countries with a low rate of income tax, or, as is the case in some countries in the Middle East, without income tax, it may be the first chance they have had to accumulate a substantial amount of money, and this may indeed be the whole object of the exercise. Expatriates are therefore an obvious target for firms and individuals offering financial advice on such matters as tax, mortgages, insurance schemes, school fee funding, income building plans and stock and 'alternative' investments. Most of them are honest, but some are better than others, either in choosing investments wisely or in finding schemes that are most appropriate to the needs and circumstances of their client, or both. At any rate the expatriate with money to spend is nowadays faced with a wide variety of choices, ranging from enterprising local traders proffering allegedly valuable antiques, and fly-by-night operators selling real estate in inaccessible tropical swamps, to serious financial advisers and consultants. The internet might also help independently minded investors in remote locations, and provides another source of advice.

UK expatriates live all over the world, 95 per cent of them in Australia, Hong Kong, Canada, Spain, South Africa, New Zealand, Germany, Ireland, France, the United States, the UAE, Argentina, Cyprus, Italy and the Netherlands. Some people will love their new environment and may stay on for longer than originally antici-pated. Some may loathe it and can't wait to get back.

When moving to a country that has a totally different culture and way of life you will need to respect and adhere to differing tradi-tions and customs. Not only will the language be 'alien' but so too will be the culture and the general way of life. Before you 'up sticks' you need to spend some time in methodical planning. After all, the key to any successful move is to be well prepared and organized. Limiting potential problems or issues will help you to settle in and adjust quickly to your new 'homeland'.

A good starting point is to research your destination so you know what to expect. There may be a British or expatriate community where you are moving to, which will help you to understand what help and support are available to you and your family. Assistance may also be available from your employer or more widespread support organizations.

OFFSHORE BANKING

Awareness of offshore banking services is traditionally low within the UK, with many people asking their local banking branch to refer them to the relevant specialist department, logging on to the internet or relying on good-quality money-management media for guidance. Others may rely on word of mouth from a colleague who has already opened an offshore account. Good financial planning should start by establishing a sound offshore base for your finances before leaving your country of residence.

There are a number of banks offering international coverage, both British and foreign, although not necessarily with a physical presence in the country to which you are moving. The full range of services that each provides varies considerably and you should study the alternatives carefully.

Whichever bank you choose, you need to be reassured of its probity and expertise. A choice of currencies, 24-hour internet banking and telephone banking are probably minimum require-ments. Lloyds TSB International, for example, has a long history of assisting international customers with all aspects of their financial planning and is now helping tens of thousands of customers all over the world.

Lloyds TSB International has welcomed a wide range of customers to its innovative International Personal Banking Service. For further information, see pages 79–83.

Whether you are taking up a new posting overseas and require a personal/business account, or you are retiring to sunnier climes, ensure that you make your banking arrangements in plenty of time. You can then concentrate on the real reason for the move, be that work or relaxation.

FOREIGN CURRENCY

If you're intending to work overseas it's important that you don't forget about the impact that foreign exchange can have on your finances, both before you go and once you arrive. Exchange rates are constantly moving and as a result can have a big impact on the amount of money you have to start your new life abroad.

Foreign currency specialists, such as No1currency, remove all the worries and complications associated with moving your finances and provide you with:

- bank-beating exchange rates;
- no commission charges;
- guidance and support;
- a fast, efficient, secure service.

Once you have moved, a foreign exchange specialist can also help with regular overseas payments. If you have an income that you would like to be transferred on a regular basis, they can arrange to have the transactions processed on specific dates set by you. It is also possible to secure a rate for a fixed period of time, thus ensuring that you are not exposed to negative foreign exchange rate movements.

When it comes to transferring hard-earned assets, everyone wants to get the best rate possible. The choice usually comes down to either your high street bank or a foreign currency specialist such as No1currency. But what exactly is the difference?

Steve Smyth is married with a 10-year-old daughter. He was working in the RAF and was offered a senior position that involved emigrating to New Zealand:

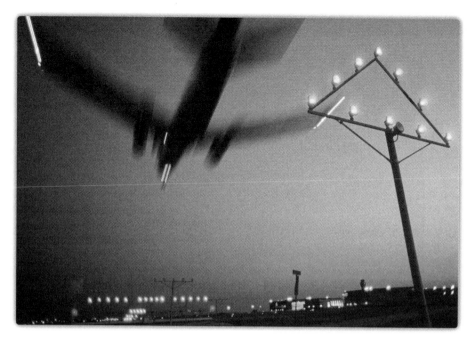

Looking for a safe place
for your savings abroad?

When you're living and working abroad, it's really important to find a safe place for your savings. Lloyds TSB has a range of products that help you make the most of your savings. From great returns with our Fixed Term Deposit Accounts offering up to 5% AER,** to instant access with our International Bonus Saver Account offering up to 2% AER.**

To find out how to make the most of your savings abroad, get in touch.

 Lloyds TSB | International

Call +44 (0)1624 641 823 or visit
lloydstsb-offshore.com/save

Wherever life takes you, we're here for the journey

Working abroad can be an attractive, tempting and rewarding proposition, but how will you manage your finances during this exciting journey?

Whatever you want from banking or investing worldwide, Lloyds TSB International is here to help you every step of the way. We've lots of ways to safeguard and make the most of your money, from premier international banking services or building a property portfolio to looking after your hard-earned savings.

Part of Lloyds Banking Group, we have truly worldwide reach, expertise and resources. So no matter where you are, we're easy to contact – and easy to do business with.

Working Abroad Checklist – Before You Leave

Before your journey's even begun, there's an incredible amount of financial matters to attend to:

- Inform the tax authorities of your plan to work abroad.

- Inform your mortgage provider that you will be out of the country.

- Find out about the tax and social security system in the country you're going to.

- Get advice on the legal status of your will in the country you're going to.

- Establish whether you need to take out medical, personal injury or other insurance.

You also need to determine the type of bank account that will most effectively meet your needs once you've made the move abroad.

Choosing a Bank Account

There are two main options for getting your overseas salary paid into a bank account. Some people ask for their salary to be paid into a local bank native to the country they've gone to work in. However, opening a bank account in a foreign country can be a long and sometimes difficult process. This is because you'll not only need a local address, a social security number and identity documents. You might even need knowledge of the local language from day one to communicate with bank staff and complete all their forms!

The other, perhaps easier option is to open an international account with Lloyds TSB before you go.

Opening a Lloyds TSB International Account

Designed to match the unique demands of global life and living, with 24/7 access, no matter what time zone you're in, opening an international account with Lloyds TSB will help you make the most of your money and build your future.

Available in a choice of up to 3 currencies – sterling, euro or US dollar – you can access your money 24/7 thanks to our Internet Banking and PhoneBank services. To ensure worldwide access to your money, we'll provide you with a debit card in the currency of your international account, plus a cheque book if you're a sterling account holder. You can also send and receive money worldwide with confidence via our easy and secure international money transfer service.

Additional Financial Services for Ex-pats

As your financial partner worldwide, we can also offer you much more than a day-to-day bank.

The award-winning International Mortgage Service is definitely worth investigating. Offering flexible mortgages in a choice of 10 major currencies for purchases in 11 countries, the International Mortgage Service is designed to take the worry of securing finance away from you so that you can enjoy the benefits of owning your dream home abroad. International Account customers also benefit from an incredible 50% reduction on mortgage arrangement fees!

International Mortgages are provided by Lloyds TSB Bank plc offices in Hong Kong and Singapore.

When you're living and working abroad, it's really important to find a safe place for your savings. From the competitive rates on Fixed Term Deposits to the instant access of our International Bonus Saver or the higher potential returns of Offshore Limited Edition Deposits, we are ideally placed to help you look after your hard-earned savings.

And if it's investment advice you're after, speak to one of our Financial Advisers. They can provide advice on a suitable strategy and service for you.

Globally At Your Service, 24/7

Our network of offices spans the globe from the west coast of the United States to the east coast of China. You'll also find us in many international financial centres across North America, Europe, Africa, the Middle East and Asia, making it simple to bank with us, talk to us and meet us face-to-face.

Always available online and on the phone, 24 hours a day, 365 days a year, challenge us to show you how we can make your financial life smoother and more straightforward, whatever time zone you plan to work in.

Four simple steps to opening a Lloyds TSB International Account

1. Confirm your eligibility:

You're eligible for an international account if:

- You are a personal customer aged 18 and over
- You have either:
  - A gross annual income of £50,000 (or currency equivalent)
  - Or over £25,000 (or currency equivalent) to invest with Lloyds TSB within 3 months of account opening.

2. Make sure you have the following information at hand:

- A valid email address
- Passport or ID card
- Income details
- Your addresses for the past 3 years
- Your current account details if you're an existing Lloyds TSB customer
- If you need a joint account, all of the above for the second applicant.

3. Complete an application form:

Complete an international account application form, available online at:

http://www.lloydstsb-offshore.com/international/account/apply/

Simple to complete, this should take you no more than 15 minutes!

We'll send you a confirmation email upon receipt, plus details of the supporting documents that you will need to send to us.

4. Forward your supporting documents:

Once we've received your supporting documents, if your application is successful, we will then:

- Open your account and send you a welcome letter within 5 working days
- Send your debit card within 10 working days.

For further information about our range of financial services for overseas workers, please contact our team of International Banking Advisers on **+44 (0)1624 638000** or visit **www.lloydstsb-offshore.com**

Issued by Lloyds TSB Offshore Limited and Lloyds TSB Bank (Gibraltar) Limited.

PO Box 160, 25 New Street, St. Helier, Jersey JE4 8RG. Registered in Jersey, number 4029. Regulated by the Jersey Financial Services Commission. We abide by the Jersey Code of Practice for Consumer Lending.

Deposits held with Lloyds TSB Offshore Limited are covered by the Jersey Depositor's Compensation Scheme which came into effect on 6 November 2009.

The scheme compensates people who have money in current and deposit accounts in Jersey, up to a maximum of £50,000 of deposits per individual depositor, per Jersey banking group. The compensation is payable, irrespective of which country the customer lives in. The Minister for Economic Development has designated that accounts held with the Jersey branches of Lloyds TSB Bank plc, Lloyds TSB Offshore Limited and Bank of Scotland plc will be regarded as one bank for the purpose of paying compensation to depositors. This means that where a depositor has accounts with more than one bank in the same group, collectively deposits in those accounts will only be protected up to £50,000 in total. Customers should refer to the International Finance section of the States of Jersey website for further information.

www.gov.je

The Isle of Man branch of Lloyds TSB Offshore Limited is licensed by the Isle of Man Financial Supervision Commission. Business Address: PO Box 111, Peveril Buildings, Peveril Square, Douglas, Isle of Man IM99 1JJ.

Lloyds TSB Offshore Limited is a deposit taker licensed by the Isle of Man Financial Supervision Commission (FSC). Under the terms of the license, deposits are covered by the Isle of Man Depositors' Compensation Scheme (DCS).

The DCS compensates people who have money in current or deposit accounts in the Isle of Man with up to £50,000 of net deposits per individual depositor, per licensed deposit taker.

This means that a maximum of £50,000 compensation is payable per individual depositor. The DCS covers all individuals irrespective of which country they live in and non individual depositors (including charities, trusts and businesses) to a maximum of £20,000.

Further details can be obtained from the Isle of Man FSC website: http://www.gov.im/fsc/investor/dep_comp.xml

Lloyds TSB Offshore Limited is a Jersey registered company that is a wholly owned subsidiary of Lloyds TSB Bank plc. Lloyds TSB Bank plc is incorporated in the United Kingdom, regulated by the UK Financial Services Authority and is part of the Lloyds Banking Group. Lloyds TSB Offshore Limited places funds with Lloyds TSB Bank plc. Prospective depositors should satisfy themselves as to the financial standing of Lloyds TSB Offshore Limited and its parent based upon publicly available information. An abridged version of Lloyds TSB Offshore Limited's latest annual financial statements is available on our website at www.lloydstsb-offshore.com

Lloyds TSB Bank (Gibraltar) Limited. Registered office: 323 Main Street, Gibraltar. Registered in Gibraltar, no 99982. Regulated and authorised by the Gibraltar Financial Services Commission for the conduct of banking, investment and insurance mediation business. Lloyds TSB Bank (Gibraltar) Limited is a participant in the Gibraltar Deposit Guarantee Scheme ("the Scheme") established under the Deposit Guarantee Scheme Act, 1997. Details of the Scheme are available on request.

The information contained in this advertorial does not constitute an invitation to buy or the solicitation of an offer to sell securities or accept deposits or to provide any other products or services in any jurisdiction to any person to whom it is unlawful to make such an offer or solicitation, nor should it be construed to constitute any investment advice.

Legislation or regulations in your home jurisdiction may prohibit you from entering into such a transaction with us. We reserve the right to make final determination on whether you are eligible for any products or services.

Residents or Nationals of certain jurisdictions may be subject to exchange controls and should seek independent advice before entering into any transactions with us.

Rules and Regulations made under the Financial Services and Markets Act 2000 for the protection of investors, including the Financial Services Compensation Scheme, do not apply to the Financial Service business of companies within the Lloyds Banking Group carried out from offices outside of the United Kingdom.

The currency of your mortgage must either match the local currency of the property's location or the currency of your primary income.

This product and service is not available to residents or nationals of countries where not permitted by local laws or regulations. It is your responsibility to ensure you comply with relevant laws. The International Mortgage Service is not applicable to certain types of properties and is subject to us being able to obtain an independent valuation.

Please note that the service is principally designed for customers planning to purchase properties outside their country of residence. We can provide mortgages for owner occupation in Hong Kong and Singapore, but not in other countries. Legislation or regulations in your home jurisdiction may prohibit you from entering into such a transaction with us. We reserve the right to make final determination on whether you are eligible for any products or services.

Residents or Nationals of certain jurisdictions may be subject to exchange controls and should seek independent advice before entering into any transactions with us.

YOUR HOME IS AT RISK IF YOU DO NOT KEEP UP REPAYMENTS ON A MORTGAGE OR OTHER LOAN SECURED ON IT.

The paid up capital and reserves of Lloyds TSB Offshore Limited was £439m as at 31st December 2008.

Lloyds TSB Offshore Holdings Limited has registered the business name of Lloyds TSB International in Jersey and has licensed it to Lloyds TSB Offshore Limited. Lloyds TSB (Gibraltar) Limited has registered the business name of Lloyds TSB International in Gibraltar.

As soon as we started planning the move last March, I began to consider the financial implications. I visited NZ in July and a former RAF colleague there gave me advice on a range of brokers, and said that, in his view, No1currency were the best.

Establishing a base involved lots of financial planning: I had to set up a new house, buy a car and transfer my family's belongings. No1currency provided an absolutely top-class personal service.

Overall, they saved me a significant amount of money, especially in comparison with the high street banks, in terms of charges and foreign exchange rates. The best financial advice I can offer anyone considering emigrating is to look at the market and remember that you do have an alternative to the high street banks.

To find out how a foreign exchange specialist can benefit you, you can visit No1currency online at www.no1currency.com or speak directly to a specialist on 0800 840 2887.

ALTERNATIVES FOR INVESTING SURPLUS INCOME

There are really only three types of objectives in investment: growth, income, and growth with income. The choice of one main objective usually involves some sacrifice in regard to the other. A high degree of capital appreciation generally implies a lower level of income and vice versa. Growth with income is an ideal, but generally it means some growth with some income, not a maximization of both. Ultimately, the objective is the preservation of capital in bad times and the increase of wealth in good ones, but your adviser cannot perform miracles. If they are lucky enough to catch the market in an upward phase, as in the case of the buoyant equities market at the beginning of 2010, they may be able to show quick results, but normally investment is a process that pays off over a longer period and through the course of varying market cycles.

The prolonged 'bear' market in equities, which preceded the last pre-financial crisis bull market, exposed the fallibility of fund managers. Few foresaw the length or depth of the decline in equity prices, or reacted by switching their clients' funds into stable fixed-interest securities before heavy losses were incurred. History may be repeating itself: this is hardly the moment to be considering stock exchange investment until you are satisfied that share prices have bottomed out.

INVESTMENT THROUGH UK OR OFFSHORE MANAGED FUNDS

There are many investment opportunities in the offshore fund markets, from specialized funds in individual countries to international ones spread across many industries. There are equally many ways of investing: regular investments, lump-sum purchase of units, periodic and irregular investments. It is also possible to invest in commodity markets and there are specialists trading in gold, silver, diamonds, sapphires and metals generally. Another innovation is the currency fund referred to earlier, which regulates holdings of foreign exchange and aims to predict fluctuations in exchange rates.

Your consultant should be able not only to inform you of the various schemes available, but also to advise on the degree of risk, the quality of management available and the combination of investments most likely to achieve your aims.

In the meantime, the alternative of simply putting your money on deposit with a bank or building society is hardly attractive with present interest rates. However, there is now a concession to non-residents – interest is paid without tax being deducted at source. You will have to inform your bank about your non-resident status. A building society may also require you to open a separate, non-resident account.

You may still be assessed for income tax on any interest earned in the year of your return to the UK. For this reason, there are a number of advantages in taking up the facilities that UK banks offer non-residents to open an account in one of the established tax havens, notably the Channel Islands and the Isle of Man.

In all cases, though, there are important tax considerations before you return to the UK. You should discuss these with your adviser at least six months before then if you can, so that the necessary plans can be drawn up in light of the current and pending taxation regime.

SCHOOL FEES PLANNING

There are many schemes available for school fees planning. These schemes aim to provide you with a tax-free income at a specified date for a predetermined length of time. They need not necessarily be used for educational purposes, and some readers may feel that if the employer is paying school fees, as is often the case, there is no need to take out such a policy. However, parents should bear in mind that it is highly advisable not to interrupt children's education, and taking out such a policy would obviously be a good way of ensuring that your child could go on with their education at the same school, even if your employment with that employer ended.

BASIC PLANNING POINTS

There are a number of basic planning points for expatriates to bear in mind, whatever their nationality of origin or place of work.

Two tax regimes

Usually there will be two tax regimes to consider: the home tax regime and the host tax regime. Almost invariably these will operate in different ways. The interaction between the two can be complex, but it is a vital part of sound financial planning.

Advice based on only the host or home country's rules is best avoided; what works in the UK may not work over there and vice versa. Therefore, potential British expats should read and understand the advice provided in Chapter 5 relating to the UK taxation aspects of working abroad and review carefully the summary of the taxation regime to which they plan to transfer (contained on the website for which you have a password).

Fundamentals that do not change

While tax rules will vary from country to country, many of the fundamentals of financial planning apply across the globe. For example, it will always make sense to hold a rainy-day cash reserve in a readily accessible deposit account. For expatriates, that might mean two cash reserves – one in their host currency and one in their home currency.

While being an expatriate may offer tax advantages, tax must not become the only reason for doing something. So, for example, investment decisions should firstly be made on investment grounds, with tax then being considered only in terms of the structuring of the investment, eg whether the chosen investment fund is set up onshore or offshore.

Regular professional reviews are vital

All financial plans must be reviewed regularly. Laws can change with great speed, rendering last year's tax-efficient plan this year's no-go area. The UK has seen plenty of examples of this in recent years, some of which have had a direct impact on expatriates. No doubt there will be more to come in the next year or so. It is particularly important to review plans a year or so before returning home – if sufficient advance warning is available.

If in doubt, the expatriate should always seek professional advice. The combination of different legal and tax regimes can make what would be a simple matter for the ordinary UK employee subject to UK tax highly complex for the expatriate counterpart. As a general rule, only the larger financial and accountancy firms will possess the necessary expertise.

PLANNING FOR DEPARTURE FROM THE UK

The sooner the would-be expatriate takes professional advice on financial planning the better. There will usually be a number of decisions to be made and changes to be undertaken, all of which are best not handled hastily. These are covered in the following sections.

Dealing with the home

As a general rule, leaving a property empty while overseas is best avoided, as there will always be a concern about vandalism or occupation by squatters. From a financial planning viewpoint, an empty property is a poor use of capital. It will yield no income but continue to generate costs such as general maintenance and, probably, mortgage interest. If the home will not be occupied by family members while the employee is working overseas, the real choice is whether it should be sold or rented out.

The case for selling is that it removes the problem of looking after a property from a distance and clears an outstanding mortgage debt. Some people will prefer to sell rather than have strangers (ie tenants) in their home. Selling property will also produce a lump sum to invest, but this may create its own problems in terms of investment risk, as the money will normally be earmarked for future property purchase on return to the UK. Of course, selling your home in today's market is hardly attractive.

Conversely, the major advantage of renting out property is that it allows the expatriate to retain a foothold in the UK residential property market. There are plenty of cautionary tales of expatriates who sold up only to find that, on their return several years later, they could not afford to buy the equivalent of their former property because of price increases during their absence. The case for letting and insuring your house while you are away is stronger today than before the 'credit crunch' wreaked havoc on property values, and some explanation on how to do this with professional advice is presented later in this chapter.

Pension benefits

In this area it is important to determine how the expatriate's employment will be structured. Will they be employed by the UK employer or will the contract of employment be moved to an overseas employer, possibly a subsidiary?

If the expatriate remains employed by the UK company, then the employee can remain in that employer's occupational pension scheme unless the transfer abroad is permanent. An expatriate working for an overseas employer may retain membership of their UK pension scheme, subject to a number of conditions specified by HMRC. The most notable of these is that the pension entitlement must be based on the remuneration that would have applied had the employment been in the UK.

Expatriates with personal pensions are less favourably treated. If they are not resident for tax purposes, then neither they nor their employer can make personal pension contributions in respect of their overseas earnings. This could mean that pension-linked life cover has to be cancelled. Any remuneration package for the expatriate will need to take account of the pension position in terms of the impact on benefit entitlement and any foreign tax liabilities that might arise.

Ancillary employee benefits

Alongside pension rights, there will also be other benefit entitlements that need to be addressed as part of the expatriate's financial planning. The most significant of these is adequate private medical insurance, and the provision of expatriate medical cover is discussed in detail in Chapter 10. Permanent health insurance (income protection cover) should also be reviewed in the context of overseas employment.

Existing investments

As a broad rule, existing investments do not need to be disturbed ahead of departure from the UK, other than as part of normal financial planning:

- ISAs can continue to be held by non-UK residents with unchanged tax advantages.
- Unit trusts, shares and life insurance policies can all be retained. Although these may give rise to a UK tax liability (at no more than the basic rate), for a non-UK resident what limited potential tax savings are available by moving offshore would probably be offset by the costs of sale and reinvestment.
- Deposit accounts are an exception to the general rule. A non-UK resident can request to receive interest without declaration of tax from UK bank and building society accounts. Strictly speaking such interest is not tax-free and would be taken into account by HMRC when considering how any claim to use personal allowances was applied. For this and other tax-related reasons, the normal advice is that the expatriate should open an offshore bank account – typically in the Channel Islands or Isle of Man – and close UK-based deposits. Interest from offshore accounts is paid gross and will be free of UK tax while the expatriate is non-UK resident.
- New investments ahead of departure should only be made after seeking professional advice. There may be opportunities to structure fresh investments to ensure that profits arrive only once the investor is free of UK tax liabilities.

FINANCIAL PLANNING WHILE OVERSEAS

Provided that the advance preparation has been satisfactory, the best financial planning action that the new expatriate can take in the first few months overseas is to do nothing. The reason for this is that it will take the new expatriate at least this period to adjust to the new life and pattern of expenditure. Once settled into a routine, the expatriate will be much more aware of what they can save on a regular basis.

Existing investments

A change introduced by the 1998 Budget significantly reduced the capital gains tax advantages of being an expatriate. As a general rule, for the expatriate who has been resident and UK ordinarily resident for at least four out of the seven tax years before departure overseas and who will be non-UK resident and not UK ordinarily resident for less than five tax years, any capital gains realized on investments held before leaving the UK will remain subject to UK capital gains tax. For these 'short-term' expatriates, the 1998 change limits the scope for realizing large gains, as might, for example, have accrued from the exercise of share options. Even for the expatriate who expects to be abroad for five or more tax years, caution is necessary until the five-year point is reached; a premature return to the UK could occur for any number of reasons, including health, business or even war. Be aware also of changes in the indexation rules relating to capital gains.

Income from UK shares and unit trusts will usually continue to be subject to UK tax, which will generally not be reclaimable. There may also be a liability in the host country, although this will often be reduced or eliminated as a result of double taxation agreements.

New investments

Aside from monies placed in Channel Islands/Isle of Man deposit accounts (see above), professional advice should always be sought before making investments while overseas. Ideally the advice should be from a firm regulated in the UK by the Financial Services Authority (FSA). Any advice should take into account potential host-country tax liabilities – a point sometimes overlooked by UK-based advisers.

The obvious first port of call for new investments is the offshore financial centres, including Luxembourg, Bermuda and Dublin, as well as the islands closer to home. While certain offshore investments can offer tax benefits to expatriates, these may be offset by higher charges than apply in the UK. Investments made while overseas will usually escape UK capital gains tax provided that gains are realized before the tax year of return to the UK.

Consideration must always be given to what happens to the investment on return to the UK because the tax-efficient investment for the non-UK resident can turn into a tax-inefficient investment for the UK resident. This can be a particular problem if an overseas employment is terminated at short notice.

Expatriates should avoid committing themselves to fixed-term savings contracts as a way of accumulating funds while non-resident. Lack of flexibility can be a serious drawback in many of these schemes, although they are heavily promoted.

Share options

The tax treatment of share options held by expatriates is a highly complex subject. For example, under an unapproved scheme, a UK tax liability will arise on exercise by a non-UK-resident employee if the option was granted when the employee was UK resident. Professional advice should be sought before any action is taken, including the initial grant of an option.

THE UK EXPATRIATE – PLANNING FOR RETURN

In an ideal world, every expatriate would spend the year before return to the UK putting their financial plans in order. In practice, there may be a last-minute rush, either because the expatriate was too busy with other matters or because the return home was earlier than originally intended.

Pre-return planning is as important as pre-departure planning. The aims should be to minimize the overall tax liabilities on investments before arrival in the UK, and to ensure that any new plans put in place are appropriate upon return to the UK. This will require professional advice, which should begin in the tax year before that in which the return to the UK will take place.

The planning will need to consider UK tax rules alongside host-country tax rules. It may be better to suffer UK tax – currently at a maximum rate of 40 per cent – rather than host-country tax. In some instances, it could even be worth spending a few days in a third country and realizing profits at that interim stage, before becoming UK tax resident but after ceasing to be host-country tax resident.

For 'short-term' expatriates, there will only be scope to avoid UK capital gains tax on investments acquired while overseas, provided that they are not sold in the tax year of return to the UK. The old planning trick of 'bed and breakfast' – selling one day and buying back the next – to realize a gain but to retain the investment is no longer effective. However, the same result can be achieved if one spouse sells and the other buys.

If offshore deposit accounts are used, usually these should be closed immediately before return to the UK so that all interest is crystallized free of UK tax. UK deposit accounts will automatically give rise to taxable interest in the tax year of return, even if interest is paid before the date of physical return.

LETTING AND INSURING YOUR HOME WHILE ABROAD

Most home owners going to live abroad for a limited period will be looking for a tenant to live in their house or flat while they are away. There is, of course, an obvious alternative, which is to sell, but then there is the question of storage of your effects – the average storage charge for the contents of a typical three-bedroomed house will be more than £75 per week – and, more to the point, the fact that when you do return to this country you will have no place of your own to go to. Even if you do not intend to return to the house you lived in when you come back, it may be advisable to retain ownership because your house represents a fairly inflation-indexed asset. Conversely, if you believe that the UK housing market in 2009 was so overheated that the easing in house prices from the 2008 high is likely to degenerate into an even more serious decline while you are abroad, there is a strong case for selling up if you are leaving now.

The case for letting, as opposed to leaving your home empty, hardly needs to be put today when crime and vandalism are constantly in the headlines. Long ago, the government, recognizing the difficulties for owners leaving their homes and wishing to encourage the private landlord, introduced the Assured Shorthold Tenancy (AST) in the 1988 Housing Act, making letting safer and easier. The 1988 Act was further amended by the 1996 Housing Act, making an AST the market 'default' type of tenancy agreement as long as certain criteria are met. An AST guarantees possession to a landlord at the end of a tenancy. Lettings to large companies where the occupier is a genuine employee being housed by the company temporarily are excluded from the Act and are simply contractual tenancies (referred to as Company Lets); these types of tenancy are quite common in bigger cities, particularly in central London. It is not possible here to define the various differences between these two forms of tenancy. It should be noted that a letting to a member of the Diplomatic Corps based in the UK has some risks and complications. Generally a court order for possession can be executed but successfully imposing any type of monetary court order (for rent arrears or damages) can be very problematical as the individual would be outside the jurisdiction of British courts and may well have returned to their country of origin. It is essential, therefore, for the owner to obtain proper advice before deciding which form of tenancy to choose.

Assured shorthold tenancies

1. These can be for any length of time if both parties agree, although it is most common to start with either 6- or 12-month fixed-term tenancies. However, the landlord will not be able to seek a court order for possession before the end of 6 months unless there has been a breach of the tenancy agreement.

2. The rent will be a market rent, although the tenant may apply to the Rent Assessment Committee during the first 6 months if they feel it is too high. However, on the expiry of the original term, the owner is entitled to request the tenant to pay a higher rental and the tenant is not entitled to go back to the Rent Assessment Committee. It is common to have rent increase clauses within longer-term tenancy agreements.

3. Two months' notice has to be served that the landlord requires possession on a certain date (but not before the end of the fixed term); if the tenant refuses to leave, the courts must grant possession.

Additional and amended provisions (grounds) for a mandatory possession order were included in the 1996 Act, such as two months' arrears of rent, and there are a number of discretionary grounds on which possession can be granted, even if the owner does not wish to return to the house. However, there is one specific disadvantage if the owner is unfortunate enough to have a tenant who refuses to leave when the owner wishes to reoccupy and the landlord then has to apply to court. The judicial system in the UK can occasionally take some time to operate, particularly if a local court happens to be busy. This unfortunately can extend the period needed before a possession order is granted by the court and owners would be well advised to take out one of the various insurance policies now available to cover hotel costs, legal fees, etc and, as a minimum, to make sure that either alternative accommodation is temporarily available in the event of an earlier than expected return home, or that the procedures for terminating the tenancy are instigated well before the projected date of return.

As must now be obvious to the reader, the complexity of the rules does nothing to encourage owners to attempt to let the property or manage their home themselves while away, and the need for an experienced property management firm becomes even more important than in the past. A solicitor might be an alternative but, although possibly more versed in the legal technicalities than a managing agent, they will not be in a position to market the property to the best advantage (if at all) and solicitors' practices do not usually have staff experienced in property management, able to carry out inspections, deal with repairs, arrange inventories and to handle the many and various problems that often arise.

Having obtained advice to ensure that you have the correct form of tenancy, you now need to find an experienced and reliable letting and management agent. Ideally, they should be a member of the Royal Institution of Chartered Surveyors (RICS), the Association of Residential Letting Agents (ARLA) or the National Association of Estate Agents (NAEA) specializing in property management, who will be well versed in both the legal and financial aspects of the property market.

Property management

Property management is a rather specialized role and you should check carefully that the agent you go to can give you the service you need, that they are not just an accommodation broker, and that they are equipped to handle the letting, collection of rent and management of your property, as well as the more common kinds of agency work. Your solicitor should be able to advise you here, but to some extent you will have to rely on your own judgement of how ready and satisfactory the agent's answers are to the sort of questions you are going to ask. There are several specialized firms well equipped to deal with your affairs, but it is best to stick to members of RICS, ARLA and NAEA as they and their activities are all regulated by their professional bodies.

In the first place the agent you instruct should have a clear idea of the kind of tenant you expect for your property, and preferably be able to show you that they do have people on their books who are looking for rented accommodation of this kind. Obviously the rent and the tenant you can expect will vary with what you have to offer, and an agent who understands the local market well will be able to advise on what additional fixtures and equipment you need to install in order to maximize the rental value. Equipping your house or flat to be a desirable 'let' and, therefore, marketable at a high rent can be an expensive exercise. For example, a business executive will expect wi-fi internet connection as well as a plasma TV set. A normal family house in a good area should attract someone like the executive of a multinational company who is in a similar, but reverse, position to your own: that is, someone working here on a contract basis for a limited period of time who may well provide a stable tenancy for the whole or a substantial part of your absence. A smaller house or flat would be more likely to attract a younger person who only wants the property for a limited period or who, at any rate, might be reluctant to accept a long-term commitment because of the possibility of a change in professional circumstances or marital status. Equally, if you are only going to be away for a shortish period like 6 to 12 months, you are going to be rather lucky to find a tenant whose needs exactly overlap with your absence. You will probably have to accept a slightly shorter period than your exact stay abroad.

For your part you should bear in mind that tenants, unlike house purchasers, are usually only interested in a property with almost immediate possession, but you should give the agent, wherever possible, at least four to six weeks' warning of your departure in order that interest may be built up by advertising, mailing out details, etc, over a period of time.

Rent

How much rent you can expect will also vary with what you have to offer and where it is, but the point to bear in mind is that rents are not usually subject to bargaining like the price of a house. Bargaining, if there is to be any, is more likely to occur over the terms of the lease, which are set out below. Do not, therefore, ask for an unrealistically high figure in the expectation that the tenant will regard this as a starting point for negotiation. Your agent, if they know the job, will be able to advise you on the rental you should ask, though if you have not had previous dealings with them it might be advisable to ask the agent to give you some instances of rentals being achieved in the market for similar accommodation. An offer that is a bit less than you had hoped for, but from a good tenant, might be worth taking in preference to a better one from somebody who, for various reasons, looks less reliable.

Terms of agreement

A property management agent should have, or be able to produce fairly quickly, a draft agreement to cover the specific situation of the overseas landlord. Member agents of the three professional bodies all have access to model agreements that take account of the various pieces of legislation and will have been drafted taking account of the Unfair Terms in Consumer Contract Regulations which impact heavily on what can and cannot be said in such agreements. You should show this to your solicitor if in doubt, and how well it is drafted will again be a pointer to how effective the agent concerned is likely to be. The document should cover at least the following points:

1. The intervals of payment – monthly or quarterly – and the length of lease.
2. How much the tenancy deposit is to be and where it will be held, and the process for dealing with damages disputes at the end of the tenancy.
3. An undertaking by the tenant to take steps to reasonably maintain the garden.
4. An undertaking by the tenant to pay for telephone and other services from the commencement of the lease, including council tax.

5. An undertaking to allow the landlord, or the agent, access to the property (upon lawful notice) for inspection and repair; and two months before the expiry of the lease to allow them to take other prospective tenants or purchasers round the property.

6. A clause stating that the lease is terminated if any of the other clauses are broken, although the wording has to be carefully drafted to avoid invalidating the agreement.

7. What you, as landlord, are responsible for in the way of repairs: usually the maintenance of the structure and furnishings of the property together with anything left in the property (eg the central heating boiler). You can exclude some items, such as the television, from your responsibility, but generally the tenant is only liable for specific damage to items left in the house and not for their general maintenance. The government has tightened up safety laws in respect of gas appliances. In November 1994 the Gas Safety (Installation & Use) Regulations 1994 were introduced, forcing landlords to take greater responsibility for the safety of their tenants by regularly servicing and repairing any gas appliances through a British Gas- or Corgi-registered company. A landlord has to provide a tenant annually with a Gas Safety Record. Heavy penalties will be enforced for failing to comply.

8. Any special restrictions you want to impose: if, for example, your house is full of valuable antiques you may wish to specify 'no small children'.

9. Notice under Sections 47 and 48 of the Landlord and Tenant Act 1987. The former should be on all rent demands; the latter, notifying the tenant of an address in England or Wales at which notices can be served on the landlord, need only be served once on a tenant at the beginning of a tenancy.

Although the agreement is probably the central document in the transactions involved in letting your house, it does not bring to an end all the things you have to think about. For instance, there is the important matter of the contents insurance. Letting your home to a third party is probably not covered in your policy and you will have to notify your insurers (and the people who hold your mortgage) that this is what you are doing. In many instances, insurance companies will not insure the contents if the property is to be let and you will need to check carefully that you have cover and switch to another company if it becomes necessary. (This is covered in greater detail on pages 102–03, under Insurance.) At the same time you would be wise to check that the contents insurance covers the full value of what you have left in the house. This check could be combined with making a proper inventory of the contents, which is in any case essential before tenants move into a furnished property. Making an exact inventory is quite a time-consuming business and you should bear in mind that it will also have to be checked at the end of the lease, when you may not be there. There are several firms that provide a specialist inventory service at both ends of the lease, covering dilapidations as well as items actually missing, for quite a modest charge which, incidentally, is deductible from the tax due from the letting. Any good management agent should be able to put you on to one of them or will provide an in-house inventory service.

It is also essential that landlords are aware of important fire regulations that have come into force concerning the supply of furniture and furnishings when letting out accommodation. The Furniture (Fire) (Safety) Regulations 1988, introduced for all landlords on 1 January 1997, make it an offence to supply furniture which does not comply with the regulations concerning fire resistance. Essentially, it covers all upholstery and upholstered furnishings, including loose fittings and permanent or loose covers. These must comply with the following three tests, each of which measures the flame-retardant properties of the furnishings: Cigarette Test; Match Test; Ignitability Test. Heavy penalties will be enforced for failing to comply. Your managing agent should be able to provide details of exactly what furniture should be removed or replaced and when.

Finding the tenant and getting a signature on the agreement marks the beginning rather than the end of the property management firm's responsibilities. Broadly, these fall under two headings: the collection of rental and the management of the property. The rent is collected from the tenant, usually on a standing order basis, under the terms – monthly or quarterly – as set out in the agreement; and, in the event of persistent non-payment, the agent will instruct solicitors on your behalf to issue a County Court summons, or if you have taken out rental or legal insurance, the agent will contact the insurance company.

What can you expect from the agent?

The letting and residential managing agent should be regulated. Most commonly this means being a member of the Association of Residential Letting Agents, ARLA. This is the only professional body that is solely concerned with letting and renting and the management of residential property. To be a member of ARLA, the agent must be fully compliant with client accounts, professional indemnity insurance and the ARLA bonding scheme. Every ARLA member office must employ staff with relevant qualifications. Should it be felt that the agent has not performed satisfactorily, ARLA operates an independent redress system.

To check whether or not an agent is an ARLA member, or to find one, or for advice on letting your property or buying to let, visit www.arla.co.uk.

Management is a more complex subject, but an experienced property management agent should be able to supply you with a list of the services that they can undertake. It is, therefore, also a checklist of the kind of eventualities that may crop up in your absence which, broadly speaking, relate to the collection of rent, the payment of charges such as service charges and insurance, arrangements for repairs to the fabric of the building and its contents, garden maintenance, and forwarding mail.

Thus, apart from the basic business of collecting the rent, the agent can also pay, on your behalf, any charges on the property (eg ground rent, water rates and insurance) that your contract with the tenant does not specify should be paid by them. There may also be annual maintenance agreements to pay in respect of items like central heating plant and the washing machine.

Then there is the question of what to do about repairs. As we have indicated earlier, whatever you manage to get the tenant to agree to take care of under the terms of the lease, there are certain responsibilities for maintenance and repair that you have to accept by virtue of your status as a landlord. If repairs are necessary, you will simply have to trust the agent to obtain fair prices for you.

On the other hand, except in the case of essential repairs that affect the tenant's legal rights of enjoyment of the property, you can ask your agent to provide estimates for having the work carried out, so that your approval must be obtained before the job is put in hand. Bear in mind, though, that in certain parts of the world the postal system may not be all that reliable. You may, therefore, find it a good idea to put a clause in the management contract giving the agent freedom to proceed with the best estimate if they do not hear from you within a specified period. For the same reason it is also wise to ask the agent to send you a formal acknowledgement of receipt of any special or new instructions you have given. An example of this might be an instruction to inspect the property at regular intervals.

To summarize, the responsibilities of a property management agent are as follows:

- collection of rent;
- day-to-day tenant liaison;
- general supervision of the property;
- payment of service charges and insurance;
- arranging repairs to the building and contents;
- payment of charges on the property;
- payment of maintenance agreements;
- obtaining prices/estimates for repairs.

Depending on how many concessions you have to make to the tenant to get them to sign the lease, there may be other articles for which repair and maintenance remain your responsibility. These may include the washing machine, TV and the deep freeze. Such responsibilities should be set out in the management contract and you should give the agent the details of any guarantees or maintenance contracts relating to them and photocopies of the actual documents for reference. If no such arrangements apply, you should list the manufacturers' names and the model number and age of each item so that the agent can get the manufacturer to send the repair people along equipped with the right spares.

It is very important that a third party, other than you and the tenant, should be in possession of all this information, particularly when there is likely to be more than one tenancy during your absence; and it is a competent management agent, rather than friends, relatives or even a solicitor, who will be best equipped in this case to find new tenants, to check their references, to draw up new agreements and supervise the handover of the tenancy.

Costs and tax

The costs of all these services vary according to the nature of the package you need. For example, the charge for letting and collection is usually 10 per cent of annual rental. In the case of management services, expect to find additional charges made (usually 5 to 7 per cent of the annual rent). These are reasonable fees for the quite considerable headaches involved. We have shown enough of them here to indicate that not only is it virtually impossible to administer a tenancy yourself from a distance, but also that these are not matters to be left to an amateur – friend or relative – however well intentioned. In real terms the agent's charges may be diluted because they are deductible against the tax levied in the UK against rental income.

Expatriates letting their homes also derive a further benefit in respect of capital gains tax. Generally, if you let your principal residence, when you come to sell it you can claim exemption from CGT only for those years in which you lived in it yourself. However, if you let it because you are absent abroad this does not apply, provided you come back to live in the house before you sell it.

Finally, in this context, it is worth pointing out that some mortgage lenders are now prepared to consider giving mortgages to expatriates for the purchase of a property in the UK and to allow them to lease that property for the period of their stay overseas. Up to 90 per cent of the purchase price is available at normal rates of interest. This is an attractive proposition for expatriates, particularly for young executives and professional people who have not yet bought a home in the UK but are earning a substantial income in, say, the Middle East, and for older expatriates perhaps thinking of a retirement home in the UK.

Some agencies supply details of the lenders offering this facility, or you could approach a lender directly and explain your position. Should you buy a house as an expatriate and then let it until you return, the earlier recommendation that you leave the management of the property to an experienced and competent agent still applies. If a UK property is bought purely as an investment, you would have to time its sale carefully to avoid liability for CGT.

Taxation is too complex a subject and varies considerably in its effects on the individual, preventing any practical advice being offered other than to state the importance of employing the services of an accountant in your absence, but it must be stressed that rent received in the UK is considered unearned income, and is subject to UK tax laws. A scheme now operates whereby letting agents, or where there are no letting agents, tenants of a non-resident landlord, must deduct tax at the basic rate from the rental income, and pay tax quarterly to Her Majesty's Revenue & Customs. Those landlords who wish to receive their income with no tax deducted can apply to CNRL for approval. Forms are available from: CNRL (non-residents), St John's House, Merton Road, Bootle, Merseyside L69 9BB; tel: 0151 472 6208/6209.

Insurance

One important point that is often overlooked by people who let their house or flat is the necessity of notifying the insurers that a change of occupancy has taken place. Insurance policies only cover occupancy by the insured, not the tenants, though they can be extended to do so on payment of what is usually only a small additional premium. As many insurance companies will not cover properties that are or will be let, notifying the company concerned becomes essential.

What worries insurance companies much more is if the house is left unoccupied for any length of time. If you look at your policy you will see that it lapses if you leave your house empty for more than 30 days or so – a point that is sometimes forgotten by people who go away on extended holidays. If you are going abroad and leave the house empty – maybe because you have not yet succeeded in finding a tenant – the insurers will usually insist that you turn off the main services and that the premises are inspected regularly by a qualified person. That means someone like a letting agent, not a relative or friend. Even if you have let the house without an agent, it may still be advisable to get one to look after the place. A situation could easily occur where the tenant moves out, leaving the place empty and without satisfactory steps having been taken from an insurance point of view. Furthermore, if the worst happens and the house is broken into or damaged, it is imperative that the insurers are notified right away. The effects of damage can be made worse if they are not rapidly attended to, and insurers do not hold themselves responsible for anything that happens between the time the insured eventuality occurs and the time they are notified of it. For instance, if your house is broken into and, a few days later, vandals get in through a broken point of entry and cause further damage, you would not be covered for that second incident unless the insurers had been notified of the first break-in.

Valuable contents are best put into storage and insured there. Pickfords, for instance, charges a premium of 12.5 per cent of the storage charge, inclusive of insurance premium tax (IPT). For contents worth more than £25,000, a reduction may be negotiable. For very high-value items, safe deposit boxes are becoming popular, but from an everyday point of view, the important thing is to make sure you are insured for full values. If you insure contents for £15,000 and the insurer's assessors value them at £20,000 you will only get three-quarters of your claim. To keep insured values in line with rising costs, an index-linked policy would be the best buy for anyone contemplating a long stay abroad. A policy specially written for expatriates is available from Europea-IMG Ltd: the Weavers Homeowners Policy. It also offers expatriate motor insurance on private cars being used overseas. All insurance premiums are now subject to IPT.

Insuring at full value, incidentally, is equally important when it comes to insuring contents and personal belongings in your residence abroad. Many items will cost much more locally if you have to replace them than they did at the time they were originally bought. There are a few such policies available in the UK; so it may be possible to insure in the country concerned.

Finally, but most importantly, you should insure against legal and hotel costs when letting your house. Although in principle the legal instruments for quick repossession exist, events have shown that a bloody-minded tenant with a committed lawyer can spin things out to their advantage for almost an indefinite period. Premiums, which can be offset against rental income, are in the region of £85 a year.

Also recently introduced are rental protection policies, some providing limited cover at a relatively low premium, others covering the higher rental amounts, which are naturally more expensive. In addition, these policies will normally cover legal and other costs. However, due to the wide cover involved, the insurance companies usually insist on their own credit check and the employment of a managing agent, as well as the usual references.

The same companies will add, as an extra, buildings and/or contents cover when the property is let, often at rates that are competitive to the premiums charged when the property was owner-occupied.

Checklist: Financial planning and the expatriate

1. Check out your financial adviser's credentials.
2. Consider the pros and cons of offshore funds.
3. Check your life assurance policy to make sure that there are no restrictions about overseas living.
4. Consider tax-efficient ways to save for school fees.
5. If your company has a pension scheme in the country of residence, make sure you become acquainted with its rules and local legislation through your financial adviser.
6. Notify your financial adviser at least 12 months before the tax year of your return so that they can mitigate tax liabilities.

Checklist: Letting your home

1. Take professional advice about the most appropriate type of tenancy and the likely rental level, terms, etc.
2. Remember to take account of notice periods when planning your return.
3. Ask your property management agent to explain to you what kinds of people they have on the books.
4. Try to give the agent six to eight weeks' warning prior to the rental date.
5. Seek advice from your solicitor concerning the agent's draft contract.
6. Inform your insurance company (and your mortage lender) of your intention to let your home and check that your contents insurance covers the full value of what you have left in the house.
7. Make a full inventory of the contents.
8. Ensure that your furniture complies with fire regulations.
9. Provide your agent with details of any guarantees or maintenance contracts.
10. Put valuable possessions into storage.
11. Consider insuring against legal and hotel costs.

The section in this chapter on foreign exchange was provided by No1currency. The editor expresses his thanks for use of the material.

7

National Insurance, Benefits and Pensions

The desire to earn more money – and to pay less of it in tax and other deductions – looms large for many as a motive for going to work abroad. People who take this step are often temperamentally inclined to be strongly individualistic and self-reliant and, as such, many feel that they would rather fend for themselves when circumstances get difficult rather than rely on what they regard as 'state handouts'. Whatever the virtues of this attitude of mind may be, those who have it are more to be commended for their sense of independence than their common sense. The fact is that during your working life in the UK you will have made compulsory National Insurance contributions and you are therefore eligible for benefits in the same way as if you had paid premiums into a private insurance scheme; drawing a state benefit you are entitled to is no more taking a handout than making an insurance claim.

National Insurance has another feature in common with private insurance: you lose your entitlement to benefit if you fail to keep up your contributions, though the circumstances under which this would happen are different from, and more gradual than in private schemes. Furthermore, you cannot immediately reactivate your eligibility for benefits in full if, your payments having lapsed for a period of time, you return to this country and once again become liable to make contributions. For instance, in order to qualify in full for a UK retirement pension you must have paid the minimum contribution for each year for at least 90 per cent of your working life. In the case of other benefits too, in order to qualify to get them, there must be a record of your having made a certain level of contributions in the two tax years governing that in which benefits are being claimed.

DWP AGENCIES

National Insurance provisions are handled by Executive Agencies of the Department for Work and Pensions (DWP) (website: www. dwp.gov.uk). The Contributions Agency deals with all contributions and insurability matters, while the Benefits Agency deals with all matters relating to social security benefits. Both Agencies may be accessed through the DWP website.

NI contribution matters for persons working abroad are handled by the Contributions Agency's International Services, Longbenton, Newcastle upon Tyne NE98 1YX; tel: 0845 915 4811. The International service can provide you with information on your National Insurance liability, voluntary contributions, retirement pension forecasts, health care and other benefits. Visit the website at www. inlandrevenue.gov.uk/nic/intserv/osc.htm. Matters relating to benefits are handled by the Benefit Agency's Pensions and Overseas Benefits Directorate at Tyneview Park, Newcastle upon Tyne NE98 1BA; tel: 0191 218 7777.

Leaflet NI 38, or for European Economic Area countries leaflet SA29, available from either agency at Newcastle, or from a local social security office, sets out the basic conditions relating to National Insurance and benefits abroad.

LIABILITY FOR CONTRIBUTIONS
WHILE ABROAD

If your employer in the UK sends you to work in another European Economic Area country or in a country with which the UK has a reciprocal agreement (these are listed in leaflet NI 38) for a period not expected to exceed that which is specified in the EC regulations or the reciprocal agreement (RA) involved, you will normally continue to be subject to the UK social security scheme for that period and you will be required to pay Class 1 contributions as though you were in the UK. (The specified period can vary between one year where the EC regulations apply and up to five years depending upon the reciprocal agreement involved.) If your employment unexpectedly lasts longer than 'the specified period', then for certain countries you may remain insured under the UK scheme with the agreement of the authorities in the country in which you are working. Your employer will obtain a certificate for you from the Contributions Agency, International Services, at Newcastle upon Tyne confirming your continued liability under the UK scheme, which you should present to the foreign authorities if required to confirm your non-liability under their scheme. This form, E101, is issued with European Health Cards which provide health care cover abroad for you and your family for the period of employment in another country.

If you are sent by your UK employer to an EU member state or to a country with which there is a reciprocal agreement in circumstances other than the above, eg for an initial period expected to exceed 12 months or for a period of indefinite duration, then normally you will cease to be liable to pay UK contributions from the date you are posted and will instead become liable to pay into the scheme of the country you are working in. Leaflet SA29 tells you about the European Community (EC) Regulations on social security and their effect on EU nationals. If you would like a copy of leaflet SA29 or would like more information, you can telephone or write to International Services. Alternatively you can get a copy of leaflet SA29 from your local social security office.

If you are sent by your employer to a country other than those in the EU or with which there is a reciprocal agreement, you will be liable to pay Class 1 contributions for the first 52 weeks of your posting provided your employer has a place of business in the UK, you were resident in the UK immediately before you took up employment abroad, you remain 'ordinarily resident' in the UK while you are abroad and you are under UK retirement age (currently 60 for women and 65 for men). If you are self-employed you must obtain forms E101/E102/E128.

MAKING VOLUNTARY CONTRIBUTIONS

For non-EU and non-RA countries, when your period of liability for Class 1 contributions ends, you may wish to pay voluntary Class 3 contributions to the UK scheme in order to protect your UK retirement/widow's pension entitlement. We will deal with the mechanics of this later, but at this stage it should be pointed out that if you are going abroad for a British-based firm you will be liable to make the same contributions as if you were employed in this country. For the 2009/10 tax years, if you earn more than £110 per week and up to £844 per week, you pay 11 per cent of the amount between the two. You can also pay an extra 1 per cent of any earnings over £844 per week. Your contribution will be deducted from your salary, as if you were still working in the UK. Payment of these contributions for the first 52 weeks of your employment abroad will make you eligible to receive incapacity or unemployment benefit and, in the case of a woman, maternity allowance, under the usual conditions applicable to those benefits, on your return to the UK – even though this may be some years later – because Class 1 contributions will be deemed to have been paid in the tax year(s) relevant to your claim. This is subject to the proviso that you remained 'ordinarily resident' in the UK during your absence. If you did not intend to sever your connection with the UK when you went abroad, continuing ordinary residence will usually be accepted. To establish ordinary residence you may need to show that you maintained a home or accommodation in the UK or stored your furniture in the UK during your absence. To maintain entitlement to UK retirement pension or widow's benefits, however, it will usually be necessary to pay Class 3 contributions after the Class 1 period has expired although this may not be necessary for the balance of the year – April to April – in which Class 1 liability ceased. The Contributions Agency, International Services, Room BP1303, Longbenton, Newcastle upon Tyne NE98 1ZZ can advise you about this. Remember always to quote your National Insurance number and the country involved when you write.

Class 1 contributions are not payable at all in respect of employment abroad if your employer has no place of business in the UK. However, if you work for an overseas government or an international agency such as the UN, you will be able to pay your share of the Class 1 contribution for the first 52 weeks of your employment abroad and so qualify on return to the UK for the benefits named in the previous paragraph.

You may, of course, have been a self-employed person paying the Class 2 rate of £2.40 a week for the 2009/10 tax year. These contributions also cover a more limited range of benefits – Jobseeker's Allowance (previously unemployment benefit) and injury or death caused by an industrial accident or prescribed disease are excluded

– but like Class 3 contributions, they can also be paid voluntarily if you go to work in an EU country or countries with which the UK has an RA agreement, provided you are gainfully occupied there. However, you need not pay Class 2 contributions just because you were self-employed before you went abroad. You can go to the voluntary Class 3 rate (which is a flat rate of £12.05 a week for the 2009/10 tax year), but if you want to qualify for incapacity benefit when you return to the UK, provided you were employed abroad you can switch back to Class 2 payments for the two tax years governing the benefit year in which you are due to return. Advice for those who are self-employed is available from the National Insurance Contributions Office, Self-Employment Services, Benton Park View, Newcastle upon Tyne NE98 1ZZ, or by ringing the Helpline (0845 915 4515) and quoting your National Insurance number.

These rates and conditions apply, of course, as much to women as to men. The right of married women to pay reduced rate contributions has been phased out. If you get married while working abroad you should write to International Services for leaflet CA13, which explains in more detail your National Insurance position as a married woman. A married woman may consider paying contributions in her own right (eg for retirement pension purposes). See leaflet NI 38.

Leaflet NI 38 contains a form at the back (CF83) which should be filled in when you want to start making voluntary payments. You can pay by annual lump sum, by arranging for someone in the UK to make regular payments for you, or through direct debit if you have a bank or building society in the UK or Channel Islands.

Class 2 and Class 3 contributions can be paid before the end of the sixth tax year following the one in which they were due. However, although you have six years in which to pay there is a limited period in which to pay at the relevant year's contribution rates. International Services can advise you about this. Whatever method you choose it is important that your contributions are paid on time. For further information see leaflet CA07 – *Unpaid and late paid contributions*. Also see CF411 *How to protect your State Retirement Pension*.

GETTING NI BENEFITS ABROAD

Thus far we have only mentioned the range of benefits available to you once you return to the UK. But is there any way you can become eligible for benefits while still abroad? Generally, the answer is that you can only receive retirement pensions and widow's benefits, but there are important exceptions in the case of EU countries and some others – a full list is given in leaflet NI 38 – with which the UK has reciprocal agreements. How those agreements affect you varies somewhat from country to country, but in essence they mean that the contributions you have paid in the UK count, for benefit purposes, as if you had paid them in the reciprocal agreement country, and vice versa. This is usually advantageous if you do become eligible for benefit while abroad because in relation to the cost of living – or even in absolute terms – UK benefits are lower than many foreign ones. You will, in general, have to pay contributions to the scheme of the country you are working in, so by the same token if you are going to a country with which the UK has a reciprocal agreement, you will have to decide if you want to pay voluntary contributions to the UK in order to maintain UK pension entitlement when you return here. The Contributions Agency can advise you on this. If you have not yet come under the scheme of a foreign country and are paying Class 1, 2 or 3 contributions to the UK while working abroad, then, if you think you are eligible for benefit, you should write to the Benefits Agency, Pensions and Overseas Benefits Directorate immediately the contingency governing your claim arises. One important point to bear in mind in this case, though, is that if benefit can be paid, you will only get paid at the UK rate, not that of similar welfare schemes of the country in which you are living. In many cases the latter may be much more generous than UK rates; furthermore, UK rates may bear very little relationship to the cost of living abroad.

In this connection it is also worth pointing out that the UK is by no means the top of the world league table when it comes to the percentage of the pay packet taken up by contributions to social services. In many of the EU countries, in particular, it is significantly higher. This is an important detail to discuss with a prospective employer, because the 'social wage' and what you have to put in to get it obviously have a bearing on the real value of the remuneration package you are being offered.

THE NHS AND HEALTH CARE BENEFITS

In one important instance UK benefits are actually more generous than those of many other countries. We refer here to the UK

National Health Service. But medical expenses incurred abroad are definitely not refunded by the NHS, which is only available to people living in this country; so, contrary to popular belief, you will no longer be able to get free NHS treatment in this country once you become permanently resident abroad. Many overseas countries do have reciprocal health agreements with the UK – once again a list is given on the HMRC site – but the services they provide are not exactly comparable with those of the British NHS. European Health Cards are available from the DSS or post offices and are essential documents in being able to access this reciprocal care. See also leaflet T5 – *Health Advice for Travellers Anywhere in the World*. The range of treatment provided free of charge varies considerably and it is advisable to take out private health insurance to cover eventualities where free medical attention is not, or is only partially, available. Leaflets giving information on the procedures you need to observe, both in the case of temporary spells and permanent residence abroad, are available from the Contributions Agency's International Services (tel: 0845 915 4811 or 44-191-225 4811 if calling from abroad).

CHILD BENEFITS WHILE WORKING ABROAD

There are various situations which, in different ways, affect your entitlement to receive child benefit while working abroad:

1. If you go abroad permanently, taking your children with you, your child benefits cease from the date of your departure. When you arrive in the new country you can only rely on that country's family benefit.
2. If you go to work in another EU country you will generally be insured under its social security legislation and so entitled to the local family allowances. If you are insured under another EU scheme but leave your children behind in the United Kingdom, you may still be entitled to family allowances from the EU country in which you are insured. If you remain insured under the UK scheme, child benefit may still be payable whether your children are in the United Kingdom or with you. If your children are not with you, you would have to maintain them by at least the weekly rate of child benefit after the first 56 days. If your children live with you but your spouse or partner is

insured under another EU scheme, you will be entitled to local family allowances. However, you may be paid a 'supplement' equal to the difference between the local rate and the UK rate of benefit if the UK rate is higher.

3.   If you have been sent abroad to work temporarily, for a period of not more than eight weeks, and you return within that time, benefit will continue to be paid whether or not you take your children with you. Child benefit orders cannot be cashed outside the UK, but you will be able to cash them when you return, provided each order is cashed within three months of the date stamped on it. After eight weeks of temporary absence, your eligibility for UK child benefit ceases unless you happen to be in one of the reciprocal agreement countries.

4.   You can also continue to be eligible for UK child benefit, even after eight weeks of absence, if in the relevant tax year at least half your earnings from the employment which took you abroad are liable to United Kingdom income tax. However, in this case your entitlement cannot be decided until your tax liability has been assessed.

5.   If a child is born abroad within eight weeks of the mother's departure from the United Kingdom and she is abroad only temporarily, child benefit may be paid from then until the end of the eight-week period of absence. If you wish to claim in these circumstances you should write to the Child Benefit Centre (Washington), PO Box 1, Newcastle upon Tyne NE88 1AA, quoting your child benefit number if you are already getting child benefit for another child.

6.   Special rules exist in respect of serving members of the forces and civil servants; persons falling into these categories should consult their paying officer or Establishments Division.

Full details of these schemes, including the form CH 181(TO) which you have to fill in before your departure, are set out in leaflet CH 6, available from your local Social Security office. Alternatively, you can get a copy by writing to the Information Division, Leaflet Unit, Block 4, Government Buildings, Honeypot Lane, Stanmore, Middlesex HA7 1AY.

UNEMPLOYMENT BENEFITS FOR JOB HUNTERS WITHIN THE EU

Under EU law you can go jobseeking for up to three months in most EU countries, provided you have been registered as unemployed in the UK for four weeks before departure. You are entitled to receive Jobseeker's Allowance on the day of departure and you actually register for work in the new country. While you are in the other country, you can continue drawing UK Jobseeker's Allowance via the employment services of the country you are in provided you follow their control procedures.

You should inform your local unemployment benefit office *in person* of your intention well in advance of your departure, and obtain from them leaflet UBL 22. The Pensions and Overseas Benefits Directorate of the Benefits Agency will then issue the authorization form E303 to you if you are going to France, Greece, Portugal, Spain, Germany or Italy and there is enough time before your departure. Otherwise, it will be sent to your address there. If you are going to another EU country, the form will be sent to a liaison office in the country concerned. Regardless of which country you are going to, ask your local unemployment benefits office to issue you with a letter of introduction. You should give this – and form E303 if you have it – to the employment services when registering for work in another EU country.

In practice, many EU countries have blocked this progressive move by putting obstacles in the way over such matters as residence permits – France is particularly bad in this respect – because the UK is not alone among European Union countries in having an unemployment problem. The good news is that if you do succeed in getting a job in an EU country, in some states not only are wages and salaries higher but so also are unemployment benefits. If you are unlucky enough to lose your 'new' job after being insurably employed under the social security scheme of an EU country, your previous UK insurance may be taken into account to help you become eligible for unemployment benefits which are very much higher than those in the UK.

All Jobcentres now handle vacancies in the EU and can give further details on relevant legislation and social welfare provisions. The Employment Service issues a useful leaflet on these matters, called *Working Abroad*, as well as others detailing conditions in individual countries.

UK PENSION SCHEMES AND THE EXPATRIATE

UK pension schemes have been affected by changes in the state provisions introduced since July 1988. Many pension experts think that employees of companies contracted in to the state earnings-related pension scheme, known as SERPS, which was in operation from 6 April 1978 to 5 April 2002, might be better advised to set up a personal pension scheme which the new legislation now allows them to do, on an individual basis. The value of such a step would depend on a wide variety of circumstances, such as age, whether the expatriate has taxable income in the UK, and, if the employer has a contracted-out pension scheme, just how good the benefits of its scheme are. Under the Welfare Reform and Pensions Act 1999, UK employers who do not provide either a final salary scheme with defined benefits or a money purchase pension under a defined contributions scheme are obliged to offer access to a stakeholder pension scheme. The issues are very complicated and the taxation rules are subject to change. You should seek advice from a reputable financial management firm with experience of expatriate problems.

Checklist: Working abroad and National Insurance

1. Contact both the Contributions Agency and the Benefit Agency for relevant literature on working abroad and National Insurance contributions.
2. Consider paying voluntary contributions to maintain your benefits entitlement on your return and organize payment through direct debit from your bank or building society while you are away.
3. Check to see if you are still entitled to be paid Child Benefit.
4. If you are looking for work and claiming Jobseeker's Allowance, inform your local unemployment benefits office well in advance of your departure.
5. Take advice on your pension scheme arrangements while working abroad.

Part Three

Preparing the Family

8

Partner Issues

The success or failure of longer-term foreign assignments nowadays is more often than not affected by the family's willingness to relocate, and the pressures on an expatriate family should not be underestimated. Many families are organized around a dual-income couple with equal weight given to both careers. The problems of accommodating two careers, or for one partner to give up theirs for the sake of the other, are considerable. Moreover, there is less willingness to send children to boarding school and many employees are accompanied by both partner and offspring to a new location. Creating a fulfilling experience for both partner and children is the key to a successful assignment and this chapter looks at some of the ways in which this may be achieved.

COMPANY ATTITUDES

Enlightened organizations have accepted that the days when the partner was a 'wife', and that a wife did not work, are long gone. Unmarried and dual-earning couples are now frequently the case and, as such, the partner status has become an increasingly urgent problem to sort out. Many partners are unwilling to put their careers on hold. Furthermore, those that do will need help to turn the experience into a worthwhile venture if the employee is to complete the assignment.

It is perhaps no surprise that partners show reluctance to relocate. In a recent survey, relocation company ECA found that, while 65 per cent of expatriates were accompanied by a partner on assignment, of the partners, 60 per cent had worked prior to the assignment but only 16 per cent worked during the assignment. It is quite reasonable to presume that a number of the 44 per cent who didn't work chose not to; however, it is also safe to assume that many would have liked to work, but were not given the opportunity to do so.

With this in mind, larger companies are beginning to recognize the need to provide support to partners. However, these are still a minority, for according to an ECA International survey several years ago only 12 per cent of companies have established a uniform policy, and of that number, 35 per cent deal with partner careers on a case-by-case basis. Job searches, career counselling, network contacts and educational assistance are some of the ways in which these companies are trying to help partners. Table 8.1 shows the range of company assistance on offer or being considered by organizations.

However, companies with a long-established tradition of expatriation have also begun to develop strategies that see the partner included in the relocation process right from the very start, including the initial selection interview. The inclusion of the partner at this stage not only secures an understanding of their needs and expectations but gives a good indication of whether employees have thought through the impact a foreign assignment might have on their personal relationships.

Employees will have the support and structure of the company to help settle in to their new location. The partner, on the other hand, might well be giving up a job, and certainly a social network,

Table 8.1 Assistance with partner careers

	Current practice (%)	Considering (%)
Networking contacts	50	10
Work permits	41	11
Education/training assistance	38	22
Career consultancy advice	33	18
Cost of career enhancement	25	12
Access to recruitment specialist	26	17
Arrange employment within company	24	10
Arrange employment with partner's company	6	3
Intra-company database/job swap	2	10

Source: ECA International

to move to a foreign location without any structure or obvious objective. Recruiters have recognized that it is a false economy not to try to help partners either to find a job or to have a local support network. Failed assignments are costly and many founder on the trailing partner's desire to return home.

Elisabeth Marx has written about the problems faced by partners in *Breaking Through Culture Shock* and suggests that the pressures are twofold. First, couples experience major problems and crises on international assignments because of the unique situation they find themselves in. Faced with the unpredictability of their situation and having to depend on each other, they are without their social network and normal social controls. Furthermore, Marx points to the fact that in most cases the female partner has to deal with the challenges of settling into a new place. These include organizing schooling for the children, sorting out a home and the daily basics, and supporting a partner through the early stages of a new job. Additionally, she will have to try to tap into a social network for the children, and for her and her partner. Add to this the possible demands of her new job, for those who have found one, and one can see why enlightened companies are keen to involve partners from the earliest stage.

Professor Cary Cooper has written extensively about the pressures on dual-income families, and occupational stress. He believes that companies can avoid problems by communicating honestly and inclusively with couples: 'It would seem reasonable that the spouse should be given the "option" to get involved in the decision-making and information-sharing process concerning any move that may impinge on the family. At the moment, organizations are contracting with one element of the family unit, but making decisions which radically affect the unit as a whole. By operating in this way they often cause conflict between the individual and his/her family' (Cooper and Lewis, *The Workplace Revolution*, Kogan Page).

FINDING WORK

The biggest problem for companies is in trying to find career opportunities for the partner in the new location. Apart from being able to find a suitable job to match up to the partner's skills in the new location, there are many parts of the world that will not allow couples to work on one work permit.

If you are a citizen of the European Union original 15 countries (ie live in Austria, Belgium, Denmark, Finland, France, Germany, Greece, Ireland, Italy, Luxembourg, the Netherlands, Portugal, Spain, Sweden or the United Kingdom) and you are being relocated within its borders, there are no such restrictions and partners are allowed to work without a permit.

Outside the European Union, however, work permits for EU citizens are hard to come by, as are permits for non-EU citizens to work in the European Union. In most cases work permits are provided only for the employee who has the backing of an international organization and a specified job to go to. Dependants are generally allowed resident visas but the opportunity to work on their partner's permit is arbitrary and on the whole limited. For example, Australia allows dependants the right to work on an employee's permit, as does Sweden. Japan, on the other hand, allows part-time work. Islamic countries, such as Saudi Arabia, do not issue work permits to females unless they are in the teaching or nursing professions. Perhaps the most difficult country of all for which to obtain a work permit is the United States, which operates a rigorous immigration policy, unless the partner can show that they have unique and rare skills to offer.

Large companies are able to negotiate limited reciprocal arrangements on work permits with other countries, but these tend to be used up by employees. 'In some cases they can go with a joint work permit,' explains John Thompson of PricewaterhouseCoopers, 'in other cases there is a real problem and virtually prohibitive because if you have an unmarried partner, for example, some countries will not give visas. They would not be recognized as a de facto spouse. In some cases we have to say, well, it won't work. As far as we are concerned their status is what it is and if they are going together as an established couple, provided the immigration authorities in the country we are dealing with recognize that, we will do so as well. But we have to look at the practicalities of what can be done.'

Given the difficulties, a few companies will try to find work within their own company for partners with appropriate skills and relocate them in their own right. Others might begin communication with a partner's company to see if there are possibilities for relocation to the same destination within their existing organization. However, both these, as seen by the ECA survey results, are the least favoured options. Barry Page from Accenture points to further problems, caused by the changing workforce profile, in trying to relocate working partners. 'I have come across organizations where the spouse or partner has a more senior position than the employee and that creates more problems. Also, one cannot presume that the spouse or partner is a female either.'

Many companies find it easier to help partners obtain work permits in their own right rather than to try to do so as a dependant, and to do this have set up network systems and recruitment search facilities to help look for new opportunities. For example, Shell International has set up its Outpost website, www.globaloutpostservices.nl, which provides information to partners who wish to work or develop their skills during and after expatriation. Others provide advice through a career consultancy agency for partners seeking jobs, and advice is given on academic and professional qualifications, and whether training is needed to pursue their career abroad. However, partners looking for work should also think about taking up some of the suggestions in Chapter 1, Independent Job Opportunities, in their search for a job in their own right. Further useful websites are listed at the back of this book.

It is quite possible to look for work once relocated and in situ. However, work permit restrictions might, once again, cause problems and it is worth finding out the situation before leaving for your foreign destination.

FROM EXPAT TO EXPERT

Jonathan Wix, Teacher Recruitment Section, British Council

If you find yourself with time on your hands in a foreign city, your ability to speak English at native fluency is potentially one of your greatest assets. Demand for teachers of English as a Foreign Language (EFL) is high all over the world, and shows no sign of declining. The British Council owns and manages premises equipped for language teaching in almost 50 countries around the world. We offer our students access to great high-tech facilities and resources, but they consistently tell us the best resource we provide is their teacher.

We employ qualified EFL teachers on full-time, part-time and hourly-paid contracts, and from a wide variety of backgrounds. Someone who comes to teaching as a second or third career brings valuable skills and life experience to the work we do. Most of our students are individuals who want English for their work or leisure, but we regularly win contracts from large organizations and businesses that commission us to teach language and other professional skills through English to their staff. There is also high demand for teachers who have the skills to manage a class of school-age children. If you've already taught children or had teacher training, then you have valuable skills for an EFL institute abroad.

Students at the British Council expect to be taught by experts, and we aim to employ the best-qualified candidates. The typical EFL teacher used to be a backpacker or gap-year student, but it's now a credible profession and big business. Without some training, leading to a recognized qualification, your chances of working for a good employer are slim.

The best training courses are those that lead to qualifications that are recognized across the globe. As a guide, we use the Cambridge ESOL Certificate in English Language Teaching to Adults (CELTA) or the Trinity College London Certificate in Teaching English to Speakers of Other Languages (Cert. TESOL), or any course that is their equivalent, as one of our entry-level requirements for all recruits. You can take these courses in many different cities around the world. Go to the relevant websites below for the provider locators. Some British Council centres offer the CELTA course, where your fellow trainees could be local English language teaching specialists from the state system or ex-pat novices.

You don't have to be British to work for the British Council, but you do need to speak English to native ability in order to teach. If you don't have a UK passport, in some countries we would only be able to hire you on a local contract, but the work you do, your status and the rate of pay are the same as for teachers appointed from the UK. Managers will advertise vacancies for local-hire teachers in the local English language press, and maybe on the local British Council website. Since many students have day jobs they come for English lessons after work or at weekends, so the working hours for most teachers are unconventional. If you are looking after family or want to spend time with your partner who's working too, it's important to bear this in mind.

Students are motivated and eager to share their culture as much as learn about others, and through learning English they are learning much more than when to use the present continuous. Our teachers equip their students with skills and attitudes that make them international citizens. With the skills and experience of an EFL teacher you can work pretty much all over the world. If you're not one when you start, it's not long before you become an international citizen yourself.

Websites:

British Council teacher recruitment: http://trs.britishcouncil.org

University of Cambridge ESOL qualifications:

www. cambridgeesol.org

Trinity College London ESOL qualifications:

www.trinity college.co.uk

Helpful resource for TEFL qualifications: www.cactustefl.com

FURTHER EDUCATION

If finding a job or obtaining a work permit proves too difficult, the time spent abroad might be a chance to explore other avenues. There are several options available to a trailing partner. For example, investigating educational opportunities in a new location could be one avenue for a trailing partner. Universities and business schools might offer an alternative structure and social network to a job. Furthermore, taking a local qualification might aid the process of finding a job in the new location. For example, INSEAD, the French Business School, provides a career service to holders of its MBA.

The internet is also becoming an invaluable educational tool. There are an increasing number of distance-learning courses available through the web. As mentioned in Chapter 1, the Open University Business School is one institution that is using electronic means to fully explore educational potential and offers a range of six-month courses on a distance-learning basis. Professionals might also use this opportunity to take postgraduate professional qualifications. Professional associations and regulatory bodies will advise you on the availability of distance-learning courses. Non-professional education might also be available. For example, learning the language of your host country will provide both practical help and intellectual stimulus.

NETWORKING AND CONSIDERING
THE CHILDREN

An invaluable aid to partners is the network of contacts that an employee's company can provide before expatriation. This is not just a way to find out what the location is really like but also provides invaluable contacts on arrival. Shell International has recognized the importance of this and has set up a worldwide information network, Outpost, of Shell expatriate families, which is run by volunteer Shell partners and spouses. Likewise, PricewaterhouseCoopers encourages contact with expatriates already in location and tries to link up non-working partners.

Once again, the internet has come into its own when considering the opportunities of contacting other expatriate partners. The plethora of websites for expat spouses is too numerous to mention here and is listed in the back of this book. However, apart from the Shell Spouse Centre already mentioned, there is also the *Electronic Telegraph's* expatriate website at www.telegraph.co.uk, Expat Resources for Spouses at www.thesun.org and Expat Forum at www.expatforum.com. Numerous nationality-, location- and occupation-specific forums also exist on the internet and, again, are listed at the back of the book. Furthermore, if your partner's company has not got an expat partner's website, it might also be a good time to enquire as to the possibilities of setting one up.

The focus of settling children in to a new country tends to be placed on schooling, and this will be dealt with in depth in the next chapter. However, it is also important to consider the effect that expatriation will have on their psychological and social development. Each child is, of course, uniquely different and will deal with new situations in their own way. For some children the opportunity to experience a new place and meet new people will be regarded as an adventure and will be welcomed. For others, it could be a profoundly disturbing experience, with family and friends disappearing from their daily lives. Older children will also present problems and before relocating it is worth considering how they might find living in a more restrictive or more liberal environment and what kind of freedoms they might expect in comparison to their home culture. Harsh punishments can be handed out for the use of 'soft' drugs and other such misdemeanours in many parts of the world. The example of the flogging of a US teenager for vandalism in Singapore should act as a warning. However, the advice remains consistent. As companies need to include partners in the decision-making process, so too children should be included in preparatory discussions and be given information about their new home. An inclusive process for the whole family might well ease some of the anxiety and stresses of relo-cation. Likewise, new technology might provide the answer to homesick children who can keep in contact with friends and family through the use of e-mail and the internet. As in other situations, children can act as conductors for the emotional highs and lows of a family and if there are tension and anxiety surrounding the decision to relocate they are also likely to pick this up. Using the time before departure to investigate and research your destination with your children could be a useful exercise for the whole family.

USING YOUR INITIATIVE

No matter how supportive a company might be, in the end the trailing-partner role is unlikely to be an easy one. Investigating all the possibilities and opportunities before you go is vital: whether it be job opportunities, further education or building a network of contacts to develop a social life. The last of these might also provide openings that will not become apparent until you have arrived in your new location, such as voluntary work or job opportunities. The stresses and strains on relationships should also be expected and a positive approach to the experience might help ease them. As with your partner's career change, relocation could add to your own career or life expectations by giving you international work experience and/or new skills – such as a language – and by opening new horizons. Having decided to make the move, a flexible approach will be the best way of ensuring that you are open to the opportunities available to you.

Checklist: Partner issues

1. Can you find work in the new location and are your quali-fications recognized?
2. Can you work as a dependant or will you have to apply for a work permit in your own right?
3. Is your new location sympathetic to unmarried partners, same-sex partners and women who want to work? All of these can affect your chances of being granted a work permit?

4. Can your company or your partner's company find work within their organization for you in the new location?

5. What are the educational possibilities in your new location and can your partner's employer help you identify them and/or training opportunities? Consider qualifying as an EFL teacher.

6. Does the company have a network for expat partners either on the internet or through telephone communication?

7. If your company does not have a network for expats, are you in a position to start one yourself?

8. Talk to other expats about the host country's environment for children and give particular thought, if you have teenagers, as to what kind of social life they might be able to have.

9. Involve your children in finding out about the new destination through different media or by making contact with expat children already in situ.

10. Encourage your children to use communications technology to keep in touch with friends and family.

9

Your Children's Education

For those contemplating a job abroad, the issue of schooling cannot be taken lightly. Not only can an unsatisfactory educational solution prejudice a child's chance of achieving academic success, it can also create tensions that have an adverse effect on the home and working environment. In some cases it may lead to the premature termination of overseas contracts.

Educational options certainly demand careful thought and planning. Among the possibilities to be considered are:

1. A boarding school in the UK.
2. A day school in the UK (with guardianships/relatives).
3. An expatriate school abroad.
4. A company-sponsored school abroad.
5. A local national school abroad.
6. Home teaching abroad.

The ultimate choice will be determined by the age, ability and personality of your child, together with the quality of education available abroad and the expected duration of the contract. It will also be based on personal financial considerations and on the education support policy of the employer.

School fees (all, or a substantial part) may be paid by major international companies and organizations, and in some cases by governmental agencies. Whether such an allowance is used to contribute towards education at a UK boarding school or at a local fee-paying school will depend on local availability and the employer's policy. Some of these organizations employ trained staff to offer advice and support. They may also cover travelling expenses to and from the school in the UK, including air fares.

Smaller British companies may indicate that the salary they offer includes an unspecified sum towards the cost of schooling. Locally owned companies, particularly in developing countries, rarely provide an educational allowance.

MAINTAINING CONTINUITY

One factor that must be considered at the outset is that few organizations can be relied upon to give any help with school fees once the assignment abroad has been completed. On return to the UK many parents may find it difficult to finance boarding school fees from a lower, and often more heavily taxed, personal income. However, it can be disruptive to move your children from one school to another and particularly inadvisable at a sensitive stage in their schooling when they have begun a GCSE or A-level course. On the other hand, if you have chosen a school abroad with a curriculum that bears little or no resemblance to that followed in the UK, your child may find it hard to cover lost ground. When selecting a school it is crucial to look ahead and to make plans which will serve your child's best interest when your overseas contract comes to an end.

Most schools will go to considerable trouble to make arrangements to see prospective parents, often at short notice. Where possible take your child with you when you visit a school and listen to the child's comments. Whatever your personal feelings about education, it is essential that those of your child are fully respected. Many children have sensible views about what is best for their own development and, where necessary, they should be persuaded rather than instructed.

Your child may be eager to make the transition from state to private school and adapt well to a new environment. However, you should be aware that moving back to the state system can be difficult for ex-independent school pupils. These difficulties can also be encountered by children returning to a local school routine after the cultural diversity of an international educational environment.

The major problem for most children of expatriates is the lack of educational continuity, particularly when they are obliged to move from country to country, and school to school, every few years. If your child is to realize their potential you must try to provide educational stability. Much can be done to ease the process of transition by providing a new school with a detailed profile of your child. Reports, syllabus information, titles of books which they have been using and levels of attainment can enable a teacher to assist your child to settle happily into life in a new school with the minimum of disruption.

CONTINUED SCHOOLING IN THE UK

Many parents find it difficult to decide whether to send their child to a day or boarding school. For parents who are working overseas boarding is an obvious choice. Indeed, some parents may opt for a job abroad in order to finance their children's education at a boarding school.

How to find a boarding school

Selecting the most appropriate school for your child can be a time-consuming and confusing process, but there are several organizations to help you make your choice.

One is the Independent Schools Council (ISC), St Vincent House, 30 Orange Street, London WC2H 7HH (tel: 020 7766 7070, website: www.isc.co.uk). The website includes an informative Daily News summary and a personalized school search service.

Another, from which advice is also available free of charge, is Gabbitas Educational Consultants Ltd, Carrington House, 126–130 Regent Street, London W1B 5EE (tel: 020 7734 0161, fax: 020 7437 1764, website: www.gabbitas.co.uk). Gabbitas invite parents to tell them as much as possible about their child, their circumstances and the type of school they are looking for. On the basis of this information they are able to recommend a selection of suitable schools from a wide range of independent boarding and day schools. Shortlisted schools are asked to send parents a prospectus. It is then up to the parents to visit the schools personally. There is no charge for this service. Gabbitas also offer detailed guidance on education at all levels (a fee of £135 + VAT per hour is charged for such consultations). Experienced consultants deal with a range of educational issues, including options at 16+ and planning for higher education and career opportunities.

How to choose a boarding school

Having shortlisted several schools, either with or without the guidance of a professional organization, parents are well advised to read the prospectus through carefully, and to prepare a checklist of questions in readiness for a visit to a school.

Many of the factors governing choice are self-evident and conclusions will be arrived at quickly. Access to an international airport, proximity to relatives, religious denomination, co-educational or single-sex, the academic aims of the school and the scale of fees are points which all parents will need to consider. Also important are:

- the academic record of the school;
- the qualifications and approach of the teaching staff;
- the staff/pupil ratio;
- the physical environment;
- the attitude to discipline;
- the quality of sports education;
- the range of information technology;
- the range of extra-curricular activities;
- the quality of pastoral care;
- costs;
- the numbers in the sixth form;
- the quality of careers counselling;
- contact with parents;
- the house system;
- school publications;
- references.

Entrance examination

To be admitted to an independent secondary school your child will normally be required to pass the school's entrance test or the Common Entrance examination, which is set for candidates of 11+, 12+ and 13+ (the appropriate examination is normally determined by the child's age on 1 September in the year of entry).

- At 11+ the subjects examined are English, mathematics, science and reasoning. Examinations take place in January and November.
- At 12+ candidates sit papers in English, mathematics, science and French (written and oral). Latin may be offered as an

optional paper. Examinations take place in February/March and November.

- At 13+ the papers are English, mathematics, science, French (written and oral), history, geography and religious studies. English as an additional language, German, Spanish, Latin and Greek may be offered as optional papers. Examinations take place in February/March, June (for most candidates) and November. Candidates for boys' schools most commonly take the 13+ examination.

Each senior school sets its own entrance standards and is responsible for the assessment of papers. Some schools require candidates to sit their own independent examinations in addition, or as an alternative, to Common Entrance. The examinations are normally taken at the candidate's own school.

Children applying to boarding schools from abroad or from state schools will be in direct competition with those who have been tutored for the entrance examinations at UK prep schools. Many schools will take this fact into consideration when making their assessments. However, in some cases it may be necessary to arrange individual coaching in advance of the examination. Consultancy and assessment, as well as tuition, are available from members of the Association of Tutors, Sunnycroft, 63 King Edward Road, Northampton NN1 5LY; tel: 01604 624171 (www.tutor.co.uk). Supportive tuition or complete coverage can be provided for primary and secondary work, as well as some university-level work. Some services are available on a distance basis, and some as intensive, holiday-period schemes. Examination advice and preparation for particular exams, like the Common Entrance, is a particular expertise.

The syllabuses for each subject, and the examination papers, are set by the Independent Schools Examinations Board. Copies of syllabuses, past papers and information are available from: The Independent Schools Examinations Board, The Pump House, 16 Queen's Avenue, Christchurch BH2 31BZ; tel: 01202 487 533; fax: 01202 473728; website: www.iseb.co.uk.

Scholarships

Many independent schools offer entrance scholarships to children of outstanding ability or potential. These may be based either on general academic standard or on particular strengths, notably musical, sporting or artistic. Individual schools will supply details on request.

A number of schools offer bursaries for means-tested families. Others make specific awards to the children of clergy and service families.

ISC runs an advisory service on scholarships and bursaries for parents seeking general advice.

Insurance and financial planning

A growing number of financial service groups and independent financial advisers are able to offer school fee plans, with obvious benefits for those who are able to plan and save well in advance. For those with a more immediate requirement, loan schemes, both equity- and non-equity-based, are available. ISC produces a useful leaflet called *School Fees*.

Many schools cooperate with insurance companies in schemes for the remission of school fees during unavoidable absence through illness. Other policies are available that guarantee the continued payment of fees in the event of a parent's death, disablement or redundancy before the completion of schooling.

Maintained boarding schools

Some local authorities run their own boarding schools or offer boarding facilities alongside day schools. Eighteen of these maintained schools have opted out and are now grant maintained (grant-maintained schools have been given a new status under government plans but this should not affect the education provided). Although any child with a legal right to attend school in Britain may seek entry to any maintained school, some authorities give priority to local children, even for boarding places. As tuition is free at these schools and parents pay only for boarding, the overall costs are approximately a half to two-thirds of the cost of an independent school. Many pupils are from service families, or have parents who work for banks or government agencies abroad.

The Boarding Schools Association at 35–37 Grosvenor Gardens, London SW1W 0BS; tel: 020 7798 1580, fax: 020 7798 1581, email: bsa@iseis.uk.net, website: www.boarding.org.uk provides an online school search tool. All publications of the Department for Children, Schools and Families (DCSF) are available on the DCSF

website www.publications.dcs.gov.uk or by e-mail to dcsf@
prolog.uk.com.

Local authority grants

Some education authorities are prepared to give grants to assist
with boarding school fees when both parents are abroad and there
are no places available in a state boarding school. Application should
be made to the director of education or chief education officer for
the area in the UK in which the family is normally resident.

Arrangements for your child

A boarding school accepts responsibility for the day-to-day welfare
of its pupils in term time, but overseas parents will naturally want
assurance that their child is being cared for at all times, including
short holiday periods and occasions when they may be in transit
between school and home. There are a number of organizations
that care for children in these circumstances.

Child supervision

Some boarding schools are able to send a school bus or driver to
collect children from, and deliver them to, the nearest airport.
Where this service is not available parents may wish to use a
commercial escort service.

* Universal Aunts Ltd, PO Box 304, London SW4 0NN (tel: 020
  7738 8937; website: www.universalaunts.co.uk) can arrange for
  children to be taken to and from school according to parents'
  instructions. They try to allot the same 'aunt' to a child so that a
  warm relationship is established. When required to do so they
  can also arrange for children to be accommodated for the night
  in the home of one of the aunts. Holiday accommodation is
  also available.

Finding a guardian

Most boarding schools require parents to appoint a local guardian
for their child. Several organizations are able to offer a guardianship
service for parents who do not wish to impose upon relations or
family friends.

Guardianship schemes have developed in response to demands from parents and schools to cover welfare, education and finance. They are provided by, for example, the following organizations:

- Clarendon International Education, 41 Clarendon Square, Royal Leamington Spa, Warwickshire CV32 5QZ (tel: 01926 316793, fax: 01926 883278, www.clarendon.uk.com).
- Guardians and Tutors, 131 Pomphlett Road, Plymstock, Plymouth PL9 7BU (tel: 01752 401942; e-mail: brian@stoyel.co.uk).
- Gabbitas Educational Consultants Ltd (www.gabbitas.co.uk) run a comprehensive guardianship service which takes care of all aspects of education, welfare and finance.

Day schools in the UK

If you feel that your child is unsuited to boarding school life, or that it would be too disruptive to move schools – for example, during the GCSE years – you may wish to consider a day place. Where relatives and friends are available to care for your child this arrangement can work smoothly, particularly when a child continues at their present school. Many older children are reluctant to leave their friends and interests behind, and are able to respond positively to a new degree of independence.

In some cases, where there are no relatives or friends to rely on and parents wish to avoid placing their child in lodgings, mothers stay behind with their children. Although this offers the child continuity it can cause strains in the marital relationship and may offset the financial benefits of the posting.

Few employers offer more than a token allowance for lodging if your child remains at a day school in the UK.

SCHOOLS ABROAD

Neill Ransom, Chelstoke International

Expatriate schools

Unlike other nations such as France, Germany, Japan, Switzerland or the United States, Britain provides no financial assistance for the creation and management of schools for British expatriates. This means that British parents moving abroad must expect to pay substantial school fees unless they choose to send their children to local national schools.

British schools

There are a large and increasing number of 'British' schools operating in many countries of the world, the majority based in the major cities, which attract large numbers of international companies and diplomatic services.

Most of these follow the British National Curriculum (beware – as there are many similarly termed 'National Curricula'). However, also beware – in many countries one can also find 'British school' used as a name for local private schools, which provide an 'old style' English school curriculum but are populated almost entirely by local national children.

While most British schools abroad are not 'government' approved or registered and as independent organizations are not subject to Ofsted inspection, the majority of the most successful and best-performing British schools nevertheless undertake inspections or take part in recognized accreditation schemes.

There are various groups of British schools, either relating to membership of an association, such as the British Schools of the Middle East (BSME – see www.bsme.org.uk) or group ownership, such as the British Schools of America (currently comprising the British Schools of Washington, Boston, Chicago, Houston and Charlotte – see www.britishschool.org). The latter were set up as a direct response to British companies and staff relocating abroad and expressing concern that local schools (even where the language was similar) did not prepare their children for the British National Curriculum and any return home. Similarly, a number of British schools, for example in Eastern Europe, are currently operated by Nord Anglia, a listed UK company. In Hong Kong the well-established English Schools Foundation (www.esf.edu.hk) operates a number of high quality primary and secondary schools and is somewhat similar to an independent LEA (Local Education Authority).

One of the most established membership groups, comprising individual British International Schools, is COBIS (The Council of British International Schools), now comprising 84 member and affiliate schools, from 39 countries. This group is uniquely recognized by the DfES and their teachers can join the UK teachers' superannuation scheme. COBIS has recently agreed to act jointly with FOBISSEA (The Federation of British International Schools in South and East Asia, representing 34 British Schools in 11 SE Asian countries). The respective websites are www.cobis.org.uk and www.fobissea.org.

A small number of British schools abroad are affiliated to UK professional associations including HMC (the Headmasters' and Headmistresses' Conference, GSA (the Girls' Schools Association) and NAHT (the National Association of Headteachers). These and other links allow headteachers and staff to keep abreast of UK educational developments.

The European Schools

Starting with the first European School established in Luxembourg in 1953, there are now 14 European Schools situated in Luxembourg, Belgium (Brussels I, Brussels II, Brussels III and MoI), Germany (Karlsruhe, Munich and Frankfurt), Italy (Varese), the Netherlands (Bergen), the UK (Culham, near Oxford) and Spain (Alicante), with the latest additions in Brussels and Strasbourg.

Linked to and supported by the European Commission, this network of schools serving some 21,000 pupils enjoys government and European Community support. A particular feature of the education provided is the European baccalaureate, specially established for this group of schools.

American Schools

American schools offer an American curriculum, but may be an option for British children because the language of instruction is English. It is important to remember that the educational approach will be quite different and that pupils will be prepared for American examinations at college entry level, such as the Standard Achievement Tests (SATs). To graduate from an American school a certain number of credits are required. Credit courses in the final two years of schooling may include Honours and Advanced Placement Sections which provide able students with special challenges. British universities are familiar with the entrance requirements of leading American universities and set similar entry requirements for applicants from American-style schools.

International schools

International schools are established in most capital cities of the world. They may be distinguished by the fact that they are independent of any state system and aim to educate children from a variety of nationalities.

Many are outstanding, offering intellectual pluralism and exceptional cultural variety – typically 50 to 60 different nationalities are represented in the student body. Some are members of international associations such as the United World Colleges and the European Council of International Schools (ECIS), others have headteachers in membership of the (British-based) Headmasters' and Headmistresses' Conference or the Girls' Schools Association.

In many respects they are as varied as their locations – large or small, monolingual, bilingual (using a foreign language as a medium of instruction for some subjects) or even multilingual (using more than one foreign language as a medium of instruction), traditional or emphatically modern. Some are subsidized by local governments, others are among the most costly schools in the world. Almost all are co-educational, and in the majority the language of instruction is English.

Curriculum options

International schools may follow a standard US college preparatory programme or a standard GCSE or International GCSE (IGCSE) programme, or a combination of these. Although a number of schools also work towards national examinations such as the German Abitur or the Spanish Bachillerato, at sixth-form level many are now preparing for the diploma of the International Baccalaureate Organisation (IBO).

A few years ago, the choice of curriculum at international schools was between an American 'international' curriculum and a British 'international' curriculum. However, there are now a range of specially designed international curriculum options available, the majority of which are well established, well supported and recognized internationally. The curriculum offered can often be a determining factor in choice of school – at least where the luxury of choice exists.

The highly successful International Baccalaureate (IB) for post-16 students has led to the development of both the MYP (Middle

Years Programme) and the PYP (Primary Years Programme) also administered and accredited by the International Baccalaureate Organisation (IBO) from its headquarters and offices in Geneva and Cardiff. IBO registered schools now total 2,832 schools in 138 countries. The PYP followed by the MYP are thematic skills-based curricula, designed to lead students through to the IB and as such are gaining popularity in increasing numbers of international schools – details on the IBO website at www.ibo.org.

The other well-established alternative at primary level is the IPC (International Primary Curriculum). This was originally developed by Fieldwork (www.fieldworkeducation.co.uk) for the worldwide Shell Group of International Schools and its success and credibility had led to its being taken up by many successful international schools. The IPC is operated by Fieldwork Education Services (see www.internationalprimarycurriculum.com), which is now a division of World Class Learning Schools & Systems Group (www.greatlearning.com).

The alternative – and somewhat less international – option at secondary level is those schools that follow a curriculum leading to the IGCSE (International General Certificate of Secondary Education), which is a derivative of the UK GCSE.

For post-16 students, the International Baccalaureate (IB) is based on a two-year curriculum that maintains a balance between the sciences, the arts and languages. The programme is broader than A-levels as all students must offer one subject from each of six groups:

- language A (first language);
- language B (second language);
- individuals and societies;
- experimental sciences;
- mathematics;
- electives (including art, music, IT).

Of the six subjects studied, three are taken at Higher level, and three at Standard level. This represents a deliberate compromise between the European emphasis on breadth and the British tradition of rigorous specialization. In effect students offer three subjects to A-level equivalent standard and three subjects to a standard somewhat above GCSE. To be eligible for the award of the Diploma candidates must score a minimum of points and meet three additional requirements: submission of an extended essay; satisfactory completion of a Theory of Knowledge Course; and compulsory participation in a CAS programme (Creativity, Action, Service).

Students holding the IB Diploma have entered more than 700 universities throughout the world. All UK universities accept the IB as satisfying their general requirement for entrance. For further information contact: The International Baccalaureate Organisation, Curriculum and Assessment Centre, Peterson House, Malthouse Avenue, Cardiff Gate, Cardiff CF23 8GL, UK (tel: +44 2920 547 777; fax: + 44 2920 547 778; website: www.ibo.org).

Another worldwide school-leaving certificate, which has been available to English-medium schools throughout the world since 1986, is the Advanced Intermediate Certificate of Education (AICE). AICE is a 'group' certificate which is awarded on the basis of a broad and balanced curriculum of five full-credit courses or their equivalent. All candidates must take at least one course from three subject groups: mathematics and sciences; languages; and arts and humanities. The AICE curriculum, which is designed to be of worldwide relevance, offers a high degree of flexibility. As there are no compulsory subjects, student programmes may range from the highly specialized to the general. Most UK universities now accept AICE as an alternative to A-levels. AICE is administered by the University of Cambridge Local Examinations Syndicate (UCLES), 1 Hills Road, Cambridge CB1 2EU (tel: 01223 553311; fax: 01223 460278; website: www.ucles.org.uk).

Special educational needs

If your child has special educational needs (SEN), then it is very important to check in detail with likely schools as very many international schools are not able to provide relevant and sufficient support for such students. This is because the support facilities and back-up agencies we rely on in the UK often do not exist abroad. It is therefore important to discuss things in detail with any possible school, so there can be no misunderstanding.

How to find an overseas school

Finding out what schools are available abroad in specific countries and cities can be done via two main routes.

The first is via the internet, where a majority of schools – especially successful international schools of every type – maintain a website presence. Indeed many of the websites are extremely professional and give enormous insight into the life of the school. A search for schools and city/country or international schools, etc will invariably bring up some options.

However, a second and perhaps more inclusive start will be via those organizations that exist to support and advise on international schools and education abroad. The most comprehensive and best established is CIS (Council of International Schools). The success of ECIS has led to the founding of a sister organization – CIS which, as a service organization, deals with the regular accreditation of international schools and headteacher and staff recruitment, in parallel with ECIS which is the related membership organization for conferences and professional support and development. Websites (www.ecis.org and www.cois.org) give full details. The membership list of ECIS/CIS in their annual *International Schools Directory* is the most comprehensive list of international schools available, with the advantage of showing which are fully accredited, or in earlier stages of membership such as affiliate members. The directory is available from John Catt Educational at www.johncatt.com with an online version via the ECIS website or via John Catt website.

Various other websites and groups give information and lists of schools, but very few are totally comprehensive and it is unclear what is being missed.

How to choose a school abroad

Depending on the city or country and its standing as a centre of international trade or diplomatic missions, there will be a degree of choice available. In smaller, developing countries, there may be only one or two appropriate schools. In the more established international cities there will be a range of schools catering for differing national and international curricula and providing healthy competition and choice. There will often also be a number of smaller private schools with names suggesting they are British or similar, when in fact they cater predominantly for local nationals. It is thus important to discover how established and successful a school is. The first step is to check whether it has accredited status – ideally from ECIS and associate organizations, or for example as an IBO accredited school.

Information from company HR departments and other colleagues may be useful, but the needs of your children and your aspirations for them may be very different. There is no substitute for actually seeing and visiting a school, to really gain a feel of its ethos and atmosphere and meet the headteacher and key staff.

For senior executives, many international companies provide the services of an educational relocation specialist as part of their HR relocation support – who can provide a service advising on school placements to individual families, suggesting schools available, advising on their standing and in certain cases arranging visits and providing a specialist consultant/adviser.

Preparation is important to get the most from any school visit, or seek answers to key questions. The list below may be a helpful starter:

1. Many employers pay for families to visit the country before their projected move. This gives them the opportunity to visit the available schools (it is useful to obtain prospectuses beforehand) in person, and to consider the alternatives with existing expatriate parents and organized parents' groups which are attached to the schools. However, it is important to remember that other people may have standards which do not correspond to your own.

    In many instances expatriate schools become both a community and a social centre for expatriate families. This can be a great help for incoming families.

2. It is advisable to link house-hunting with the choice of school so that transportation problems can be considered in advance.

3. By their nature, with families being moved by companies as their agreed contract period finishes, international schools experience a steady turnover of pupils – often with 25 to 30 per cent a year moving. Similarly there will be staff turnover, as two- and three-year contracts are often the norm. The best international schools will have strategies to minimize this potential disruption – so ask the question.

4. It is important to establish how schools overseas are controlled. Many schools are run by boards composed of leading figures from the local community, including representatives from the parent body and the organizations which use the school. The latter may be relied upon to ensure that the facilities available to their employees are of a high standard.

5. Every effort should be made to meet the headteacher, who is responsible for the quality and organization of the school. They

will be able to tell you whether there is a waiting list for admission to the school and when you need to register your child. In some instances the waiting time for admission can be a full academic year. Other schools may be ready to accept pupils at almost any time.

6. Take time to consider the curriculum. How far does it correspond to the National Curriculum in the UK? How straightforward will it be for your child to transfer back to the UK? Try to establish how much support, both pastoral and academic, is provided for individual children, to enable them to cope with the process of transition.

7. It is important to consider the type of report and record-keeping system which is in operation in the school. How much information will be available as a record of your child's achievement at the school? Pupil profiles are particularly essential for children who move from school to school frequently.

8. The language of instruction will be of key importance to your child. Find out what kind of English is used – whether it is American, British or non-mother-tongue English. How many children and staff do not have English as a first language? Are they likely to hinder your child's progress?

9. Expatriate schools are geared to accept pupils at any stage during the school year. However, the process of transition is generally easier when pupils begin school at the start of a new term.

10. If your company does not offer an educational allowance, or pay school fees – which is increasingly the case – then your homework needs to include fee levels. School fees tend to vary with age, with secondary and post-16, where subject specialisms increase, attracting the highest fees. In London these can be up to £16,000 for the more expensive day school fees; across Europe the fee can be €16,000 or more. While the fee may be payable in local currency, many schools operate in the more stable currencies of pounds sterling or US dollars and so exchange rate fluctuation may be a consideration. In addition to the tuition fees, it is common practice to charge a one-off registration fee and also an initial or more often now, an annual building or development fee – the latter put towards new development or buildings either planned or recently completed.

Company-sponsored schools

In more remote countries or areas where initial development is occurring, such as new oil or gas fields, there may be no schools available. In such cases some companies will sponsor and develop a school. The trend, however, is to bring in specialist operators to operate the school on their behalf. The original worldwide network of Shell Schools, for example, is now supported and, for many aspects managed, by Fieldwork Educational Services (www. fieldworkeducation.co.uk).

Local national schools

Within Europe there are significant advantages to be gained in sending your child to a local national school, not least an opportunity to acquire proficiency in another language and to absorb a new culture. Although the standard of educational provision may vary there is no doubt that in some countries, such as France and Germany, it is excellent. However, a complete immersion in another language and culture is demanding and it will depend very much on the age and ability of the children as to how successfully they can adapt.

Learning the full range of school subjects in a new language can be exacting, particularly where no provision is made for extra language tuition. Parents who do not speak the necessary language themselves must remember that they will be able to offer little advice and assistance to their child, who may feel isolated as a result.

For those on short-term contracts it is important to consider how well such schooling will prepare children for the next stage in a UK education. Certainly, a child working towards GCSE examinations could expect to be disadvantaged. The experience may also pose difficulties for younger children returning to the UK.

Transfer into and out of school systems in other parts of the world can also pose problems. Traditional teaching methods which rely on rote learning are still applied in many developing countries, where schools are frequently ill-equipped and crowded. As education is so highly prized as a route out of poverty, expatriates will not be encouraged to supplant a local child. However, where no alternative exists, parents may need to compensate for a restricted curriculum by providing supplementary lessons at home.

Differences in attitudes to schooling are particularly marked in countries where religious and political beliefs have shaped the curriculum. Even in other parts of the English-speaking world there are fundamental differences in approach. For example, in Australia formal schooling starts at age 6 and secondary education at 12.

This section has been edited and revised by Neill Ransom, Chelstoke International (tel: 07860 212109, e-mail: neill@chelstokeinternational.com).

Checklist: Your children's education

1. Consider the options in relation to your child's age, ability and personality, and in relation to the quality of education in your new location.
2. Consider whether your organization will contribute towards your child's education.
3. Does your host country's education system bear any resemblance to your native country's?
4. If you are considering using the independent sector, what are the financial implications, particularly when you return from your assignment?
5. If your child is to go to boarding school, what arrangements can be made for a local guardian?
6. What are the local alternatives and can you speak to other expat parents to find out what educational facilities are like in your new location?
7. Are the qualifications offered by your local national or international schools compatible with your domestic ones?
8. Can you team up with other expat families to provide a home teaching group?
9. If not, will your company provide support in setting up a company school?
10. If your child has special needs, contact support agencies for advice.

Health, Security and Welfare

HEALTH RISKS

Whether you are relocating to a new country by yourself or with your family, one of the most important pre-trip considerations is what health hazards might be encountered in your host country. You might feel that developed countries might not represent too many risks to a visitor. However, it is always advisable to seek expert advice, regardless of your destination. This advice should include information not only about local health risks but also about the health service and access to medical care in your host country. While the emphasis is on developing countries, travellers should also be aware that risks in non-Third World countries are still prevalent, for example the hepatitis virus in areas of Turkey, and an outbreak of diphtheria in Russia.

A useful book that can be thoroughly recommended is *Travellers' Health* by Dr Richard Dawood (published by Oxford University Press). This provides detailed information and guidance on every conceivable medical area and is essential reading before departure.

The risks to children will also need to be identified. Some illnesses, such as gastroenteritis, present a far greater risk to children than to adults and it is essential that you arm yourself with information concerning symptoms and medical treatment, such as the administration of a fluid-replacement solution. You will also need to make sure that your child's immunizations are up to date and to identify any specific vaccines that may be required. Seek advice for babies under six months who are not able to have these immunizations.

Specialist organizations

Good general advice on health preparations before departure is available from the website of the Medical Advisory Service for Travellers Abroad (MASTA) at www.masta.org and is shown below:

- Make sure you are up to date with your immunizations such as tetanus and polio, and check which others you might need for your destination.
- Allow six to eight weeks to undergo a full course of immunization.
- Malaria tablets should be taken one week before entering a malaria area or two to three weeks before if taking Mefloquine.
- Find out what your blood group is to ensure prompt treatment in an emergency.
- Find out how you can contact emergency services in your new location.
- If you are taking medication, make sure that you have adequate supplies and make a note of the medicines you are taking and the dosage to inform a doctor in an emergency.
- Do not take any drugs to a Third World or developing country unless they are prescribed and labelled.
- Keep a record of your medical history and briefly note down the relevant details of treatment and medication.
- Note down any pills or medicine to which you are allergic.

MASTA also offers health briefs on 230 countries. Information can be obtained direct from MASTA on 0113 238 7575, and from their Traveller's Health Line on 0906 8224100 (charged at 60p per minute). A particular feature is a personalized health brief, combining a personal medical check-up with very up-to-date information on the country (or combination of countries) to be visited, from the MASTA database, which covers more than 250 countries and includes the latest data from the Foreign Office. Central billing for companies can be arranged to cover all their employees who travel abroad. One MASTA service particularly geared to the intending expatriate is a detailed health brief and an extensive individual health report on the country concerned.

Other organizations specializing in travel medicine are as follows:

- The Malaria Reference Laboratory at the London School of Hygiene and Tropical Medicine, which runs a helpline on 09065 508908 (charged at £1 per minute).

- The Travel Clinic, Hospital for Tropical Diseases, Mortimer Market, Copper Street, off Tottenham Court Road, London WC1E 6JB (website: www.theGtd.org), which offers preventative advice and has an extensive range of health products and immunizations available. For information, call their Healthline on 020 7950 7799; to make an appointment, telephone 020 7388 9600.
- British Airways no longer operates its own travel clinics and refers its passengers to the MASNA network.

However, one major international health hazard that has come to the fore since earlier editions of this book is the problem of acquired immune deficiency syndrome (AIDS). It has reached epidemic proportions in some parts of Africa and other developing countries. It is no longer sufficient to warn expatriates against the dangers of promiscuity. People can become infected through transfusions of infected blood or treatment with instruments that have not been properly sterilized. Expatriates are now advised to contact the local British embassy or high commission, which keeps a register of reliable blood donors among the expatriate community. It is also inadvisable in many countries to attend local doctors' or dentists' clinics unless they are known to enforce the highest standards of hygiene. Medical kits should also be top of the packing list. Organizations such as MASTA can advise on the appropriate contents.

Those working in Saudi Arabia should note that they will have to produce a doctor's certificate to show that they are HIV negative. It has been pointed out that this can raise problems when applying for medical insurance. Even the answer 'yes' to the question 'Have you ever been HIV tested?' can raise the suspicion that your lifestyle exposes you to the risk of AIDS. Thus, if you have been HIV tested in connection with an assignment to Saudi Arabia, you should point this out if the question arises on a medical insurance form.

An extremely useful leaflet, *Travellers Guide to Health*, which covers prevention and planning, emergency care and international health care agreements, and contains an application for a European Health Insurance Card (EHIC) for free or reduced-cost emergency medical treatment in most European countries, can be obtained from your GP, or through the Health Literature Line on 0800 555 777. A comprehensive guide is available in the form of *Health Information for Overseas Travel* (published by The Stationery Office,

£7.95, tel: 0870 6005522, website: www.tsonline.co.uk). This detailed work is primarily intended for reference by GPs, but serious travellers will find it most useful, as it provides a thorough guide to disease risk, immunization and other hazards, as well as child-specific information.

EXPATRIATE MEDICAL INSURANCE

Most of the countries that expatriates go to do not operate a national health service like that of the UK. It comes as something of a shock to find oneself paying £100 or more for a routine visit to a doctor or dentist and the costs of hospitalization can be such as to wipe out the savings of months, or even years. In places like the EU, South Africa, Australia or other developed Commonwealth countries there are established local methods of medical insurance, and in many cases the cost of this is included in the remuneration package. If not, it is certainly a matter which should be clarified while you are negotiating the job offer.

Some OPEC and similar resource-rich countries do have state medical schemes, and as a matter of fact their hospitals are, in many cases, better equipped than our relatively rundown institutions. They are, however, established primarily for the benefit of local nationals, which means that the customs and culture of medical care are different from those which most Westerners are used to. For this reason, most expatriates in those countries arrange for attention in private hospitals which, needless to say, tends to be very expensive indeed. There are a lot of health legislation changes taking place in the UAE currently. People who go to the Middle East should check the health insurance legislation of each country they are going to. In Saudi Arabia and Abu Dhabi, for example, it is now required by law that employers provide all expat employees with health insurance. Medical insurance for anyone going to these places is therefore essential, and a number of plans have now been developed specifically for expatriates by AXA PPP healthcare, BUPA International and others. The health insurance business is fiercely competitive; if you are paying your own insurance you should ask your broker for a complete list of all the plans that are available, so that you can compare them in detail. You will need to establish whether quoted premiums include or exclude insurance premium tax and how long companies take to settle claims. You will also want to check that the plan you choose includes, as do AXA PPP healthcare's and BUPA International's, the typical health services that every expat has come to expect, such as medical evacuation, 24-hour helpline, translation services and arranging for direct payment in nearly every hospital throughout the world.

AXA PPP healthcare

AXA PPP healthcare is one of the longest established and largest medical insurers in Britain and has nearly 2 million customers worldwide. Its International Health Plan has three different levels of cover, of which the benefits are detailed in Table 10.1 (see page 152–54):

- **Prestige.** A top of the range plan, providing all the benefits of AXA PPP healthcare's comprehensive and standard options but with the addition of routine pregnancy cover, adult health screen, disability compensation cover and annual travel insurance.
- **Comprehensive.** As the name suggests, the plan provides comprehensive cover, in-patient, day-patient and out-patient treatment and, in addition, covers non-routine dental treatment.
- **Standard.** A plan specifically designed for members who do not require out-patient cover but which offers similar in-patient and day-patient treatment cover to the comprehensive option.

Depending on where you reside, travel to or wish to receive treatment there are three geographical areas of cover:

- Area 1 – worldwide;
- Area 2 – worldwide except the United States and Canada;
- Area 3 – Europe and specified countries.

AXA PPP healthcare defines Europe as: Albania, Andorra, Armenia, Austria, Azerbaijan, Belarus, Belgium, Bosnia and Herzegovina, Bulgaria, Channel Islands, Croatia, Republic of Cyprus (including Akrotiri and Dhekelia SBAs), Czech Republic, Denmark, Estonia, Faroe Islands, Finland, France, Georgia, Germany, Gibraltar, Greece, Greenland, Hungary, Iceland, Ireland, Isle of Man, Italy, Kazakhstan, Kyrgyzstan, Latvia, Liechtenstein, Lithuania, Luxembourg, FYR Macedonia, Malta, Moldova, Monaco, Netherlands, Norway, Poland, Portugal (including Madeira), Romania, Russian Federation, San Marino, Serbia and Montenegro, Slovak Republic, Slovenia, Spain, Sweden, Switzerland, Tajikistan,

We can't afford a cheap health plan – so we pay less for a great one!

When you've got loved ones to care for, nothing but the best healthcare protection will do. And you can be sure our award-winning international cover won't let you down. You can rely on expert English-speaking medical help and advice; prompt access to treatment in a choice of hospitals; plus our plans are made to be portable – so you can be covered wherever you travel.

You'll also discover our prices˙ are less than our leading competitors. But don't just take our word for it, put us to the test…

To save on your international health cover call AXA PPP healthcare today on

+44 (0)1892 550817 quoting reference WA2006 or visit
www.axappphealthcare.co.uk/wa

PPP HEALTHCARE

Table 10.1 AXA PPP healthcare – summary benefits table

The three options you can choose from	Prestige	Comprehensive	Standard
Policy benefit limit	Up to £1,250,000 each year	Up to £1,000,000 each year	Up to £750,000 each year
In-patient and day-patient treatment including surgeons', anaesthetists', physicians' and consultants' charges, diagnostic tests and physiotherapy	No annual maximum	No annual maximum	No annual maximum
Out-patient surgical procedures	No annual maximum	No annual maximum	No annual maximum
Radiotherapy, chemotherapy, computerized tomography, magnetic resonance imaging and positron emission tomography (brain and body scanning). Received as an in-patient, day-patient or out-patient	No annual maximum	No annual maximum	No annual maximum
Parent accommodation. Charges for one parent staying with a child member under 18	No annual maximum	No annual maximum	No annual maximum
International emergency treatment (evacuation or repatriation service)	No annual maximum	No annual maximum	No annual maximum
Outside area of cover. Emergency treatment, or treatment of a medical condition which arises suddenly while outside your area of cover.	Up to 10 weeks' treatment in any year	Up to six weeks' treatment in any year	Up to six weeks' treatment in any year
Separate limit for United States/Canada	£20,000	£15,000	£10,000

Table 10.1 *continued*

The three options you can choose from	Prestige	Comprehensive	Standard
Dental care. We will pay up to 50% of the costs incurred. The maximum we will pay in a year is:	Area 1 £600 Area 2 £500 Area 3 £400	Area 1 £400 Area 2 £320 Area 3 £240	Area 1 £400 Area 2 £320 Area 3 £240
Accidental damage to teeth	Up to £10,000 each year	Up to £10,000 each year	Up to £10,000 each year
Cash benefits for each night you receive free in-patient treatment	£100 a night	£100 a night	£100 a night
Ambulance transport for emergency transport to or between hospitals	Up to £500 each year	Up to £500 each year	Up to £500 each year
Health at Hand	Included	Included	Included
Doctor, Dental, Optical Helpline	Included	Included	Included
Interpretation service helpline	Included	Included	Included
The International Travel Plan	Included	Optional	Optional
Out-patient treatment i) Medical practitioner charges for consultations ii) Consultations and treatment for psychiatric illness iii) Complementary practitioner charges iv) Diagnostic tests and physiotherapy v) Travel and childhood vaccinations administered by a medical practitioner	Complementary practitioner charges limited to £300 each year	Complementary practitioner charges limited to £300 each year	Not included Not included
Combined overal limit	£5,000 per year	£3,000 per year	Not included

Table 10.1   *continued*

The three options you can choose from	Prestige	Comprehensive	Standard
Hospital-at-home	Up to 28 days each year	Up to 14 days each year	Not included
Day-patient radiotherapy and chemotherapy cash benefit	£50 a day	£50 a day	£50 a day
Out-patient drugs and dressings prescribed by a medical practitioner	Up to £500 each year	Up to £200 each year	Not included
Optical cover	Up to £100 each year	Up to £100 each year	Not included
Eyesight test cover	Paid in full for one eyesight test each year	Paid in full for one eyesight test each year	Not included
Adult health screen	Up to £300 each year towards a health screen for each adult on the policy	Not included	
Disability compensation cover	Up to £50,000		
Pregnancy and childbirth (after 10 months' cover)	Up to £10,000		

Turkey, Turkish Republic of Northern Cyprus, Turkmenistan, Ukraine, United Kingdom of Great Britain and Northern Ireland, Uzbekistan and Vatican City State.

As well as the private health care aspect of its plans, AXA PPP healthcare also gives members access to its overseas evacuation or repatriation service, which provides emergency medical advice and assistance worldwide, 24 hours a day, 365 days a year.

BUPA International

Bupa International has 38 years' expertise in caring for the insurance needs of expats and their families around the globe. Covering over

800,000 people in more than 190 countries, Bupa International is the largest international expatriate health insurer in the world, supplying quality individual and group medical cover to people who are in their home country or living abroad for six months or more, with a network of 7,500 hospitals. The company is part of the leading international health and care group, Bupa.

In 2008, Bupa International received the Best International Private Medical Insurance Provider award at the UK's Health Insurance Awards, for the ninth time since 1999.

Expat understanding

Understanding that expats want peace of mind about their health while abroad Bupa International has developed an extensive worldwide network of over 7,500 participating hospitals and a 24-hour helpline, open 365 days a year, manned by a team of experienced advisers who, between them, speak 34 languages. Bupa International processes over 15,000 claims a week, provides a prompt turnaround of claims and direct settlement of bills where possible; claims can be paid in any of 80 currencies.

Tailored products are offered to suit the needs of differing groups. For the oil and gas industry for example, there are policies covering employees both offshore and onshore, as well as a maritime policy, designed for crew employees who live and work aboard yachts, super yachts or ocean-going vessels.

Medical expertise

The Bupa International emergency medical team, available around the clock to customers, consists of highly-trained doctors who are experts in high altitude diseases, tropical infections, patient evacuations and home transportations. They also have extensive experience of diagnosing and treating cancer, heart disorders and musculoskeletal conditions. The medical team ensures that immediate and correct treatment is provided, when the need arises.

Cover alternatives

Three benefits packages are defined in pages 156–58. Worldwide Medical Insurance provides cover up to a maximum of £1,500,000 for each registered member in any one year. Worldwide Medical

What is covered?

Worldwide Medical Insurance – annual overall limit £1,500,000/€1,875,000/$2,550,000

Benefit	Level of cover	£ Sterling	€ Euros	$ US	At a glance	Notes
Staying in hospital overnight or as a day-case	Paid in full				Room and board costs when staying in hospital overnight or as a day-case	0.0
Parent accommodation	Paid in full				Room and board costs when staying in hospital with your child	0.1
Nursing care	Paid in full				Nursing services provided in hospital	0.2
Operating room, medicines and surgical dressings	Paid in full				Operating room, recovery room, medicines and dressings when you have surgery	0.3
Intensive care, intensive therapy, coronary care and high dependency unit	Paid in full				Room and board costs when staying in hospital or intensive care, intensive therapy, coronary care or high dependency unit when required as part of your treatment	0.4
Surgery, including surgeons', anaesthetists' and assistants fees*	Paid in full				Includes operations performed whether staying in hospital overnight, as a day-case or as an out-patient	0.5
Specialists' consultation fees	Paid in full				Meetings with or treatment by a specialist in hospital	0.6
Pathology, X-rays, diagnostic tests and therapies	Paid in full				Investigations such as blood or urine tests and diagnostic X-rays,* or therapies	0.7
Rehabilitation	Paid in full for 30 days each condition				A combination of therapies aimed at either restoring full function or the ability to live independently	0.8
Advanced imaging	Paid in full				Diagnostic imaging whether staying in hospital overnight, as a day-case or as an out-patient	0.9
Psychiatric treatment overnight in hospital, including room, board and treatment costs	90 days lifetime limit				Treatment of mental health problems, including eating disorders	0.10
Psychiatric treatment as a day-case, including room, board and treatment costs	Paid in full for 20 days each membership year					0.11
Prosthetic implants and appliances	Paid in full				An artificial body part which is designed to form a permanent part of your body or is a medically necessary temporary part of your body	0.11
Prosthetic devices	Each device	2,000	2,500	3,400	An external artificial body part, such as a prosthetic limb or prosthetic ear	0.12
Childbirth and treatment in hospital	Each membership year, up to	6,500	8,100	11,050	Available once the mother has been a member for 10 months or more. Hospital charges, obstetricians' and midwives' fees for normal and complicated delivery	0.13
Childbirth at home	Each membership year, up to	650	810	1,105		0.14
Newborn care	Paid in full	75,000	93,750	127,500	All treatment within first 90 days following birth	0.15
Cancer treatment	Paid in full	150,000	187,500	255,000	All treatment you receive for or related to cancer whether staying in hospital overnight, as a day-case or as an out-patient	0.16
Transplant services	Each condition, up to	150,000	187,500	255,000	All costs for treatment in hospital, including donor expenses for organ harvesting if the recipient is a Bupa International member	0.17
Hospice and palliative care	Lifetime limit	20,000	25,000	34,000	Expenses following the diagnosis that your condition is terminal when treatment can no longer be expected to cure your condition	0.18
Local road ambulance	Paid in full				Medically necessary travel by local road ambulance when related to covered hospitalisation	0.19
Local air ambulance	Each membership year, up to	5,000	6,250	8,500	Medically necessary travel by local air ambulance, such as a helicopter, when related to covered hospitalisation	0.20
Home nursing	Paid in full for 30 days each membership year				Payable for home nursing after a covered stay in hospital	0.21
Hospitalisation cash benefit	Each night for a maximum of up to 30 nights each membership year	100	125	170	Payable for each night you stay in hospital without charge	0.22
Emergency dental treatment	Paid in full				Dental treatment in hospital after a serious accident	
Treatment of congenital and hereditary conditions	Each membership year, up to	20,000	25,000	34,000	Payable for treatment received after the first 90 days' following birth	

Worldwide Medical Plus –
annual overall limit £25,000/€31,250/$42,500 (excluding transplant benefits)
These benefits are only available if you have chosen this option and it is listed on your membership certificate.

Benefit	Level of cover	£ Sterling	€ Euros	$ US	At a glance	Notes
Specialists' consultation and **doctors'** fees	Paid in full up to 35 visits each **membership year**				A meeting with your **specialist** or **doctor**	1.0
Physiotherapy, osteopathy and chiropractor treatment	Paid in full up to 30 visits each **membership year**				Physical therapies	1.1
Consultations and treatment with complementary therapists	Paid in full up to 15 visits each **membership year**				To include acupuncture, homeopathy and Chinese medicine	1.2
Psychiatrists' and psychologists' fees	Paid in full up to 30 visits each **membership year**				**Treatment** for mental health conditions	1.3
Speech therapy	Paid in full				Provided on a short-term basis following a condition such as a stroke	1.4
Pathology, X-rays and diagnostic tests	Paid in full				Investigations such as blood or urine tests, diagnostic X-rays and hearing tests	1.5
Young child care	Each **membership year**, up to	1,000	1,250	1,700	Routine preventive care for children covered under this option	1.6
Maternity	Each **membership year**, up to	2,000	2,500	3,400	Pre and post natal care	1.7
Accident-related dental treatment	Each **membership year**, 80% up to	500	625	850	An accident resulting in a need for dental **treatment** only, which is received as an **out-patient**	1.8
Transplant services	Each condition, up to	50,000	62,500	85,000	Costs for transplant related **treatment**, before and after the transplant	1.9

Worldwide Medicines and Equipment
These benefits are only available if you have chosen this option and it is listed on your membership certificate.

Benefit	Level of cover	£ Sterling	€ Euros	$ US	At a glance	Notes
Prescribed medicines and dressings	Each **membership year**, up to				Medicines and dressings prescribed for you by your **medical practitioner**	2.0
Durable medical equipment rental	Up to 45 days each condition each **membership year** up to	1,500	1,875	2,550	Such as crutches, a wheelchair or **hospital bed**	2.1
Long-term prescription medicines	Each **membership year**, 80% up to	10,000	12,500	17,000	Medicines prescribed for long-term use of six months or more	2.2
	Lifetime limit	60,000	75,000	102,000		

What is covered?

Worldwide Wellbeing - annual overall limit £5,000/€6,250/$8,500

These benefits are only available if you have chosen this option and it is listed on your membership certificate.

Benefit	Level of cover	£ Sterling	€ Euros	$ US	At a glance	Notes
Screening and prevention:						
Full health screen					A range of tests performed to review your general overall state of health and fitness	3.0
Mammogram					Breast X-ray to detect signs of disease	
Papanicolaou (PAP) test					Smear test to detect signs of cervical cancer	3.1
Prostate cancer screen	Each membership year, up to	500	625	850	A blood test and/or digital rectal examination to detect signs of prostate cancer	
Colon cancer screen					A test such as a colonoscopy or an X-ray such as a barium enema to examine the large bowel for signs of colon cancer	3.2
Bone densitometry					A scan to determine the density of your bones	3.3
Four dietetic consultations					Meetings with a dietician	3.4
Vaccinations					Vaccinations and immunisations	
Dental						
Preventive	Each membership year, 100% up to				Routine check-ups and hygienist services	3.5
Routine and major restorative	Each membership year 80% up to	3,500	4,375	5,950	Treatment of a dental problem	3.6
Orthodontic	Each membership year 50% up to				Treatment of misaligned teeth: under-bite, over-bite	3.7
Optical						
Eye test (including consultations)	One each membership year 100%				Meeting and tests with an eye specialist to assess your sight and vision	3.8
Spectacle lenses	80%				Prescribed lenses only	3.9
Contact lenses	80%					
Spectacle frames	Once every two membership years, 80% up to	150	185	255	Only available if you have prescribed lenses	3.10

What is covered?

Worldwide Evacuation

These benefits are only available if you have chosen this option and it is listed on your membership certificate.

Benefit	Level of cover	£ Sterling	€ Euros	$ US	At a glance	Notes
Medical evacuation	Paid in full				Transfer to a hospital either in the same country or another country if the treatment you need is not available locally	4.0
Medical repatriation	Paid in full				Option to transfer to a hospital in your home country	4.1
Travel cost for an accompanying person	Paid in full				A friend or relative can accompany you on your transfer, if there is a reasonable need for someone to go with you	4.2
Travel cost for the transfer of minor children	Paid in full				If minor children will be left without a parent or guardian in the event of an evacuation or repatriation of a parent	4.3
Living allowance	For a maximum of 10 days each membership year, each day up to	100	125	170	A daily allowance towards living expenses for an accompanying person	4.4
Repatriation of mortal remains	Lifetime limit, up to	6,500	8,125	11,050	Transfer of your mortal remains either to your home country or to your country of residence	4.5
Compassionate visit and return	Five trips lifetime limit. Each membership year, up to	800	1,000	1,360	Travel expenses for a relative's visit	4.6
Compassionate visit living allowance	For a maximum of 10 days each visit, each day up to	100	125	170	A daily allowance towards living expenses for a visiting relative	4.6

Plus provides additional cover for consultations and specialist treatment up to £25,000 for each registered member each year of cover. Worldwide Wellbeing is another optional addition which provides cover up to £5,000 per annum for health screening, vaccination and dental and optical treatment. Further options are Bupa International's Worldwide Medicines and Equipment and Worldwide Evacuation packages.

Quotations for subscription terms, according to the deductions from claims that you are prepared to take for payments by yourself, are available on application from the telephone numbers below.

For more information, visit www.bupa-intl.com. For international health cover for you and your family call +44 (0) 1273 718 304. If you're interested in group cover call +44 (0) 1273 718 308.

Another firm which issues its clients with a card is International SOS Assistance, whose medical and security schemes enable the holder, or those looking after them, to call for medical assistance at six main centres throughout the world. They specialize in emergency medical evacuation to the nearest high-quality medical facility, repatriation and return of mortal remains. AXA PPP, BUPA, Goodhealth Worldwide, Expacare, IPH, William Russell, Carecard International and other private insurers use these services. As they point out, it is only of limited use to have cover for repatriation unless it can be implemented easily. GESA Assistance provides a similar service to, among others, Falcon Healthcare.

Catering particularly for the retired expatriate, the Exeter Friendly Society does not automatically increase premium rates with advancing age, making their policies a good buy for the over-50s.

John Wason (Insurance Brokers) Ltd, founded by a former expatriate, offers a specialist 'Overseas Personal Insurance' scheme, which includes optional medical and personal accident/sickness cover worldwide. Levels of cover accord with 'units' purchased.

Finally, there is the possibility of free, or subsidized, local medical care courtesy of a reciprocal agreement with the UK health authorities. The EU and many other countries have such agreements, but the terms do vary. An EHIC is required and can be obtained from the Post Office, through the Health Literature Line on 0845 606 2030, or online via www.dh.gov.uk (your NHS or national insurance number will be required). However, this scheme is no substitute for a good insurance policy.

Some of the questions you should ask about your medical cover are as listed on page 160.

1. Does the scheme cover all eventualities?
2. Are the scheme's benefits realistic in the light of local costs?
3. Can you make claims immediately or is there an initial indemnity period during which claims are disallowed? (Some insurers insist on this to protect themselves from claims caused by 'pre-existing medical conditions'.)
4. Is there a clause providing for emergency repatriation by air, or air ambulance, if suitable treatment is not available locally? If so, who decides what constitutes an emergency and/or adequate local treatment?
5. Is the insurer's nearest office accessible personally or by telephone?
6. What is the length of the insurer's settlement period for claims?
7. Is there a discount for members of professional or other associations?
8. Does the policy continue to apply, partly or fully, while you are back in the UK?
9. What is the insurer's attitude to AIDS and HIV tests?

PERSONAL SECURITY

There are overseas countries where crimes against persons, either for gain or to make political points, are a serious hazard. Countries where Islamic fundamentalism is rampant are a case in point. Other places, notably in Africa and Latin America, qualify as high-risk locations in terms of personal safety, eg Colombia, Zimbabwe, Brazilian cities and Johannesburg. There are also corporate or national connections that may be the target of terrorists:

- Anything to do with Israel. It is still advisable to carry a separate passport if you have a visa for Israel but also travel to the Middle East.
- Employees of companies associated with pollution, nuclear waste and animal experiments.
- Nationals of countries that have recently been, or are currently, in serious dispute with countries in which an expatriate is living – or even its allies.

According to the international security consultants Merchants International Group (MIG), resident expatriates tend to be more at risk in these circumstances than visiting businessmen. However, the terrorist attacks on the World Trade Center in New York and the Pentagon in Washington of 11 September 2001 and the rigorous new entry checks and routines that the United States introduced on all incoming airline passengers in response, have brought to the forefront the constant risks from terrorism to which all business travellers are exposed, even in the most developed countries. The same is, of course, true for visitors to European cities, as the London bombing incidents in July 2005 demonstrated. MIG, which specializes in the 'grey areas' of risk often associated with developing countries, is available for advice on these matters. For more information, visit the MIG website at www.merchantinternational. com or telephone its London office on 0207 259 5060 (address: 1 Grosvenor Crescent, London SW1X 7EF). Holiday locations in countries such as Egypt, India and Indonesia are also vulnerable to terrorist attack.

ACCIDENTS

Finally, it is worth sounding a note of warning. In many countries getting involved in legal action can be disastrous – even when it is over a minor incident. It is certainly worth researching your host country's attitude to such events and what kind of ethical stance it takes on such matters – including that of bribery. Check if your company has an ethical policy on such matters.

In some parts of the world it might be wise to hire a driver rather than take the risk of getting involved in an accident yourself. It is important not to take any unnecessary risks, as many countries are unsympathetic to practices accepted as normal in other parts of the world, such as drinking alcohol or gambling.

Checklist: Health, security and welfare

1. Avoid daily routines, like taking the same route to work every day at a fixed time.
2. Remove bushes and thick vegetation around the entrance to your house or place of work – they could make a hiding place for criminals, and people tend to be least vigilant as they approach familiar places.
3. If you think you are being followed, head immediately for a place where there are as many other people around as possible. Criminals prefer not to strike when there are witnesses about.
4. Watch out for abandoned cars in the vicinity. These are sometimes dumped by criminals to test police vigilance.
5. Avoid conspicuous displays of affluence.
6. Try to have a room in your house to which you and your family can retreat if serious danger threatens. It should have good doors with stout locks, and windows that can be secured from the inside but which do not bar escape routes. If possible, get professional advice on how to prepare what is called a 'keep' in your house.
7. Using firearms as a form of self-defence is fraught with danger. You will nearly always be faced with more than one assailant and you have to be prepared to shoot to kill. That in itself is much less easy than it is made to look in the movies; furthermore, in some countries foreigners are always in the wrong in such circumstances.
8. The best form of defence and survival is to rehearse a plan of action in your mind in case you are attacked or in danger – and to stick to it if you can. The thing to avoid above all is panic, because if you panic you lose control of the situation.

11

Adjusting to Living and Working Abroad

Living and working overseas can be extremely rewarding in personal, financial and career terms. It is also likely to herald a dramatic change of lifestyle. All expatriates, no matter to which country they are posted, have to make some adjustment to life overseas, and all members of an expatriate's family will be affected by the move, whether or not they venture abroad. If, as a married person, you go abroad 'on unaccompanied status', you and your family will have to make a number of adjustments to living separately. There is much to be gained in going abroad as a couple, but in so doing you may be asking your partner to give up a career and possible future chances of employment, and, if you have children, disrupting their education, and removing your family from their normal sources of comfort and support (see Chapters 8 and 9).

For families who do decide to relocate together, a failure to adapt might mean having to terminate the contract early. Such unscheduled returns to the UK tend to cause considerable disturbance and hardship to all concerned. There is a high turnover rate among expatriates, so before you commit yourself and your family to working abroad it is important to discuss the likely consequences of the move with other members of your family.

CULTURE SHOCK

In contemplating a move overseas you have probably tried to imagine what it will be like. Most people think about the physical differences: the heat, the humidity, the dirt, etc, although they are rarely able to assess how these differences will affect their daily lives. How will working in 90 per cent humidity impair your effectiveness? Could you negotiate an important contract in an atmosphere more suited to the tropical house of your nearest botanical gardens? It is difficult to appreciate how much of the background to daily life is taken for granted; for example, drinking water from a tap, flicking a switch for light, pushing a button for instant entertainment. In underdeveloped countries many of these basics of everyday life either do not exist or function irregularly. While it is easy to imagine that things will be different, it is hard to envisage how this affects the quality of daily life and your sense of well-being.

But the differences that prove the greatest barrier to adjustment are the ones that cannot be seen and that are not normally even thought about. Despite regional differences in the UK most people have grown up with common experiences and expectations of how the world works. In any given situation, most people have a fairly clear idea of what is expected of them and what they expect of others. However, different nationalities do not necessarily share the same assumptions and expectations about life, or about how other people should behave. In Britain we share a common culture and, on the whole, common beliefs about what is right and proper. Other cultures, though, have quite different underlying values and beliefs, different expectations and concepts of 'normal behaviour'. Britain is nominally a Christian country, yet although much legislation and ordinary behaviour have their origins in Christian teaching, a relatively small proportion of the population would see Christianity as the driving force of British society.

By contrast, in Saudi Arabia, Islam underlies everything. It regulates the legal and political system and the conduct of all aspects of everyday life and is so perceived by its own nationals. It can be difficult to understand how other people operate; it is easy to assume that the motivations of others are understood, while misunderstanding them utterly. In Britain the ground rules of human behaviour can be taken for granted, but overseas they must be questioned and come to terms with. For example, in Malaysia it is not uncommon for expatriates to feel that their local subordinates are disloyal when, instead of discussing some decision with which they disagree, they simply choose to ignore it. Yet to the Malaysian it would be unpardonable to cause a superior to lose face by questioning them in public; far more polite simply to ignore what is considered to be a poor suggestion.

Even unconscious behaviour is open to misinterpretation. For example, in the UK an individual who avoids eye contact would usually be categorized (unconsciously) as shifty or guilty. In Nigeria the same individual would be seen as respectful, because to avoid eye contact with an older person is a mark of respect. The classic example of how the smallest physical cues are subject to different interpretations is one of distance. The British tend to feel comfortable standing two to three feet apart when chatting; the Saudis prefer to stand closer together. A Saudi and a Briton talking to each other will each unconsciously try to establish the distance at which each feels comfortable. The Briton will feel threatened when the Saudi edges nearer and the Saudi will feel rebuffed as the Briton sidles backwards. Neither will appreciate the impact of their unconscious behaviour on the other. This kind of disorientation is experienced constantly by the fledgling expatriate, causing many expatriates to respond aggressively when no hostility was intended.

The expatriate experiences considerable anxiety when faced unknowingly with the loss of minor cues: the familiar signs and symbols that are taken for granted in the UK but are open to different interpretations in the host country. This constant disorientation is unnerving and can cause considerable stress. The syndrome is so common that it has been given a name – culture shock.

Doctors have long recognized that changes in normal lifestyle can result in stress, and ultimately physical and mental illness. Change of home, change of friends, change of job, change of lifestyle, loss of or separation from the marital partner may all be experienced by the expatriate, who may be deprived of their traditional means of support and solace. A new job is always stressful, but when the job is in a new (and seemingly hostile) environment, the tensions are even greater. Symptoms associated with culture shock include heightened anxiety and worry, feelings of isolation and helplessness, and a poor performance at work. Most expatriates eventually settle down, more or less successfully, but there is a predictable cycle to the adjustment and three main stereotyped responses to adaptation.

First, there is the chauvinistic expatriate, whose response to their predicament is to try to create a mini encapsulated UK or 'Little England'. This expatriate's attempts to understand the local way of doing things, or local colleagues, are minimal. Faced with the difficulties of this new environment they retreat from what is perceived as a hostile host country and people. The blame for misunderstandings is never anything to do with themselves, but is always the fault of the 'stupid' locals. This expatriate falls into a trap of denigrating everything local and idealizing everything from home, ultimately provoking real hostility from local counterparts and making a reality of their view of themselves alone against the world. Local expatriate clubs are full of this kind of expatriate, who often indulge their aggression over more drinks than are healthy.

The chauvinistic expatriate is experiencing culture shock. They are disorientated by the environment and feel constantly at sea. The symptoms of this state are incessant complaining, glorification of the UK, alcoholic over-indulgence, marital difficulties and general aggression. At this stage the expatriate will find it hard to work with local colleagues or clients and will be permanently miserable. It is at this stage also that expatriates tend to terminate their contracts, prior to completion, with major repercussions for their families and their own careers. Fortunately for most expatriates, this is a passing stage and after their first home leave, when the realities of life in Britain are forced upon them, they manage to adapt successfully.

The second, much rarer, response is to 'go bush'. This expatriate eschews the company of their fellow expatriates, and tends to over-idealize all things local. They identify totally with the host culture, which many of their local colleagues find both patronizing and suspect.

The third and probably most appropriate response, but the most difficult to achieve, is that of the 'open-minded expatriate' who, without abandoning their own values, is able to accept the new culture and attempt to understand it. This involves understanding how the host society's values are reflected in everyday behaviour. Decisions are made without the necessity for qualitative judgement. While differences are acknowledged, they are not categorized as better or worse.

If, prior to arriving abroad, you can come to terms with the idea that there are real cultural differences which need to be understood, you will find it much easier to adjust. These cultural differences affect work and home life. Often at work the differences are hidden because on the surface the work to be done is the same as at home, but local colleagues may have different ways of doing business and different attitudes to time and concepts of loyalty.

Management styles may differ and motivation and discipline have quite different connotations. For example, many other nationalities find Western haste in business negotiations unpalatable; it is good manners and a useful way of assessing a business associate to chat seemingly inconsequentially before getting down to real negotiations. The Westerner considers it a waste of time, even insulting. In many parts of the world ethnic loyalty is a salient feature of everyday life, and a member of one tribe may be under an obligation to find jobs not only for his extended family, ie sons and daughters of aunts, uncles, cousins, and children of his father's other wives, but also for members of his own ethnic group. Outside the West, age is still considered to bestow authority and seniority, even at work. Social adjustment can also be difficult. Business is often conducted at social events; business entertaining at home may be the norm. Social life can be restricted, as in many areas expatriates make little attempt to get to know local people and mix almost entirely in expatriate circles. This can cause considerable pressure, as any minor upset at work or at home is common knowledge and long remembered.

The married expatriate living alone abroad often has the most difficulty in adjusting, both when working and when on leave. Single people often feel excluded from much social activity, which revolves around the family. Single women suffer especially, as other expatriate women may resent or even fear them, and friendship with local colleagues can be misinterpreted. However, it is often the partners who bear the brunt of culture shock and have the greatest difficulty in adapting, as discussed in a previous chapter.

PREPARING YOURSELF FOR THE CHANGE

So how can you, as a prospective expatriate, prepare yourself and your family to make the appropriate adjustments? First, you and your family should try to find out as much as possible about the country before you accept the assignment, and preferably before you go to the job interview. Once you have accepted a job offer, some employers will give you a briefing of some description. Relatively few employers seem to appreciate that the cost of staff turnover, in money, time, effort and damage to relationships with their clients, merits an outlay on briefing expatriates and their families before their departure.

You will need to know something about your employer, the nature and responsibilities of your job, the terms and conditions of your contract and whether the benefits offered match the prevailing conditions in the country. You will want to learn about the country, its history, geography, climate, politics, economics, form of government, people and religion, etc. Much of this basic or factual information will be available in standard publications from the national embassies and tourist offices (although most countries naturally like to present a favourable picture of themselves). There are a number of specialized directories available in public reference libraries containing this information and some banks, such as HSBC, produce factual booklets. The BIS produces a vast range of publications aimed at business abroad, many of which contain information of value to intending expatriates.

The financial problems of expatriate life, such as personal taxation, insurance, etc, and other aspects of interest to expatriates are covered on several websites catering specifically for their needs.

Among these, Expat Network offers a total support service for expatriates on www.expatnetwork.co.uk. It is a leading expatriate membership organization which enjoys a firmly established reputation within the overseas recruitment sector. The expatriate community and the overseas employment market need a level of understanding which can only be achieved over time. Most things are different, from the way in which contracts are negotiated, the job search itself, the problems involved with tax, personal finances, currency, locations, social security, pensions, etc. Expat Network can offer advice for each and every eventuality. A number of services are offered. The website deals with expatriate issues, offers in-depth industry features, contractual news and advice on money matters and financial security.

Some companies run their own courses; others use outside organizations. If your employer will not pay for you to attend a course, it would be worthwhile paying out of your own pocket. Ideally, both partners should attend, and children can also benefit.

The International Briefing and Conference Centre provides residential programmes and training for men and women taking up long-term appointments or short-term contracts abroad, and for home-based managers responsible for international personnel. Cultural and business briefings cover all major regions of the world, include all aspects of living and working, and allow a rapid transition to the destination country. Customized programmes provide training in international negotiation and communication skills, intercultural communication, international team building and skill transference in a foreign culture. Language tuition is also available, and the Centre's Language Plus programme combines intensive language and communication studies with business and cultural briefings. Details of programmes are available from the Customer Services Department, The International Briefing and Conference Centre, Farnham Castle, Farnham GU9 0AG; tel: 0845 3660313, fax: 01252 711283; website: www.farnhamcastle.com.

For expatriates going to Japan, China, Korea or other East Asian countries, individually prepared briefing and language sessions are available from East Asia Business Services at the University of Sheffield. Contact the EABS at 317 Glossop Road, Sheffield S10 2HP; tel: 0114 222 8060, fax: 0114 272 8028, e-mail: EABS@Sheffield.ac.uk; website: www.eastasia-business.com. These briefings are tailor-made and can be residential or in-company, according to the client's requirements. Family participation is encouraged. Sister organizations in destinations can provide further services. Briefings are modular and designed to provide new skills and practical knowledge. Sessions are conducted by business people with specific experience of the region.

The External Services Division of the School of Oriental and African Studies within the University of London provides a wide range of briefing and language services for business/government and private individuals. Open briefings on Japan and China are offered on a regular basis, including the two-day Japan Business Orientation Programme and the China Business Orientation Programme. Briefings may be integrated with language tuition if required and are offered on a tailor-made basis for most of the countries or regions of Asia and Africa. Details are available from the coordinator, Ms Dzidra Stipnieks, SOAS External Services Division, University of London, Thornhaugh Street, Russell Square, London WC1H 0XG; tel: 020 7898 4034.

These courses, and some employers, arrange for you to meet recently returned expatriates, and this is particularly useful if you can work out in advance, preferably in the form of a checklist, what you and your family really need to know. Such a checklist can also be helpful if you are offered, as has become increasingly common for senior positions, the possibility of a 'look-see' visit to the location in question.

Some expatriates have reported that the British Council is often helpful in terms of overcoming entry shock and giving advice and information about local amenities and activities.

LEARNING A LANGUAGE

A further aspect of learning about the host country is to master a few basic greetings in the local language. Even when it is not strictly necessary, familiarity with the sound of a language makes everything seem less strange and it is appreciated locally.

The traditional picture of the Englishman who expects all foreigners to speak English or hopes to get by with schoolboy French has disappeared. In the modern world of fast-moving communications, language proficiency is an essential tool. It is true that English is the world's leading language for business and commerce and, in non-English speaking countries, is taught in most schools as the second language. But in many countries knowledge of the indigenous language is essential and often a prerequisite of employment. It is vital where a job involves contact with local people, particularly in administration or industry, where orders and instructions have to be given and understood. Even where a job is technical and does not involve direct communication, it is an advantage to be able to join in conversation and be more fully integrated with local society.

Anybody working in the EU should be proficient in French and/or German. In Spain and Latin America, Spanish is essential (except in Brazil, where Portuguese is spoken). In the Third World, and in the Middle East, knowledge of indigenous languages is not so essential but it is useful to speak Arabic or Swahili, particularly in more remote areas. So the best thing you can do if you are going to work overseas is to learn one or more languages or brush up on your existing knowledge.

The increasing demand for languages is being met in a number of ways. There is the 'do-it-yourself' approach which can include:

1. Learning at home, using Linguaphone courses or other self-study materials.
2. Hiring a private tutor. Try to find a native speaker, who is prepared to conduct most of the lessons in the foreign language rather than waste valuable time talking about the language in English.

3.   Open learning courses at your local college of further education
or university. Many have established 'drop in' centres where
you have access to a language laboratory, and possibly also
computer-assisted learning, with back-up from a tutor when
you need it. This form of learning can be very effective for
those whose time is limited and who need a flexible programme
of study.

For those at the adult beginner level, *Oxford Beginner's Dictionaries*,
published by Oxford University Press, offer all the words and
phrases a beginner needs, as well as lots of extra help with learning
including grammar, culture and travel information. *Beginner's
Dictionaries* are available in French, German, Spanish, Italian,
Russian, Chinese and Japanese and are exceptionally easy to use
because they move away from the traditional dictionary layout. All
main translations are preceded by an equals sign so that they are
instantly identifiable, and all parts of the entry are spelt out in full,
avoiding confusing jargon and abbreviations. Grammar and usage
notes throughout the text warn of possible translation pitfalls, and
thousands of example phrases show how language is used in the
context. The centre section of the dictionary gives background
information on lifestyle and culture, tips on etiquette and interaction in the language, as well as a phrase finder, which provides
useful travellers' phrases.

You may prefer to attend a language class, and these are run by
most local authority adult education institutes and colleges.
However, learning on the basis of one or two sessions a week is not
the most effective way of getting to grips with a foreign language –
you will make a lot more progress on a more intensive course.

Private language schools generally offer intensive or 'crash'
courses. Be careful to check the bona fides of a course before you
enrol. An example of the type of tuition available is Berlitz (UK) Ltd
(Lincoln House, 296–302 High Holborn, London WC1V 73H; tel:
020 7611 9640; fax: 020 7611 9656; website: www.berlitz.co.uk/
london), which offers language programmes to suit the linguistic
needs for all in both the business and non-business fields. Berlitz
offers crash courses, private lessons and semi-private courses for
two to three people in most languages. The full-time Total
Immersion® course lasts from one to six weeks for those wishing to
improve their existing ability quickly. In-house courses for
companies are also available.

Conrad Executive Language Training (53 Queen's Gardens, London W2 3AF; tel: 020 72400855; fax: 020 7402 7175; website: www.conrad-languages.com), founded in 1974, is specifically geared towards meeting the linguistic needs of business people. Tuition is structured to suit both the schedule of each client and specific language requirements. Classes can be held at Conrad's London West End centre, in-company or privately, after a thorough language evaluation and needs analysis. Conrad is registered to ISO 9000 by BSI. Courses available: the Crash Course (9 am–4 pm), suitable for all levels and held over five days (not necessarily consecutively); and the Extensive Course, also suitable for all levels, which can be taken between 8 am and 8 pm – classes last at least one hour and are at times to suit the client. Conrad also offers cross-cultural training programmes for groups and individuals for all countries, and the Corporate Group Course (ideal for companies requiring language training for a small group of executives who have the same objectives and similar background knowledge).

Fees at language schools are high, but there is general agreement that they represent a worthwhile investment. Administrators of language schools sometimes complain that too few companies attach real importance to language proficiency and often leave it too late for effective action.

The European Network of Excellence in Human Language Technologies (ELSNET) is a professional body for providers of language training and related services for business. It aims to establish and maintain quality standards and help organizations and individuals to improve their performance in international markets, mergers and acquisitions, with language training and consultancy geared to the needs of business, including: language training for business; translation and interpreting; country, cultural and trade briefings; needs analysis and language audits. It provides online language courses in Spanish, French, Italian, German and Dutch, as well as English (website: www.language-learning.net).

Other options include foreign cultural institutes, such as the Alliance Française or the Goethe Institut, which run well-established courses, and organizations running courses abroad (nothing can beat learning a language in the country where it is spoken). Courses abroad are advertised in *The Times* and *The Guardian*.

Further information and advice are available from CILT (the Centre for National Languages), 3rd Floor, 111 Westminster Bridge Road, London SE1 7HR; tel: 08456 125885; fax: 08456 125995;

website: www.citt.org.uk. NATBLIS, the National Business Language Information Service (tel: 020 7379 5131, fax: 020 7379 5082), which provides information on business language training and on providers of business language services – training, cultural briefing, interpreting and translation – is also accessible from the same address.

TAKE IT EASY

Once you arrive overseas you should take it easy, adjusting to climatic changes, as they will affect your physical and subsequently your mental state. Coping with so many new stimuli all at once is overpowering and you will need time to find your bearings. Tiredness and depression make it hard to react positively to your new situation. It is part of the adjustment cycle to feel frustrated and depressed, but if you can make the effort to understand the underlying cultural reasons for your frustration, you will be well on your way to adjusting successfully and enjoying your life abroad. After that you just have to cope with the culture shock of returning to the UK at the end of your assignment.

Checklist: Adjusting to living and working abroad

1. Try to find out as much as possible about your host country – not just the physical conditions but its culture, values and beliefs.
2. Become familiar with the ground rules for behaviour towards colleagues and with attitudes to age and gender.
3. Be aware of the symptoms of stress and culture shock.
4. If you experience culture shock, find someone to talk to, perhaps an experienced expatriate, and seek professional help for prolonged symptoms.
5. Use the internet, public libraries and specialist services to find out as much information as possible about your new location.
6. Ask your employer to send you and your family on a briefing course before departure.
7. Try to learn the language of your host country – it will help you integrate into your local society.
8. Be aware that you might well experience culture shock on your return to your home country.

Part Four

Making the Move

12

Moving Out

WHAT TO TAKE AND REMOVAL

Whatever agonizing variables you feed into your mental computer about what and what not to take, you will certainly find that in the end you are left with two basic choices – either to take very little other than clothes, books, favourite possessions and whatever small items you and your family need to feel at home, or to take virtually everything.

It clearly depends on where you are going, how long you are going for, and who you are going to work for. If you are taking up an appointment in a sophisticated European capital or in North America, obviously you will not need the same kind of things as you would in a developing country, say in Africa or Asia, where everything tends to be scarce and expensive. If you are going to a tropical country, or the Middle East, clothes and equipment will be very different from what you will need in a temperate or northern area.

As a rule, travelling reasonably light is the best course of action. Even if you are going to be away for a long time, it seldom pays to take large items of household equipment, such as sofas, beds or wardrobes; the cost of shipping bulky items is very high. In any case, it can take quite a long time to clear them through customs when they arrive, so you will either have to send them ahead or find yourself arriving in a new place without any furniture.

Such situations are apt to be inconvenient and will probably result in your having to buy some things simply to tide you over. Clothes, bedlinen, crockery, kitchen equipment and so forth are cheap to transport – shipping companies usually convey some baggage free of charge – and usually expensive to replace at the other end. Furthermore, these items lend themselves to being sent ahead, and you can usually make do, or borrow, in the meantime.

Antiques are always worth taking, since they are vastly expensive in most places outside the UK, but remember that old furniture and pictures can be sensitive to climatic change. Such problems may also exist with electronic equipment, and your CD player or food mixer may have to go through costly adaptations to fit in with foreign voltages. Records, tapes and musical instruments deteriorate in hot climates. There can also be problems over import controls, though most authorities have special dispensations for personal possessions.

As far as household equipment is concerned, much depends on the terms of your contract. Most commercial firms in developing countries will provide a fully furnished house or apartment (possibly also a car). Fully furnished means that everything, down to the last lampshade, is provided and you only need your personal effects. National governments and public corporations usually supply 'hard furnished' accommodation. Hard furnished is what it implies. Only the bare necessities such as tables and chairs and a bed are provided, and you will need to supply curtains, cushions, linen, loose covers, cutlery, crockery and kitchen gear. Often you can buy these things from an outgoing tenant or returning expatriate, but you have to be on the spot for this.

It is strongly recommended that where a family is going out to a developing country the employee should travel out alone in advance, unless furnished accommodation is assured, and only send for the family when this has been fixed up. It may mean staying in a hotel or hostel for a time, but it is worth the inconvenience to be able to learn the ropes at first hand and decide what will be needed from home. Some companies arrange for both partners to go out in advance for a 'reconnaissance' visit.

In some cases, especially if the contract is a short-term one, in a difficult country, it is recommended that the employee should go out alone, leaving their family in the UK. This may sound heartless, but it does minimize the upheaval and avoids disrupting the children's education.

If you are going to a tropical country where conditions are difficult, you may not be able to buy such items as a deep freeze, food mixer, sewing machine, hairdryer and electric iron except in the main centres. A portable electric fan is useful if the house is not air conditioned. An electric kettle is a must and so is a torch. There may be power cuts, so stock up with candles.

If you have very young children with you, take pram, carrycot, pushchair and plenty of toys. Camping equipment, eg tents and sleeping bags, may be useful, and so may gardening tools, as many houses have quite large gardens. Take golf clubs, tennis rackets, photographic equipment, etc, since these leisure and luxury goods may be unobtainable or very expensive overseas, though this will again depend very much on where you go.

Stock up with cosmetics and toiletries, drugs and medicines since everything in this line is expensive and difficult to obtain. Find out the voltage and type of electric plug in use and, before you go if possible, check with the appliance manufacturer about any adaptations. A useful website address is www.kropla.com, which is a comprehensive listing of worldwide electrical and telephone information and provides details of electric plugs and voltages used in different countries throughout the world.

Don't rely on somebody sending you something from home. Postage can be exorbitant, mails are slow and the contents liable to be pilfered. It may be possible to get your children, or your neighbour's children, to bring things out when they come on leave from school.

The best way to handle the question of actual removal is to consult one of the big removal firms. Overseas removal is not a job you should take on yourself, nor is it a good thing on which to try to save money. Moving abroad is a very different proposition from moving in this country and, in choosing your remover, it is better to ask for a good name than a good quote. The bigger removers are well informed about living conditions in overseas countries – check, though, that any printed literature they give you is fully up to date.

Removers are knowledgeable about what you can and should take with you, and most have agents at ports of entry who can help with the sometimes interminable business of clearing your belongings through customs. Another advantage of a 'name' remover is that they can generally get a better insurance deal than with a smaller firm. You should, incidentally, increase your insurance to cover replacement costs at the other end. If you cannot get any specific information about this, an increase of 50 to 80 per cent over UK values will serve as a rough guideline.

An alternative to using one of the 'big names' is to contact one of the specialist consortia of overseas removal companies. These are made up of hand-picked, privately owned companies specializing in overseas removals. As a team, members provide the strength and capacity of a large international concern; individually they are able to provide a local, personal service that many customers prefer.

All members conform to standards of service that are the same all over the world. So a remover operating out of the UK will provide the same level of service as their counterparts in Italy, for instance. Using the consortium method is rather like using a removal company with branch offices all over the world.

In the past there has been extensive publicity over the sudden demise of overseas removal companies, which – having received payment in advance – have left their customers' belongings either in the warehouse or, worse still, languishing in an overseas country. This usually resulted in families having to pay twice over for their household effects to be delivered, and many who could not afford to pay again had to abandon their belongings altogether.

Protection against this sort of disaster is now available through the Advance Payments Guarantee Scheme operated by the Overseas Group of the British Association of Removers. The scheme provides that customers who have paid removal charges in advance to a firm participating in the scheme are guaranteed that, in the event of the removal company ceasing to trade, their belongings will either be delivered at no further cost, or they will be refunded the cost of the removal charges.

It should not be assumed that all removers are in the scheme. The safeguard provided by the scheme is available only through members of the BAR Overseas Group. The guarantee is under-written by a mutual insurance company set up by the industry.

The British Association of Removers itself will be happy to supply readers with leaflets giving advice on moving abroad and brochures on the Advance Payments Guarantee Scheme. The association also provides a list of companies participating in the scheme. Readers should send a 9in × 4in sae to the British Association of Removers, 3 Churchill Court, 58 Station Road, North Harrow HA2 7SA (tel: 020 8861 3331, fax: 020 8861 3332).

Removal costs vary according to the distance to be covered, the method of transportation (land, sea or air), the terms of the arrangement (delivery to port or home, packed or unpacked) and a range of other factors. Customers should obtain written estimates from several companies. Beware of firms that quote on the basis of approximate measures. Be specific, understand exactly the terms of the arrangement and obtain a written agreement, so that you have what amounts to a contract with which to resist 'surcharges' imposed at the point of disembarkation.

Some people like to pack their own things. If so, it is best to use custom-made cardboard boxes, which are stout, light and can be banded to withstand rough handling and exposure. These generally come with movers' details, logo and grids in which details of the contents, origin and whether fragile or not, can be entered. It is essential to make a list of contents and advisable to see that your cases or boxes are readily identifiable for when you collect them at the other end. Smaller goods can be taken with you, up to the 20 kg allowable limit. Some things may be carried as hand luggage, depending on how full the plane is. But on all these points, be guided by the experts.

MOVING SMOOTHLY TO A NEW WORKING LIFE

Geoff Watson, Managing Director, Doree Bonner

Moving overseas – whether emigrating or for employment purposes – is an exciting time, but it can also be a time of enormous stress and worry. Choosing the right removal company is absolutely pivotal to the success of your move and will also help take the stress out of the whole process. It's important therefore that you use a professional and experienced company able to deliver the highest levels of service. After all, this is no time for a man with a van or booking agency who actually subcontract the operational part of a move (the most important part) to a mover!

Selecting a reliable and professional international removal company

If you're planning a move abroad you will already appreciate how much there is to think about and organize, but one decision you really can't afford to delay – or get wrong – is choosing your international removals company. There are literally hundreds of removals companies out there and sadly some will fall far short of the exacting standards we set ourselves, so you need to start by thoroughly and methodically researching the sector. So just how should you go about finding a professional, helpful and reliable removal company?

Personal recommendation is often the best way to choose any service – and this is no different. Ask yourself if you, your family or friends know anyone who's emigrated and could recommend an international removal company? As one of the UK's leading moving companies, we enjoy a particularly high level of personal recommendations from satisfied customers – with over a quarter of our business coming via this route.

The internet is of course a fantastically useful resource, but you must look beyond the website as these days it's relatively inexpensive to produce a good quality website promoting a seemingly professional image but with no foundation or history to the company in question. Try looking at the online forums for impartial and independent advice about which removal company to use. And last, but by no means least; don't forget to use publications such as this one!

Attributes for selection

Professionalism and a breadth of experience are absolutely essential attributes when choosing an international moving company, so it's critical to look out for a FAIM accreditation. FAIM is a quality standard set by FIDI, the only worldwide organization of note for the industry. This accreditation guarantees the quality of the mover you've chosen and is held by more than 500 companies in over 100 countries world wide, so you shouldn't have any difficulty finding one suitable for your needs. And, in these credit crunch times, you need to ensure you trust your worldly goods to an established, financially stable company. Reassuringly, the FIDI audit ensures their members adhere to the highest standards with regards to a number of factors, including the financial stability of the company. You can also contact the British Association of Removers (BAR) and look for companies that belong to their overseas accreditation scheme.

Don't overlook insurance at this early stage in the process. This is often an area where people will try to cut costs, but we'd caution strongly against not insuring; although it can seem complicated, it's vital to ensure complete peace of mind for your move. At Doree Bonner we are regulated to sell insurance by the Financial Services Authority (FSA) and Doree Bonner offers a marine insurance policy specifically tailored to cover an international removal of the owner's furniture and household possessions on a 'door to door' basis.

The vital home visit

Once you've drawn up your shortlist, any removal company worth their salt will want to visit you at home. This is a really important part of the process as the removal cost is calculated based on the actual volume of goods you'd like to take with you. Don't accept a telephone quote – it's unlikely to be accurate and you could easily find yourself facing hefty additional charges.

During the home visit, do take the opportunity to fully discuss your requirements, making sure they – and you – know exactly what you'd like to take with you. Once the survey has taken place, the representative should sit with you and discuss all the options available, giving you their opinion on the best way to transport your belongings having taken both your timescale and budget into account. They should also be happy to provide a number of different quotes based on different options such as the best method of transporting your worldly goods – sole or shared use container? And best mode of transport – by air or sea?

How removal costs are calculated

We're sometimes asked to provide a rough estimate of costs over the telephone – something on which we refuse to be drawn – it's a 'how long is a piece of string?' question! So much depends on differing factors such as where you're going, how much you're taking and what method of transport you've chosen. However, we will always follow up the home survey quickly with a detailed written quotation covering everything discussed with our representative. This will include a comprehensive list of the goods for shipment, how your goods will be shipped, the services included at destination and the name and full details of our overseas partners. Once again, you should ensure that your removal company's overseas partners are also FAIM accredited as this will guarantee the services provided to you when you arrive. And remember; tempting though it is to go with the cheapest quote – and of course a competitive quote is important – don't fall into the trap of making cost the only criteria. As with so much in life – you generally find that you get what you pay for!

By now you will have made all of the major moving decisions, including whether to pack yourself or have the professionals do it. You should think seriously about using your removal company to pack for you. After all they're the professionals and it's at this stage that we often see clients bitterly regretting the decision to do it themselves!

Understand how best to approach the customs and quarantine maze

One of the most common questions we're asked is 'What can and can't we take with us?' Customs and quarantine procedures can be one of the most confusing aspects of an international move, which is why most people opt to use a removal company able to handle their move end to end – including advising and guiding you through the potentially hazardous customs maze.

You should note that there are some major differences between clearance procedures and customs clearance times across the world. A good removal company will make you aware of these and help factor them into your arrival plans. Don't be tempted to wait until your arrival to organize your destination moving company as you may well see your worldly goods held at the wharf for months, as pre-arrival security clearance has not been arranged. As a result, costly wharf storage and container detention charges are incurred, resulting in overall higher moving cost and a frustrating arrival.

Following these simple guidelines will ensure a smooth and successful move to your exciting new life overseas. Of course, we believe we offer the best possible service at the most competitive price possible and would be more than happy to demonstrate that to you. Our highly trained, courteous and professional staff are available to assist you so do please give us a call.

Geoff Watson can be contacted at Doree Bonner International on 0800 0214277 or e-mail: moving@dbonner.co.uk or visit www.emigratingoverseas.com.

You may also find the following websites useful:
FAIM accredited removal companies can be found on the FIDI website at www.fidi.com
British Association of Removers (BAR) www.bar.co.uk
www.emigratingoverseas.com
www.britishexpats.com

PETS

Pets often pose a problem. Some shipping companies and airlines require a bill of health from a veterinary surgeon. In all cases, before leaving the UK you should first obtain an export health certificate from the Department for Environment, Food and Rural Affairs (DEFRA). There are a number of specialist animal shipping services available. You will need to apply in good time beforehand to DEFRA for an information pack so that you can make the necessary arrangements. Quarantine has been replaced by a vaccination and electronic tagging procedure for animals being transported to and from rabies-free and EU countries. Details can be found on the DEFRA website www.defra.gov.uk.

Checklist: Choice of removers

1. The remover should provide a free estimate and a written quote.
2. Does the quote specify *professional* packing under your general supervision?
3. How will fragile items, furniture and articles be packed?
4. What insurance cover is offered? If there is any excess (ie a minimum figure below which you will not be reimbursed), what is it?
5. Can the removers immediately provide the name and address of the port agents at your destination?
6. Will they deliver to your residence at the other end, or will you have to arrange clearance yourself? Check that the quotation specifies whether the goods will be delivered to residence or to port only.
7. What proportion of their current business is in overseas removals?

VAT

You will almost certainly find that some of the things you want are cheaper to buy here, even allowing for shipping charges. You should make sure that you take full advantage of the various VAT export schemes under which a UK resident going abroad can escape having to pay UK VAT altogether. There are two schemes, one for motor vehicles and one for other goods.

Motor vehicles

If you will be living outside the EU

You have to purchase your new vehicle from a dealer who operates the Personal Export Scheme. They will give you VAT Form 410 to fill in, which will require you to fulfil certain conditions. The relevant notes are found in VAT Notice 705. Motorcycles and motor caravans are also covered by this scheme.

- You must personally take delivery of the vehicle, and it must be used only by you, or someone else who is also leaving the EU and has your permission to use it.
- You have to take the vehicle abroad within 6 months of delivery, or within 12 months if you have lived outside the EU for more than 365 days in the previous two years, or more than 1,095 days in the previous six years.
- You and the car must remain outside the EU for at least six consecutive months.

Alternatively, the supplier can deliver the car directly to your destination, free of VAT. See VAT Notice 703.

If you will be living within the EU

You must complete Form VAT 411, supplied by the motor dealer.

- The vehicle must be new, and you must take it to your destination within two months of delivery. Cars must not have been driven for more than 1,864 miles in this time.
- You must declare the vehicle to the member state's fiscal authority.

After you have had the vehicle abroad for at least 12 months you may re-import it without paying VAT, provided you are either a diplomat, a member of an officially recognized international organization, a member of NATO or returning UK forces personnel or you can prove that the duty and tax have been paid. Otherwise you will have to pay VAT on the value of the vehicle at the time of re-importation. If you return to the UK within six months of the date of export, the full amount of VAT on the sale must be paid. If the vehicle is found to be in the UK after the date for its export shown on the registration document (ie six months from purchase date if you are leaving the EU, or two months otherwise), you will have to pay VAT in full and the vehicle will also be liable to forfeiture. This applies even if failure to export the vehicle is due to circumstances beyond your control (eg theft or destruction). Therefore, while the car is still in the UK, before export, it is essential to insure it for its full value, including potential VAT. Obviously, it is important to license, register and insure the vehicle if you will be using it in the UK before departure.

Other goods

If you have been in the EU for more than 365 days in the previous two years and are going to a final destination outside the EU for at least 12 consecutive months, you may buy goods using the Retail Export Scheme. At participating retailers, you must ask to complete VAT Form 435 at the time of purchase. To receive a refund equal to the amount of VAT you must get this form certified by a customs authority when the goods are exported – the goods must be delivered to your shipper or freight forwarder at your final point of departure from the EU. You cannot take delivery of them in this country. The refund is then paid by the retailer, not HM Revenue & Customs (HMRC). See VAT Notices 704 and 704/1. As there is a lot of documentation involved, you may find this procedure is not worth your while unless you are making fairly large purchases and only in one or two shops.

TAKING A CAR ABROAD

British people tend to prefer right-hand drive and will therefore consider buying their car here and taking it with them. First check at the embassy of the country you propose to live in that private car imports are permitted.

Probably the best way to plan this is to make a list of what you will want your car to do. The road surfaces may be worse than those you are used to, so you may consider taking a good second-hand car rather than a brand new one. You will not then be so worried about driving through very narrow streets. In some places drivers actually park by shunting the cars ahead and behind!

If you buy a new car in the UK before going abroad, you can use it here for six months, run it in and have your first service before you take it overseas. Check the servicing facilities in the area where you plan to live. It would be unwise to take a car abroad if the nearest dealer service is 70 miles away. This factor may well limit your choice.

A big car will be expensive with petrol and difficult to park. If you will be living in an apartment and there is no garage, the car will usually be left in the street and possibly for long periods at that. Consider carefully the security of your car and what you may have in it. Choose a model with locking wheel nuts and high-quality locks so that it is hard to get into without smashing the windows. Radio thefts are prevalent in some countries; therefore you may wish to consider a demountable radio.

Should you decide to take a small car to a hot country, always buy one with a sun roof because the smaller cars tend not to carry air conditioning.

People moving to Spain will often choose diesel cars because the fuel is half the price of petrol and easily available. Lead-free petrol is now available in many countries and you should check whether your engine will take this quality. Some engines need minor adaptation.

The other possibility is to hire a car in the UK. First check whether the hire company is happy with your destination and route. Restrictions depend on insurance cover for more out-of-the-way locations. You should also have the hirer provide you with proof of ownership – in this case form VE103a. Hirers are more than happy to do business with expatriates because of the length of hire and the fact that most are credit- and trustworthy. With regard to this latter point, it will be essential to pay by credit card.

Taking your existing car abroad

If you take the car you own at present abroad for longer than 12 months, this is regarded as a permanent export and the procedure is described in leaflet V526, obtainable from your local Vehicle Registration Office.

The following procedure applies to exports from England, Scotland, Wales and the Isles of Scilly only, not to Northern Ireland, the Isle of Man or the Channel Islands, where cars are registered separately.

Complete section 2 on the back of the Vehicle Registration Document, entering the proposed date of export, and send the document to your local Vehicle Registration Office or to the Driver and Vehicle Licensing Centre. This should be done well in advance of your departure.

You will receive back a Certificate of Export (V561), which in effect confirms your vehicle registration and replaces the vehicle registration document (V5). Some countries, however, are failing to recognize this certificate as a registration document, which can cause problems when you wish to re-register your vehicle in another country.

A different procedure applies in Northern Ireland, the Isle of Man and the Channel Islands, where vehicles are registered locally; it is necessary to register and license a car taken to these places for over 12 months as soon as the current British tax disc expires, if not before. The Certificate of Export mentioned above will still be necessary, although these authorities may accept the vehicle registration document for re-registration purposes.

Motoring services in Europe

The Alliance Internationale de Tourisme (AIT) has its headquarters in Geneva, and motoring clubs throughout Europe are affiliated to it, including the Royal Automobile Club and the Automobile Association. There is also the Fédération Internationale de l'Automobile, based in Paris, of which the RAC is a member. These clubs provide a wide range of services to each other's members travelling abroad, so membership of one is worthwhile.

CUSTOMS

Regulations and procedures vary. Most customs authorities allow you to take in used things for your personal use and often let people, eg newly married couples, bring in new things duty free. Wherever possible keep receipts to show to the customs officials.

In most places, you are allowed to take in 'household and used personal effects', including refrigerators, radios, TV receivers and minor electrical appliances, but duties on new items of this kind are usually fairly steep. There are bans everywhere on guns, plants and drugs. Many Middle East and North African countries operate a boycott list, so do not take anything without checking the situation. Duty-free wines, spirits and tobacco up to a certain amount – check with the airline – are normally allowed, except in most Middle East countries.

ESSENTIALS BEFORE YOU GO

There are certain things you must see about before you actually leave. There are obvious chores, like cancelling milk and papers, etc. Have a thorough medical check for yourself and your family before you go, including teeth and eyes. Some jobs, of course, depend on physical fitness. Make sure you have the necessary vaccination certificates and check the requirements. Most tropical countries need certificates against smallpox and possibly cholera and yellow fever; other vaccinations may be advisable. If you are going to the tropics you should contact your GP about anti-malarial precautions. For the most up-to-date advice on malaria in the region where you are going, you should contact the Malaria Reference Laboratory at the London School of Hygiene and Tropical Medicine.

In many countries it is advisable to include a rabies injection in your schedule of jabs for yourself and members of your family. You should also warn children of the perils of cuddling strange animals, which may harbour other diseases in addition to the rabies threat.

Check that you have all your documents to hand – up-to-date passport, visas, cheque book, permits, health certificates, letter of appointment. Take spare passport photos – it is probably best for partners to have separate passports – and all your diplomas and references, even birth and marriage certificates. The appetite for documents is well-nigh insatiable in some countries!

Melancholy though it may sound, you should also make some provision for the unthinkable: instructions in the case of death, disablement or catastrophe while you are abroad. Contact your financial adviser or insurance company for more information.

If you have a reliable solicitor, you might also consider the possibility of giving them power of attorney. This is a simple legal transaction that essentially means that the person having that power can act in your stead. If you need a large sum of money to be sent out to you in a hurry, it is very useful to have a responsible person in the UK whom you can fax and who can raise the money from your bank. Likewise, if you have left your house in the hands of managing agents who are not doing their stuff, you need someone on the spot who can sort things out. Giving someone power of attorney obviously implies a high degree of trust, but there are occasions when it could save you the cost of a return fare home.

KEEPING YOUR VOTE
WHILE LIVING ABROAD

On moving abroad, you retain your right to vote in UK and European parliamentary elections; however, there are a number of conditions of which you should be aware. To be eligible you must be a British citizen and satisfy either of two sets of conditions:

Set 1

- you have previously been on the electoral register for an address in the UK;
- you were living there on the qualifying date;*
- there are no more than 20 years between the qualifying dates for that register and the one on which you now wish to appear.

Set 2

- you last lived in the UK less than 20 years before the qualifying date for the register on which you wish to appear;
- you were too young to be on the electoral register, which was based on the last qualifying date before you left;
- a parent or guardian was on the electoral register for the address where you were living on that date;
- you are at least 18 years old, or will become 18 when the register comes into force.

You have to register every year on or before the qualifying date and you may continue to register while overseas for 20 years from the qualifying date for the last electoral register on which you appeared as a UK resident.

---

*The qualifying date in England, Scotland and Wales is 10 October each year and in Northern Ireland, 15 September. This is for the electoral register, which comes into force on 16 February of the following year and remains in force for 12 months from that date.

How to register

To register you must fill in an Overseas Elector's Declaration form RPF 37, which you can get from the nearest British consular or diplomatic mission. The following information will be required: your full name and overseas address, the UK address where you were last registered and the date you left the UK. The first-time overseas elector will have to find someone to support the declaration who is aged 18 or over, has a British passport and is a British citizen, is not living in the UK and who knows you but is not a close relative. First-time overseas electors who left the UK before they were old enough to register will also have to provide a copy of their full birth certificate and information about the parent or guardian on whose registration they are relying.

How to vote and remain registered

You do not have a postal vote. Instead you must appoint a proxy who will vote on your behalf. They must be a citizen of Britain, the Commonwealth or the Republic of Ireland, a UK resident, and willing and legally able to vote on your behalf. The application form for appointing a proxy is attached to the Overseas Elector's Declaration form. Your declaration, proxy application and, if required, birth certificate should be returned to the electoral registration officer for the area where you were last registered. The electoral registration officer will write to tell you whether you qualify as an overseas elector and will be included on the register: if you do not, they will explain why. You will be sent a reminder each year, and another declaration form will be enclosed with this.

REMOVAL NOTIFICATIONS

Don't forget to tell the following organizations that you are moving abroad:

Your bank.

Income tax office. Notify HMRC giving the exact date of departure.

Contributions Agency, International Services (for information on National Insurance contributions and related health cover), Longbenton, Newcastle upon Tyne, NE98 1YX, or *The Benefits*

Agency, Pensions and Overseas Benefits Directorate (for advice on benefits and related health cover), at Tyneview Park, Newcastle upon Tyne NE98 1BA. Include your full name, date of birth and UK NI or pension number, together with details of the country to which you are moving and the duration of your stay.

Vehicle licence. If you are taking your vehicle abroad for longer than a year this is regarded as a 'permanent export'. In this case you should return your existing (new-style) registration document to the Driver and Vehicle Licensing Centre, Swansea SA99 1AB, filling in the 'permanent export' section. Alternatively, you can apply to your local Vehicle Registration Office for the necessary forms.

Driving licence. You will probably want to retain your British driving licence. Some countries recognize it as valid and a list of those that do not is available from the RAC and the AA.

International Driving Permit. An International Driving Permit is obtainable from the RAC or AA (even if you are not a member) and is valid for one year. The licence is not valid in the country where it is issued so you must obtain it before leaving the UK. Most countries require residents to hold a local driving licence so check whether this is the case on taking up your new residence. Contact RAC Travel Services, PO Box 1500, Great Park Road Bristol BS99 2LH (telephone 0870 333 2784; website: www.media.rac.co.uk for information), or Automobile Association (tel: 08706 000371; website: www.theaa.com).

Motor insurance. Notify your insurers of the date of your departure – your insurance should be cancelled from that date and you should obtain a refund for the rest of the insurance period. Ask your insurance company for a letter outlining your no-claims record to show to your new insurer.

Life and other insurances. Notify the companies concerned or your insurance broker if you use one.

Council tax. Notify the town hall.

Dentist and optician. Let them know you are moving, as a matter of courtesy. It will save posting useless check-up reminders.

Private health insurance. Notify subscriber records department.

Gas. If you use it, notify your local gas supplier giving at least *48 hours'* notice. They will give you a standard form to fill in with details of the move and any current hire-purchase agreements. If appliances are to be removed they require as much notice as possible to arrange an appointment; there is a disconnection charge.

Electricity. Notify your local district office or showroom at least *48 hours* before moving. Arrangements are much the same as for gas.

Water. The local water board should also be notified at least 48 hours before the move. Drain tanks and pipes if the house is to remain empty in winter.

Telephone. Notify your local telephone sales office as shown in the front of your directory at least *seven days* before the move.

Libraries. Return books and give in tickets to be cancelled.

Professional advisers such as solicitors, accountants, stockbrokers, insurance brokers, etc. Make sure they have a forwarding address.

Stocks and shares. Write to the company registrar at the address on the last annual report or share certificates.

Organizations and clubs – any business, civic, social, cultural, sports or automobile club of which you are a member. For the AA write to Membership Administration, Contact Centre, Lambert House, Stockport Road, Cheadle SK8 2DY (fax: 0161 488 7544) and for the RAC write to Membership Enquiries, PO Box 1500, Bristol BS99 2LH.

Credit card companies. Advise them that you are leaving the country.

Hire purchase and rental companies. Notify the office where repayments are made. You will need to settle your account.

Local business accounts – department stores, newsagents, dairy, baker, chemist, dry cleaner, laundry, motor service station.

Publications. Cancel postal subscriptions to newspapers, magazines, professional and trade journals, book and record clubs, etc.

National Health Service. Return your NHS card to the Family Health Services Authority for your area, giving your date of departure, or hand it in to the immigration officer at your point of departure.

Pension schemes. If you have a 'frozen' or paid-up pension from a previous employer notify the pension trust of your new address.

TV. If you have a rented set, make arrangements to return it.

Post Office. Notify day of departure and UK contact address.

Personal Giro. The Post Office has a special sae for this.

Premium Bonds – anything rather than join the sad list of unclaimed prizes! Contact Premium Bonds, National Savings, Blackpool FY3 9XR to check the current position, because in a few countries, Premium Bond holdings may contravene lottery laws.

Save As You Earn and National Savings Certificates. It is important to notify any permanent change of address. Advise the Savings and Certificates and SAYE Office, Durham DH99 1NS, quoting the contract number(s).

National Savings Bank. Notify at Glasgow G58 1SB.

National Savings Income Bonds. Notify Income Bonds, Blackpool FY3 9YP.

Your landlord. If you are a tenant, give the appropriate notice to quit.

Your tenants. If you are a landlord, that UK address you've organized will be needed.

Your employer. Give new address details, or a contact address, in writing.

Schools. Try to give your children's schools a term's notice that they will be leaving. If you wish your children's education to be continued in Britain, contact your local education authority or the Department for Education and Employment, Sanctuary Buildings, Great Smith Street, London SW1P 3BT, for advice, and see Chapter 9.

Make sure your *removers* have any temporary contact address and phone numbers for you, both in the UK and abroad, so that they can get in touch with you when the need arises. It is also useful for them if you can tell them when you expect to arrive in your new country.

Checklist: Moving out

1. Be practical about what to take and try to travel light.
2. Check what will be available in your new accommodation and consider whether it might be better for the working partner to go out ahead of the rest of the family.
3. Consult with a reputable removal firm with experience in overseas removal.
4. Increase your insurance to cover replacement costs at the other end.
5. If you have a pet, think about what will be the best arrangement in the long term. If you are taking your dog with you, be sure to arrange for vaccination six months before you leave.
6. Think carefully about whether or not you should take your car with you, as it might not be suitable for the terrain of your new home.
7. If you decide to take your car, obtain leaflet V562 from your local Vehicle Registration Office.
8. Have a thorough medical check-up before you leave.
9. Check that you have all your documents available and take spare passport photos.
10. Fill in an Overseas Elector's Declaration form RPF37 to keep your right to vote.

13

Settling In

You arrive, with or without your family, and may find you are not met at the airport. This is the first of many irritations which people going out to work for overseas governments may encounter. It does not usually happen with companies. You may have to stay in a hotel or hostel for a considerable time, so make sure in advance who is going to foot the bill. You will need money to meet such contingencies – and to pay for telephones and taxis to and from the airport.

Even if you are lucky enough to move into a house or apartment, you will find a bare larder. This is where any tins or packet foods you brought with you will come in useful. (In Jamaica, the Corona Worldwide branch will provide a loan of a 'basket' of essentials for people waiting for their baggage to be unloaded.)

One early need will be to fix up domestic help, if you want it. It is usually best to engage a house steward and/or any other staff on the personal recommendation of the previous occupant (you may inherit their staff) or a neighbour. Find out from the local labour office what the going rate is and negotiate accordingly, making it quite clear from the start what duties the staff will be expected to perform, eg in the kitchen, washing and housework. Living quarters are sometimes provided, but find out beforehand whether your steward plans to bring all their family and relatives to stay with them!

Both for insurance purposes and your own peace of mind, make proper security arrangements. Some people, either individually or in groups, employ nightwatchmen; others rely on dogs, or on special locks. The extent of pilfering and burglary in many African countries has grown alarmingly in recent years, so make sure your precautions are fully adequate. John Wason (Insurance Brokers) Ltd, founded by a former expatriate, offers a specialist Overseas

Personal Insurance scheme, which includes home contents, belongings, money and personal liability, as well as optional medical and accident/sickness cover. It is claimed to be the only such policy available on a stand-alone basis, and as such would be useful for those in rented or company property.

At an early stage it is a good idea to see to all your requirements for banking and for obtaining work and residence permits, income tax coding, and the driving licence and test requirements where necessary. Find out also about health products and medical facilities, contributions to provident funds and subscriptions to clubs. Many employers pay for these.

Finally, keep a close eye on the health of young children, particularly on persistent tummy upsets and fevers. It is advisable always to use water you have sterilized yourself, not bottled water of unknown provenance.

There is also the question of preparation, other than physical, for your move. Do you know what the country you are going to is like? What facilities are there for shopping, leisure and entertainment? What is the climate like and what clothes will you need? Are there any pitfalls you should know about or any special behavioural dos and don'ts? Nowadays, overseas countries are very sensitive about foreigners understanding that their new patterns of government and economic development are not just pale imitations of the West.

The importance of getting properly briefed beforehand cannot be overestimated. This will not only save you from possible embarrassing situations – for example, if you don't know the rules about drinking in the Middle East – but will help you to decide what you need to take with you and give you some idea of the atmosphere in which you will work and live. Companies specializing in country-specific briefings are described in Chapter 11. Details can also be found in the website directory at the back of this book.

GOING THROUGH DIPLOMATIC CHANNELS

Expatriates who work for British companies or those from other Western countries in the developing or newly industrialized world can usually expect their employers to come to their aid in case of a political upheaval, or even if they get into personal difficulties – deserved or otherwise. Furthermore, they can expect their contracts of employment to be clear-cut and to conform to Western norms.

Neither of these things is necessarily true if you work for a local employer, as is increasingly the case. The money is often better, but the risk is greater.

Some guidance on points to watch out for in taking up an appointment with a local employer in a developing country is given in the Employment Conditions Checklist in Chapter 3. Ultimately, though, you have no protection other than your own vigilance and UK diplomatic channels in the country concerned. They are generally very much criticized by expatriates as being ineffectual or indifferent, but the Foreign and Commonwealth Office claim this is because their role is not understood. For a start, they cannot intervene in contractual disputes, *unless* a British subject is being discriminated against in comparison with other employees. They can, however, recommend you a local lawyer who may be able to help you and they maintain carefully vetted lists of reliable legal firms. Best of all, they say, is to write to the British embassy or consulate nearest to your location before you leave the UK and ask them to put you in touch with someone who can give you a line on your prospective employer. Though UK diplomatic sources do keep track of known bad hats among employers, in the main they prefer such information to go through non-diplomatic channels, for obvious reasons.

The consular service of the Foreign Office is now very sensitive about the criticisms that have been made of it. If you fail to get an answer from the embassy or consulate you have contacted, or you are not satisfied with the service provided at a British embassy, high commission or consulate, you should write to: Director of Consular Services, Consular Directorate, Foreign and Commonwealth Office, Old Admiralty Building, Whitehall, London SW1A 2PA; tel: 020 7008 0223, fax: 020 7008 0152.

Primarily, of course, the role of British diplomats is to protect British subjects from the consequences of political upheavals. Any expatriate who goes to a notoriously high-risk place must take into account the circumstances there before deciding to accept an appointment. Diplomats are also not able to protect you from the consequences if you break the law of the land you are in. At most they can visit you in prison, arrange for you to be properly represented legally and intercede discreetly for an amnesty for you. A UK or multinational company would, in such cases, arrange for you to be flown out on the first available plane, usually with the connivance of the authorities.

Whatever your feelings about the efficacy or otherwise of British diplomatic protection, you should register with the embassy or consulate as soon as possible after you arrive to work in any developing country. This means they can contact you if a sudden emergency arises, whether personal or political. It cannot do any harm; and if you wake up one morning to the sound of gunfire, as has happened to many an expatriate, you may be very glad that you took that precaution.

Foreign and Commonwealth Travel Advice is designed to help British travellers avoid trouble by providing succinct and up-to-date information on threats to personal safety arising from political unrest, lawlessness, violence, natural disasters and epidemics. Some 650 notices are issued each year covering more than 130 countries. Notices are constantly renewed on the basis of information from posts overseas. The full range of notices is available on BBC2 Ceefax pages 470 onwards, and on the FCO's website, along with a range of Consular Division publicity material, www.fco.gov.uk. The public can contact the Travel Advice Unit direct between 9.30 am and 4.00 pm Monday to Friday on 0870 606 0290.

Other consular services information leaflets, including *Checklist for Travellers, Backpackers and Independent Travellers* and *British Consular Services Abroad* are widely distributed through travel agents, shipping companies and airlines, public libraries, Citizens Advice Bureaux and the UK Passport Agency, and can be obtained by faxing the Distribution Centre on 01444 246620.

READING MATTER

You may never have been much of a book buyer while living in the UK, but many expatriates report that not being able to get hold of books when they want them is an unexpected deprivation, especially in postings where other forms of entertainment, at any rate in English, are hard to come by.

Many places do, of course, have bookshops which stock some English titles, but the selection is often very limited (children's books are particularly hard to get) and prices are always much higher than the UK price shown tantalizingly on the jacket. You can, however, import your own books at standard London prices through the admirable Good Book Guide (website: www.thegoodbookguide.com; e-mail: enquiries@gbgdirect.com) or order books on the internet from Amazon.com or www.amazon. co.uk. The guide is a mail order book service with a substantial trade among expatriates all over the world. You can choose your books from the monthly guide, for which there is a modest annual subscription, but the service can also get any book in print for you, including paperbacks. There are also regular video and audio listings offering a wealth of entertainment: drama, documentary, comedy and children's programmes.

The choices in the guide are accompanied by brief, helpful notes written by outside experts (eg Chris Bonington on travel) and the selection of titles is broad, covering both highbrow literature and commercial best sellers, all chosen on merit alone. The subject areas are broad too, ranging through all kinds of interests. However, the Good Book Guide is not a book club – there is no obligation to buy. A free trial issue can be requested.

Payment is on a cash with order basis or by credit card and clear instructions are given with each issue of the guide on how to pay from anywhere in the world.

ENTERTAINMENT AND HOME COMFORTS

So, you've left the wonderful British weather behind, you've arrived in your new country and now it's time to settle into your new home.

Although discovering new interests and exploring new cultures will be fascinating and exciting, it can be quite hard initially and you may find that (for a short time at least) some familiar everyday links with home will really help you to adjust to your new surroundings.

This is where the internet is invaluable, especially if you are a partner based at home throughout the day and therefore without access to input and advice from work colleagues. Even if you've never used a computer before and can learn just enough to send e-mails and surf the web, then you will be able to find most of the information you need.

As well as keeping in touch easily with friends through e-mail, you can also go to the websites of most national and some local British newspapers to really keep up to date with what's happening in your area back home and, if you're a keen sports person, to follow your local football or cricket team. You can also tune into BBC radio and your local radio stations. Sometimes, when feeling a little homesick, hearing a report on your local radio station about the traffic jams on the motorways you used to travel on or the icy road conditions can be all that's needed for a cure!

There are many excellent British expat clubs around the world and, even if there is none in your local area, you can still register and join the online forums. Here you can 'chat' to fellow expats, ask for advice and generally learn about other people's experiences. This can be really helpful if you have moved to a non-English-speaking country and the culture is very different to your own or even if it is English-speaking but 'not as we know it', as in the case of the United States or Australia, for example. It can be quite surprising to learn of so many differences in the same language, and quite a few humorous books have now been written on the subject, relating some of the embarrassing moments experienced by many Brits abroad!

Once you have settled in and got used to your new surroundings, your thoughts may turn to things you miss from home, such as certain foods or particular shops. There is a huge array of products now available to order on the internet and, as long as you order from a reputable company with a secure website, this should prove to be an easy, trouble-free transaction.

Regarding food, it can be quite daunting the first time you visit the supermarket in your new country, as you view rows and rows of goods, none of which is familiar to you. Although over time most people get used to the local produce, many expats take advantage of the online shopping services offered specifically for British expats, such as Expat Essentials, which will send out British food to nearly every country in the world. It may be something to use occasionally, when you feel like a treat from home or perhaps for more essential items like baby formula, as you will probably discover that your usual brand from the UK is not available overseas. For any family with young children, this is definitely worth checking and preparing for before you leave home, as the last thing you need is an upset baby. If you plan to take a large quantity of baby formula with you, it's also worth noting that some countries restrict the amount allowed, so it would be worthwhile to check with customs first, to make sure you can import the baby products you take with you or send on ahead.

Websites like Expat Essentials (www.expatessentials.com) also have a links page for other websites of interest to British expats, so this is an easy way of finding out all sorts of other information, without the need to spend days searching on Google. There is everything from British clubs to visa consultants to buying property overseas. British embassies usually have a great selection of links on their websites too, so this is another area worth exploring.

A lot of the favourite high-street stores from Britain will only deliver within the UK, but you may be able to find a mail-forwarding company where you can have the goods delivered, and it will then charge you a small handling fee plus delivery to send them on to you. This can be especially useful for those everyday items like baby clothes, socks and underwear, where you know the quality is reliable and the fit is usually accurate. One thing to be aware of, though, is that most stores (depending on the type of goods) will not offer their usual guarantee or returns policy if the goods are being sent out of the UK. Sometimes, if it's not a particularly expensive item, it's still worth taking the risk, to be able to get the goods you're familiar with and you know that you like.

CDs are fairly universal, so you can continue to listen to your favourite music wherever you are. However, some DVDs and computer games have a different format and don't work overseas, so this is something worth checking before ordering. You may also find that a games console, such as PlayStation, Xbox, etc, taken from the UK will not play the games bought locally, so it's worth thoroughly checking the situation with any electrical or electronic items before you leave the UK or before you order from abroad. The manufacturers of these games consoles, such as Sony, can usually give you the right advice.

Lastly, wherever possible, try to learn as much as you can about the local people and their customs and their day-to-day accepted way of doing things, which may be quite different to the ways in the UK. It's always appreciated when someone tries to fit in and respects local tradition. People generally love to help too, so always ask for advice when appropriate. Probably the most important thing to remember is that, no matter how proud you are to be British (and rightly so), don't complain to your new friends about things being different from what you have at home and all the things you miss. This is where the online forums for expats are so good; you can let off steam to your fellow Brits about the things you don't like and get some good advice, without the risk of offending someone locally.

By following these simple guidelines, you should find that you'll settle into your new country in no time at all and then you can relax and enjoy all the wonderful new experiences you'll encounter.

After a while, you'll probably wonder why on earth you missed Marmite or PG Tips so much, as you discover lots of fantastic new tastes to enjoy.

While your new home is likely to be a source of varied and new experiences, you might like to maintain some of the interests that you developed at home. The internet can provide an invaluable link for this. Football fans can follow their team's progress through the season by logging on to both official and unofficial websites. Chat forums can also keep you in contact with fellow fans. The internet might also be a way to find out if there are other expatriates or host-country fan clubs in your region, which could be a good way to meet people and set up a social network.

Using the internet to keep informed with both world and local news is also a new innovation. Many radio and TV companies now use it to broadcast. For example, CNN, Reuters and the BBC all have news information. Furthermore, you can listen to some radio programmes through the internet. The BBC has recently launched an audio online version of its news and entertainment programmes which can be found on the BBC site. National newspapers also use the internet and some, such as the *Daily Telegraph*, publish the whole day's paper on their website. Furthermore, local newspapers are also setting up websites, so it is quite possible to keep in touch with your local news – including football reports, and local issues such as education and government. A listing of websites can be found at the back of this book.

Sending for goods through mail order catalogues can make up for deficiencies in local shops when working abroad. Although many companies that provide goods by mail order confine their activities to the UK and will not send goods abroad (no doubt because of potential payment problems), there is nothing to stop you making arrangements to get catalogues through UK friends or relatives and ordering through them. Expatriates with young children are reported to find the Mothercare catalogue very useful. Harrods and Fortnum & Mason will send goods anywhere in the world and you can pay by credit card. Harrods also operate worldwide accounts, and franchise outlets in airports in some surprising places. However, e-commerce also means that receiving home comforts is no longer the complicated process it used to be and many large retail companies now have ordering facilities set up on their websites.

Checklist: Settling in

1. Try to organize domestic help as soon as possible and bring a few necessities with you.
2. Brief your domestic help as clearly as possible and identify duties from the start.
3. Make proper security arrangements and check that you have all your legal requirements for work, banking, medical help, etc.
4. Find out emergency numbers, including those of your consulate or embassy, and if you are relocating to a developing country, register with them as soon as possible.
5. Identify sources from where books and home comforts can be obtained, whether locally or internationally.
6. Seek out social networks through expatriate organizations, your employer or through the internet.
7. If you have not used the internet before, now is the time to become acquainted – it will be an invaluable source of information and support!

14

Coming Home

Having completed a foreign assignment you might feel that your return home will be an uncomplicated affair. However, increasingly both companies and individuals are paying attention to the practical and psychological issues involved in repatriation. Not only do domestic issues, such as finding accommodation or dealing with tenants, need to be tackled, but career considerations and family issues need to be addressed. Furthermore, although you might feel confident about fitting back into professional and social networks, surprisingly some expatriates do experience a reverse culture shock on their return.

PERSONAL POSSESSIONS

If you are to reap the full benefit of a spell as a non-UK resident, planning for your return requires forethought and preparation, particularly in the matter of bringing back personal possessions. Price differentials between countries are no longer as great as they used to be, but there are still quite a number of places where, even taking freight into account, it is worth buying things like electronic or audiovisual equipment, even cars, locally and shipping them back home. In countries that operate exchange controls this may also be a possible way of taking out assets in the form of goods. But beware of the catch: unless you can show that an article has been used and owned for six months, you are liable for import duty – and VAT on top of that. It is no use asking an obliging vendor to provide backdated invoices, because if you are unlucky enough to come under investigation, customs officials check serial numbers as well as documents. Another thing to be aware of is that once your personal possessions, including cars, are imported without payment of import duty and VAT, they cannot be sold or disposed of within 12 months, or they become liable for both these taxes.

Even with well-used goods, you can be in for unforeseen costs unless you get your timing right. The problem is that possessions shipped back to the UK will not be released until their owner arrives home. You can get a relative to clear them on your behalf, but that person would be liable for provisional duty on their value, which is only repaid when you yourself get back. It takes about a fortnight to clear goods through customs anyway, so you will need expert advice at the other end if you are to steer the difficult course between paying warehouse charges in the UK because the goods have arrived too soon, and finding yourself without the basic necessities of life because you have sent them off too late.

The most important thing, though, is that they should actually arrive. The cheapest form of shipping may not be the best. The right course of action is to find a local firm that has a reputable agent in the UK, and to make sure you get door-to-door insurance cover.

ACCOMMODATION

Providing you have gone through the correct tenancy arrangements, reclaiming your property should not be too complicated. However, be aware that if you return earlier than planned, and your tenants have time left on their agreement, you might have to find alternative accommodation for the outstanding tenancy period. In particular, under an Assured Shorthold Tenancy – unless your tenant agrees to move earlier – you will have to wait until the contract runs its course with two months' notice given after that period.

You should try to give the letting agents who are looking after your UK property at least three months' notice of your return, so that they can give due notice to the tenants. However, should you be unfortunate enough to come across a tenant who is unwilling to move on, it is possible to insure against legal and hotel costs.

FINDING A NEW JOB

Unless you have been sent out by a UK employer, the biggest problem in returning home can be in finding another job. Well before that point you should be sending your CV round to head-hunters who are always on the lookout for those with specialist qualifications. If you feel that you might have difficulty placing yourself on the job market on grounds of age or lack of specific skills, it may be worth consulting a career counsellor. They cannot 'find' you a job – and you should be wary of those who imply otherwise – but their advice, though not cheap, has been found to be a good investment by many mid-career jobseekers.

Returning employees are also faced with career dilemmas. An Arthur Andersen Survey as long ago as 1999 reported that 21 per cent of companies expect their returning employee to initiate the search for their next position. The proportion of companies offering help is unlikely to have risen. Of those companies that do offer help, under 10 per cent begin to look for a position for the expatriate a year before return and approximately 40 per cent used to do so 6–12 months before the end of the assignment, but the latter percentage has probably fallen. Indeed, this is precisely what stops many employees taking on a foreign assignment in the first place: a lack of career opportunities on their return. Employees who are unable to return to their former job have a number of options available to them, which are shown in Table 14.1. The outlook today for returning expatriates is significantly worse than in 1999.

Chapter 4 deals with this subject in some depth. However, it is worth repeating at this point that the issue of reintegration should be raised before taking on an assignment. An employer who values the skills that have been developed abroad will also be thinking about how best to use them on your return. Leaving this to chance, though, is not a good idea. At least a year before your return you should be entering into a dialogue with your employer about career opportunities for your return. If your company provides a mentor, they should also be able to help create a constructive dialogue and repatriation process.

Table 14.1   Post-assignment options

Redundancy	50%
Re-assignment to another expatriate position	31%
Extension of current assignment	32%
Appointed 'special projects' in the home country	57%
Other	8%

Source: Arthur Andersen Expatriate Survey 1999

If you are able to settle back into your former job or one of equivalent status, it is also worth bearing in mind that time will have passed since you were last part of your home office team. Different faces, work practices and projects should be expected and it might take some time to readjust to your altered office environment. Do not expect that you will necessarily be welcome, as you will probably be affecting other people's career prospects.

The same 1999 Arthur Andersen Survey found that a mere 11 per cent of companies offered some form of post-repatriation support during the 12 months after return, and this tended to be with tax compliance rather than personal support. None of the companies gave any form of help with readjustment to home-country living and working, which, as the report's author Barry Page commented, 'is interesting, since inability to re-adapt to home-country office culture is ranked as the most common reason given by returning expatriates for leaving their company following their repatriation'.

Of course, returning expatriates have the option of moving into self-employment and this may be particularly attractive to those who have the opportunity to take early retirement on favourable terms. Since 2005, as final salary pension schemes are increasingly curtailed and changed to the 'money purchase' variety for the remainder of an employee's period of service, or where the employer requires increased contributions from pension scheme members to maintain benefits, it may make good sense to work for yourself and take your pension rights with you. As a returning expatriate, you may well have acquired skills and experience of foreign markets and industries that make you valuable as a consultant to companies that don't want to relocate their own staff – with the inevitable learning curve you went through when you took up your own assignment.

If you find that self-employment beckons, you should start researching the business opportunities and planning well before your return. In this day and age, there is no such thing as job security for life, and anyone over the age of 30 should have a 'Plan B' in the briefcase for self-employment or starting their own business. You might make a start by reading my book *Working for Yourself*, published by Kogan Page, and available at www.koganpage.com.

REVERSE CULTURE SHOCK

One of the most surprising aspects of returning home is the experience of reverse culture shock. Again, the passing of time needs to be taken into account. While you have been away things will have moved on in your home country and not only friends and family will have changed but your international experience will almost certainly have changed you as well. Your expectations might well have undergone a radical change abroad and coming home might mean that you, once again, have to re-adapt these to suit your circumstances. Much like any other major move, returning home requires a readjustment to new circumstances and time should be taken to absorb this process.

Fitting back into an office environment is one thing but it is also worth bearing in mind that partners and children might also experience difficulties settling back.

PREPARING THE FAMILY FOR RETURN

As with the move abroad, a trailing partner might well have to begin to search for another job on their return home. Beginning that search well in advance is well worth the time. Furthermore, enlightened companies are beginning to realize the need to provide information and support to enable partners to resettle. For example, Shell has 40 information centres worldwide providing information and support for partners. Children might also feel disorientated by returning home. Having to fit back into school and peer groups can be traumatic. Their experience of a different culture and returning to an unfamiliar environment might be disturbing for a period of time. Furthermore, they might not be able to return to their old school if places are scarce. Again, it is worth informing schools as early as possible about your return and to look for alternative arrangements should there be a lack of places. Children should be encouraged to keep in touch with home during a foreign assignment so that they are not completely out of step with changes on their return.

A foreign assignment is a fulfilling and life-enhancing experience. The re-adaption to home is part of that experience and its success or failure can affect the foreign experience in either a positive or negative way. Planning for your return is therefore a worthwhile process. Try to forewarn employers, tenants, schools and social contacts of your return well in advance. Keep your family in contact with friends and try to establish with your employer what job opportunities there are likely to be onyour return. Most important of all, try to be patient with the new situation. It might be home, but home can also be a 'foreign' place if you have spent some years away.

Checklist: Coming home

1. Think about what goods might be worth buying to bring home and purchase six months before returning.
2. Plan the shipment of possessions carefully to coincide with your return or look into warehousing arrangements.
3. Inform your letting agents as soon as possible of the date you are to return in order to give your tenants as much notice as possible.
4. Look into short-term rental arrangements if you are unable to move back into your property straight away.
5. Discuss with your employer well in advance what plans there are for you on your return – this should ideally take place 12 months before return. If you are returning without a job, contact headhunters and agencies as early as possible.
6. Develop a 'Plan B' for self-employment in case you find that there is no acceptable job opportunity on your return.
7. Be prepared for reverse culture shock and give yourself time to become accustomed to changes in your home and work environment.
8. Contact schools in advance and make contact with your children's friends before returning home.
9. Contact partners' support centres run by your employer to identify career opportunities.

Part Five

Website Directory of Useful Contacts

The websites listed are those identified at the time of going to print. Due to the dynamic nature of the internet, variations in content and changes of address might occur. The publishers cannot take responsibility for the content of the websites listed but have tried to ensure, where possible, that the material is of a suitable nature. However, an exemplary illustration of what can be found on the internet is the *Electronic Telegraph's* expatriate website, Global Network, which offers advice, links and country profiles. It can be found at www.telegraph.co.uk or www.global network.co.uk.

INTERNET DIRECTORIES AND SEARCH ENGINES

Alta Vista
http://uk.altavista.com
Britannica Internet Guide
www.ebig.com
Excite Search
www.excite.com
www.excite.co.uk
Google
www.google.com
Google Groups
http://groups.google.com
Search tool for finding news groups.
HotBot
www.hotbot.com
The Lists/Topica
www.lists.com
Search tool for e-mail discussion groups and e-mail publishing.
Regional Directory
www.edirectory.com
Listing of regional web directories.
UK Directory
www.ukdirectory.co.uk
Who Where
www.whowhere.com
Directory of e-mail addresses to help you keep in contact with friends, family and organizations.
Yahoo!
www.yahoo.com
http://uk.yahoo.com

JOB OPPORTUNITIES

Internet resources

America's Job Bank
www.ajb.dni.us
Extensive database of current vacancies in the United States.

Cadremploi
www.cadremploi.fr
France's leading management career site.

Career Builder.com
www.careerbuilder.com
Provides regional breakdowns of salary information.

Career Resource Centre
www.careers.org
Index of US and Canadian careers-related websites, with more than 8,000 links to related sites.

CareersInsite
www.careersinsite.org
US university site with over 1,000 links to job searching sites.

Cool Works
www.coolworks.com
Provides links to details of 'cool' jobs with the emphasis on the United States. For example, jobs in national and state parks, ski resorts and ranches. Visa restrictions are problematic for Europeans, but it is worth having a look at this site.

JobHunters Bible
www.jobhuntersbible.com
Reviews of US guidance sites with links to them.

Job Site
www.jobsite.co.uk
Directory of major UK and European recruiters, mainly in IT and human resource management.

The Monster Board
www.monster.com
Invaluable resource on international job opportunities and country-specific information. Sites in Canada, Australia, Belgium, the Netherlands and the United States.

Prospects Web
www.prospects.ac.uk
Careers information for graduates with overseas sites offering vacancy information.

The Riley Guide to Employment Opportunities and Job Resources on the Internet
www.rileyguide.com
Worldwide vacancies with emphasis on the United States.

Sciencejobs.com
www.sciencejobs.com
International scientific employment opportunities.

SYO-Guiden
www.syoguiden.com
Swedish site with links to career guidance sites worldwide.

TV Jobs
www.tvjobs.com
US TV companies offering intern or work experience or placements.

Media

BioMed*Scientist*
www.biomedscientistjobs.com
International life science and medical recruitment site. Vacancies from *The Scientist* and *BioMed* journals.

British Medical Journal
www.bmjcareers.com
Medical vacancies.

Careers in Construction
www.careersinconstruction.com
Vacancies from *The Architects' Journal, Construction News* and *New Civil Engineer,* updated weekly. Links to other sites of specialist journals.

The Daily Telegraph
www.telegraph.co.uk
Online version of full paper with recruitment vacancies worldwide.

E&P Directory of Online Newspapers
www.editorandpublisher.com
Reference resource including newspapers on the web and proprietary online services. Listed by country with search facilities for specific publications, locations or attributes. Also provides a career centre which boasts an extensive job search facility.

Emap
www.emap.com
Publishers of a wide range of trade and specialist magazines with recruitment sections.

Expat Network
www.expatnetwork.co.uk
Publishes *Nexus* and offers support service for expats and a register of those looking for work abroad which is sent to recruiters.

Financial Times
www.ft.com
Finance- and business-related vacancies.

The Guardian Unlimited
http://jobs.guardian.co.uk
Vacancies in wide range of occupational areas.

Inkpot Newspaper Links
http://inkpot.com/news/majint.html
Links to international newspapers by country and region.

Irish Times
www.irishtimesjobs.com
Searchable site for jobs in Ireland.

Nature
www.nature.com/naturejobs
International science job listings, updated weekly.

Overseas Job Express
www.overseasjobs.com
Newspaper carrying 1,500 job vacancies and information about working abroad every two weeks.

Physics World Jobs
http://careers.iop.org
Part of the UK's Institute of Physics site with job and research opportunities.

ResortJobs
www.resortjobs.com
Also produced by Overseas Job Express, a database of worldwide resort jobs. Includes ski and snowboarding resorts, national parks, cruise ships, hotels and restaurants.

Summer Jobs
www.summerjobs.com
Also produced by Overseas Job Express, a database of seasonal and summer jobs.

Recruitment consultancies and employment agencies

Au pair JobMatch
www.aupairs.co.uk
Search by country and nationality of families for worldwide au pair vacancies.

Crewseekers International
www.crewseekers.co.uk
Work found for amateur crews for leisure sailing, cruising and racing.

Engineering Production Planning Limited
www.epp.co.uk
Agency with offices in Europe, Singapore and the United States. Specializes in vacancies in aerospace, oil and gas, water, power generation, nuclear engineering, production, defence, communications, chemical processing, civil engineering and manufacturing.

Hays International
www.hays.com
International vacancies.

Malla Technical Recruitment Consultancy
www.malla.com
Specializing in engineering placements worldwide.

Michael Page International
www.michaelpage.com
Offices in the Americas, Australasia and Europe, specializing in accounting, banking and finance.

Pilot Select
www.pilotselect.com
Matches pilots with airlines looking for crews.

Reed
www.reed.co.uk
Vacancies, careers information and links to career resources worldwide.

Reed Finance
www.reed.co.uk/finance

Robert Walters
www.robertwalters.com
International accounting and finance recruitment agency.

Veterinary Locums Worldwide
www.vetlocums.com
Site for vets looking for short-term work in practices, wildlife projects or with exotic animals.

Professional Associations

British Medical Association
www.bma.org.uk
Information and advice on working abroad for BMA members.

Institute of Physics
www.iop.org
Physics-related vacancies.
Royal College of Nursing
www.rcn.org.uk
Information and advice on working abroad for RCN members.

Organizations

The British Council
www.britishcouncil.org
Teaching opportunities and voluntary work overseas. Recruits EFL teachers for its own Language Centres.
Committee on the Status of Women in Physics
www.aps.org/educ/cswp
Arm of the American Physical Society. Information on dual-science-career jobs.
Council on International Educational Exchange
www.ciee.org
Work experience, short-term jobs and worldwide exchange programmes for students and recent graduates.
Doctors without Borders
www.doctorswithoutborders.org
Opportunities for medically trained personnel to work in developing countries.
European Commission
www.cec.org.uk/work/index/htm
Commission's current vacancies for English-speaking candidates.
The International Health Exchange
www.ihe.org.uk
Health personnel for programmes in developing countries.
Search Beat
www.searchbeat.com/energyjobs.htm
Worldwide jobs in the petroleum industry.
United Nations
http://unjobs.org
Vacancy board for UN departments worldwide.

Teaching English as a Foreign Language

The British Council
See Organizations.
The Centre for British Teachers
www.cfbt.com
Teaching vacancies in Brunei, Oman and Turkey and educational specialists in Eastern Europe, Africa, Asia and India.
Council on International Educational Exchange
See Organizations.
ELT Job Vacancies
www.jobs.edufind.com
Teaching English as a Foreign Language posts worldwide.

International House
www.ihlondon.com
Recruits teachers for 100 schools in 26 countries.
i-to-i
www.i-to-i.com
i-to-i provides language courses, such as TEFL, for travellers along with volunteer placements around the world.
TEFL
www.tefl.co.uk
Teaching English as a Foreign Language courses.
TEFL.com
www.tefl.com
Teaching English as a Foreign Language job database with links to worldwide employment vacancies.

Voluntary work

British Council
See Organizations.
i-to-i
See TEFL.
Voluntary Service Overseas
www.vso.org.uk
Opportunities in 58 countries in education, health, technical trades, engineering and other fields.

International companies

BDO Stoy Hayward
www.bdo.co.uk/taxservices
A cohesive worldwide network of specialists providing immigration, tax and social security advice to expatriates and their employers.
Boeing
www.boeing.com
Aviation giant offers internships for college students at US institutions.
British Airways
www.britishairwaysjobs.com
Cabin crew, IT and sales vacancies.
GlaxoSmithKline
www.gsk.com/careers/joinus.htm
Access to both UK and US searches for current vacancies in this pharmaceutical company.
Hewlett-Packard
www.jobs.hp.com
IT giant with online application forms.
IBM
www.ibm.com
US site has links to global recruitment.

Integra Global
www.integraglobal.com
International medical insurance providers.
Lloyds TSB
www.lloydstsb.com
International banking.
Microsoft
www.microsoft.com/careers
Information vacancies at the company's different locations.
Shell International
www.shell.com
Superb website with access to expatriate information on its 'Outpost' (www.globaloutpostservices.nl) and Spouses Support Network websites (see Expat networks).
Standard Bank
www.standardbank.com
International banking.

COUNTRY-SPECIFIC DATA

Political information

Foreign and Commonwealth Office
www.fco.gov.uk
Travel Advice Unit provides up-to-the-minute information on political upheaval, natural disasters and epidemics worldwide.
United Nations
www.un.org
Information on countries in the UN.
US Department of State Travel Advisories
http://travel.state.gov/travel
Up-to-the-minute information in the same vein as the Foreign and Commonwealth Office.

Economic data

CIA FactBook
www.cia.gov/cia/publications/factbook
Country breakdown with economic, political, geographic and demographic information available.
Economics Departments, Institutes and Research Centers in the World (EDIRC – University of Connecticut)
http://edirc.repec.org
Index of economic institutions on the web.
Financial Times Country Briefs
http://surveys.ft.com
Superb country surveys providing developments and detailed information on regions and countries, including economic indicators and company activity and performance details.

Union Bank of Switzerland
www.ubs.com
Produces comparative survey 'Prices and Earnings Around the Globe' detailing costs and earnings in 53 countries.

Business guides

Department of Trade and Industry Export Publications
www.dti.gov.uk/export.control/publications.htm
Publications aimed at businesses abroad and for intending expatriates.
Hong Kong and Shanghai Banking Corporation
www.hsbc.com/businessprofiles
Publishes 'Business Profiles' aimed at companies and private individuals and contains useful information on living conditions.

General information

The Centre for International Briefing
www.farnhamcastle.com
Cultural and business briefings covering all regions of the world. Also customized programmes and language tuition.
ECA International
www.eca-international.com
Relocation company with excellent resources and country briefings worldwide.
Expat Network
www.expatnetwork.co.uk
Among other services provides location reports to members.
Expedia
www.expedia.co.uk
Many links to other travel sites.

Continent-specific information

Africa

Africaonline
www.africaonline.com
Information on African countries.
AllAfrica.com
http://allafrica.com
African news and information on countries.
Commonwealth Institute
www.commonwealth.org.uk
Information on member states of the Commonwealth.
www.kenyaweb.com
General information on the culture, history and life in Kenya.
Yahoo!
http://travel.yahoo.com/p-travelguide-191500003-africa_vacations-i
Search engine directory of information on the region.

America

US Census Bureau
www.census.gov
US statistics with links.
Yahoo!
http://travel.yahoo.com/p-travelguide-191501863-united_states_vacations-i
Search engine directory of information on the region.

Asia

Commonwealth Institute
See above.
East Asia Business Services
www.shef.ac.uk/eltc/services/eabs
Tailor-made briefings for expatriates going to Japan, China, Korea or other East Asian countries.
School of Oriental and African Studies
www.soas.ac.uk
Briefing and language service, open briefings on Japan and China, two-day Japan Business Orientation programme.
Yahoo!
http://travel.yahoo.com/p-travelguide-191500005-asia_vacations-i
Search engine directory of information on the region.

Europe

European Commission
www.europa.eu.int
www.cec.org.uk
Factsheets and information on working and living in the European Union.
Yahoo!
http://travel.yahoo.com/p-travelguide-191500008-europe_vacations-i
Search engine directory of information on the region.

Middle East

ArabNet
www.arab.net
Yahoo!
http://travel.yahoo.com/p-travelguide-191500009-middle_east_vacations-i
Search engine directory of information on the region.

Language tuition

Berlitz (UK) Ltd
www.berlitz.co.uk
Language tuition.

EXPAT NETWORKS

British in America
www.britishinamerica.com
Expats in the US link-up.

Britnet
www.british-expats.com
International site for British living abroad.

Brits Abroad
www.britsabroad.co.uk

Diplomatic Service Families Association
www.fco.gov.uk
Promotes the interest and welfare of spouses of serving and retired diplomatic service officers. Provides a link between those at home and abroad.

Escapeartist
www.escapeartist.com
Superb website with links to expat forums, country-specific data, advice on relocation and much more.

Expat Exchange
www.expatexchange.com
Comprehensive information source on moving overseas, tax and finance plus much more. Runs an expat network.

Expat Forum
www.expatforum.com
Chat forums in 24 country-specific areas, along with other areas of interest to expats.

Expatica
www.expatica.com
Well-resourced website for expatriates living in Belgium, France, Spain, Germany and the Netherlands.

Expat Network
www.expatnetwork.co.uk
Publishes *Nexus* and offers a support service for expats.

Expat Online
www.expat-online.com
Network for expats living in Belgium.

Expats in Brussels
www.expatsinbrussels.com
Interactive site for the expatriate community in Brussels.

Federation of American Women's Clubs Overseas, Inc
www.fawco.org

OUTPOST
www.globaloutpostservices.nl
Shell International's superb expat website.

Spouse Employment Centre
www.incnetwork.demon.co.uk
Shell International's website providing information to partners who wish to work or develop their skills during expatriation.

TCK

www.tckworld.com

Website for parents of 'Third Culture Kids' (TCK – expat children) which aims to enable parents to understand the culture shock their children may experience while living abroad.

EDUCATION

British Dyslexia Association

www.bda-dyslexia.org.uk

Advice on the teaching of dyslexic children.

Cambridge Education Associates

www.cea.co.uk

Provides free educational advice as well as a comprehensive guardianship service.

Clarendon International Education

www.clarendon.uk.com

Offers guardianship services.

Department for Education and Skills

www.dfes.gov.uk

Information on maintained boarding schools.

European Council of International Schools

www.ecis.org

Details of 400 international schools and website access to International Schools Directory.

Gabbitas Educational Consultants

www.gabbitas.co.uk

Advice on a selection of suitable schools. Also offers guardianship services.

Gabbitas.net

www.gabbitas.net

Excellent site that contains a fully searchable directory of English-speaking international and special schools.

International Baccalaureate Organization

www.ibo.org

OCR – Oxford Cambridge and RSA Examination Board

www.ocr.org.uk

Administers the AICE curriculum.

National Extension College

www.nec.ac.uk

Offers GCSE and A-level correspondence courses.

The New School, Rome

www.newschoolrome.com

Universities and Colleges Admissions Service

www.ucas.com

Central agency for all UK universities.

World-wide Education Service

www.wesworldwide.com

Information on overseas schools.

The World-wide Education Service (Home School) Ltd
www.weshome.demon.co.uk
Specializes in teaching children with special needs.

HEALTH ADVICE

AXA PPP healthcare
www.axappphealthcare.co.uk
BUPA International
www.bupa.co.uk
Medical insurance worldwide.
Hospital for Tropical Diseases
www.thehtd.org
For access to Health Information for Overseas Travel.
International SOS Assistance
www.internationalsos.com
Provides emergency help in a time of crisis.
Medical Advisory Service for Travellers Abroad (MASTA)
www.masta.org
Offers health briefs on 250 countries.
Reuters Health
www.reutershealth.com/en/

ENTERTAINMENT

Books

Amazon Books
www.amazon.com and www.amazon.co.uk
Delivery of over 2 million titles worldwide.
Internet Public Library
www.ipl.org
Online access to various publications.

Newspapers

The Daily Telegraph
www.telegraph.co.uk
Almost entire content of daily newspaper.
The Guardian
www.guardian.co.uk
Selected cuttings.
The Sunday Times
www.sunday-times.co.uk
Full content.
The Times
www.timesonline.co.uk
Full content.

Sport

Skysports
www.skysports.com
News on a range of sports.
Sportsweb
www.sportsweb.com
As above.
Yahoo!
http://sports.yahoo.com
Comprehensive listings of websites covering every type of sport imaginable.

Television and radio

BBC News
www.news.bbc.co.uk
BBC Online
www.bbc.co.uk
Radio and World Service programmes online with audio versions.
CNN
www.cnn.com
Soap Digest
www.soapoperadigest.com
Keep up to date with your favourite soaps.

Music, DVDs and Videos

Amazon Music, DVDs and Videos
www.amazon.com and amazon.co.uk
Delivery of over 2 million new and used CDs, cassettes, DVDs and videos worldwide.
CD Wow
www.cd-wow.com
International music, DVD and games site that delivers worldwide.
MTV
www.mtv.com
Online music site.

USEFUL MISCELLANEOUS WEBSITES

Allied Pickfords
www.alliedpickfords.co.uk
International removals.
Cybercafe Search Engine
www.cybercaptive.com
Cybercafe locations worldwide to ensure internet access.
Department for Environment, Food and Rural Affairs
www.defra.gov.uk
Advice on the transportation of animals overseas.

Expatnetwork
www.expatnetwork.co.uk
Gift service to send gifts or flowers to friends and family.

Expedia
www.expedia.co.uk
Travel links.

Fedex
www.fedex.com
Website of Federal Express for your freight needs.

Foreign Languages for Travellers
www.travlang.com/languages
Phrases in many languages.

Going-There.com
www.going-there.com
International relocation company with offices based in the UK and abroad.

Kropla
www.kropla.com
Extremely useful site with worldwide electrical and telephone information. Details of electric plugs and voltages used.

Mastercard/Cirrus ATM Locator
www.mastercard.com/cardholderservices/atm
Find automated teller machine in your new location.

MonsterMoving
www.moving.com
Comprehensive array of moving-related services and resources.

VISA ATM Locator
visa.via.infonow.net/locator/global
Find automated teller machine in your new location.

Visa Service
www.visaservice.co.uk
Specializes in processing applications for business visas and passports.

Worldwide Holiday and Festival Page
http://www.holidayfestival.com
Public holidays throughout the world.

Worldwide weather forecasts
www.intellicast.com
Local weather around the globe.

XE.com
www.xe.com
Currency converter.

Part Six

Country Profiles

This edition of *Working Abroad* is complemented by an online resource that provides updated information on more than 50 countries around the globe. The following section provides samples of 10 of those countries. All of the country profile information, including the 10 countries listed here, can be accessed online at:
www.koganpage.com/WorkingAbroad10
password: WA29006

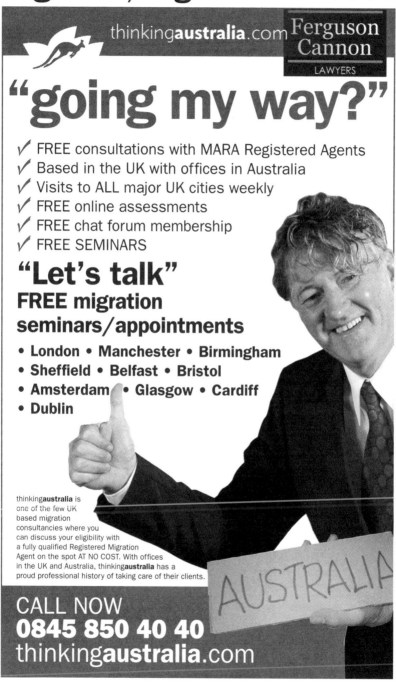

SUCCESS breeds **SUCCESS** there if you want it...

Twenty years ago, Britain's bad weather was the main reason why people wanted to Migrate to Australia.

Today, it's the economic opportunity and the desire for a better lifestyle that drives UK families and workers to seek a new life down under.

Two decades ago the UK was a leading powerhouse of growth and opportunity: today Australia has eclipsed Europe to become one of the new world's top economies.

During the BOOM and BUST 1980's the British were urged by government ministers to 'get on your bike' and go find work. Twenty years on, as the European economies suffer serious slowdown, the cycle has yet again returned with British workers, professionals and the ever growing 'Business Investors' queuing to seek the new found wealth of Australia.

As a sad reminder of the 80's, the serious are moving in droves with no turning back as the promise of the 'good life' enough to farewell their birthplace for the land they call 'down under'.

thinking**australia**.com Ferguson Cannon

LAWYERS

Over 425,000 Brits left their homeland in 2008, figures for 2009 expected higher, yet not available. But as the Recession in the UK remains very much the reality and the reminder of the 80's still very much the shadow of warning yet not heeded to, the Brits have had enough. At any one time 2.25 million are hoping to move abroad, and with Australia being the number *one* choice of destination for Brits, Australia is yet again poised to reap top skills and wealth of the migrating families.

It's not just about people wanting to get away from the UK, it's more about the endless attractions of Australia – the healthy environment, endless sunshine, bigger brighter houses for money/value, better schools, safer streets says **Darrell Todd** ceo of thinking**australia**.com

For business/investor migrants it's a *win win* situation - with all of the above plus a wealth of attractive business and commercial opportunities across fast - expanding national markets and with the range of exciting verticals - it's a no-brainer, Australia leads the way.

Australia is growing fast and with current global 'orders' of billions it's economy expanding as an influx of high quality – professional workers from the UK generate an even greater GDP and create fast expanding national consumer and services market.

You should always be mindful that Australian streets are *not* paved with gold, it still requires hard work, and for most it is the 'pick and shovel' that finds gold.

You will be out of your security zone for a couple of years, but if you plan and research as much as possible you will make the right decision.

thinking**australia**.com is a company in the UK that offers a genuine FREE service of help/information re all aspects of Australia. Their JOB EXPOS and Migration Seminars are a monthly feature to the UK circuit visiting all major cities, well worth attending, apart from being FREE they are full of information. Also visit their free ONLINE Migration HELPLINE: www.thinking**australia**.tv

Across Australia we are experiencing a 12 month waiting list for new houses says todd. Major national construction projects are being delayed because of the national shortage of skilled workers and Managers to do the work.

Mining and export quota's are not being met, it fast becoming JOBS JOBS JOBS the ' buzz ' word of today's needs. All this can only be good for those seeking a new world and the opportunity to share in this new world of wealth.

With current economic growth predicted to last for another 20 plus years, there has never been a better time for skilled/professional workers – and business migrants such as; IT and Telecoms, Property, Finance, Travel and Leisure.

Demand for workers is acute across all Australian states and now business and government agencies must compete to attract the numbers of workers needed for each state.

Simon Kinsmore, head of marketing at the ACT government in Canberra. *"We believe Australia's capital city offers the most advantages for Migrants: highest wages in the country, highest skills base, safest environment, most modern city in beautiful location - and centre of government. We have it all…"*

Bruce McFarlane, head of business development division, Western Australia government believe WA offers most to Migrants, not least it's close traditional links to the UK. *"WA and especially Perth is where many of the original Poms settled from the 50's onwards, so we've always had a very good word-of-mouth channel."* But adds; *"it JOBS JOBS and more JOBS we have on offer, we desperately need 'key' workers."*

David Neilson of Business and Investment, the leading business sales specialist in Australia and NZ; with Business Downunder a lot of things are similar but many very different, so seek expert help to find the right opportunity and the right team to support your ambitions.

To reach the top in professional or business life takes focus, drive and skill. It also takes a lot of research, expert application and teamwork. To navigate the process involved in business migration requires similar expertise', say Neilson: 'We combine individual requirement with best possible opportunities to ensure success '.

Australia is a Global focal point of new world business, sitting under the massive Asian Pacific market of enormous growth and their need for product/services to feed their growth. Australia also well placed to service these Asian markets for European/Americas trade needs, it the again winning formula, Australia has it all.

Economic growth in Australia will continue unabated, fuelled and supported by the millions of migrant workers and families that, demographically must swell the population by 20% over the next decade if Australia is to maintain it's trading position in the global market.

Currently Australia rides the economic storm well, it failed to fall victim to the recession, smartly regulated, managed well, self sufficient, but it's strength being the endless list of consumables to the market place. One of the biggest commercial orders ever placed in modern day history was to supply Gas to China, it a multi billion contract, just one of it's consumables.

This process will expand and remain self-supporting for many years to come, providing on-going opportunities for migrant workers, professionals and business investors from the UK.

thinking**australia**.com Ferguson Cannon LAWYERS

the Winning formula

Currently with 1000 new jobs per day being created now is certainly the time to consider Migration to Australia says Glenn Ferguson of FCLawyers;

The time never been better, the Australian government is making it harder to enter our county, this is due to the massive demand on our Migration intake numbers, with more and more all seeking to secure that better quality of life. To get to Australia its fast becoming JOB first then - Migration the way to it.

It's a smart country, it has it's policies right, protects it's shorelines / workers - we will never be in a situation of over supply, therefore the workforce always in demand, and where demand ensures growth and wealth, *the winning formula*

'If you have the skills, the business ambition and the ability to adapt- then we have a JOB, the lifestyle and a new home waiting for you' says Darrell Todd. With opportunities to suit everyone, it's the perfect time to start looking at your current life and prospects-and compare it to just what is possible in Australia.

thinking**australia**.com Ferguson Cannon LAWYERS

Australia

The economy

Until 2008 the outlook for the Australian economy was for continued growth, with low unemployment (around 4.4 per cent) and moderate inflation (2.3 per cent in 2007, rising to 4.6 per cent in 2008). Economic growth eased from 4 per cent in 2007 to 2.4 per cent in 2008 but recovered to 2.7 per cent in 2009. Exports which had expanded in 2008 by 4.9 per cent declined by 11.3 per cent in 2009, while imports, having increased by 11.9 per cent, also fell back by –8.3 per cent in 2009, resulting in a current account deficit ratio to GDP of 3.1 per cent in 2009. The government held a slender budget surplus in 2007 at the level of 4.4 per cent of GDP, which was reduced to 2.6 per cent of GDP in 2008 and 1.5 per cent in 2009.

The government maintains a cautious line on immigration policy. Preference is given to people with direct and close family connections, skilled and business migrants, and others accepted under refugee or special humanitarian programmes. A points system is used in some of the categories to determine a person's eligibility based on factors such as age, health, education, occupation and the level of skill required to undertake that occupation in Australia. All non-nationals must obtain a visa beforehand. (Indeed, this is the model that the British government is considering for the UK.) Additional information can be obtained from the Australian High Commission in London or the Australian Consulate in Manchester.

Working conditions

Leave entitlements

At executive and professional levels, international standards and conditions of work apply. Holidays are normally four weeks a year, and some firms pay a holiday bonus. There is also often a form of sabbatical leave after 10 years' service with a company. Flexible working hours are quite common in Australia, particularly in the public sector.

The chief difference in working conditions between Australia and other countries is that the concept of status related to specific jobs – and, even more, the social and workplace behaviour associated with it – has to be discarded. Any tendency to 'give yourself airs' is fatal!

Recruitment

Australian employers will not usually recruit from a distance, but it is possible to get a good picture of the sort of employment opportunities available from Australian newspapers and particularly from the Australian migration authorities. In general, the demand is for specific skills and professional or managerial qualifications. Most British professional qualifications are recognized in Australia; however, accreditation from the appropriate licensing board may be required for certain professions.

Entry visas

There are a number of business visas available for individuals or companies wishing to set up a branch or representative office in Australia or to engage in business activities. The following is a brief summary of some of the more commonly used visas:

- *Business visit visa (456)/electronic travel authority (ETA).* The business visit visa/ETA allows for a visit of up to three months – no extensions can be made while the visa holder is in Australia. No work may be undertaken on this visa. The purpose is to attend meetings, hold discussions, participate in short-term training, etc. Nationals of certain countries can apply on the internet or through travel agencies or airlines for the ETA. Non-ETA-eligible nationals need to apply for the 456 visa through the nearest Australian diplomatic mission.

- *Business long-stay visa (457).* This temporary visa is granted for up to four years and can be renewed or extended. It is commonly known as the work visa, as it provides visa holders with permission to work – but only for the sponsoring company. This visa is commonly used by companies overseas looking to send staff to Australia to set up and run a branch or representative office, or to establish a company in Australia, for the purposes of engaging in business. This visa is also used by companies already operating in Australia that wish to bring in specialist staff from overseas. There are three stages to obtaining a 457 work visa: 1) Sponsorship – an overseas-based company must first apply for approval as a sponsoring company. Assessment looks at company background, financials, and proposed activities in Australia. 2) Nomination – this involves assessing the position that is to be filled by the visa applicant. The position must relate to an occupation on a list of skilled occupations. The salary for the position must meet minimum thresholds. 3) Visa – assesses the visa applicants and whether they have the formal skills and qualifications for the position.
- *Occupational training visa (442).* A temporary visa for up to two years that allows an Australian company to sponsor someone from overseas to undertake work-based training. A formal training programme is essential.
- *Employer nomination visa.* This is a permanent residence visa. It requires a company to sponsor someone and is similar to the 457, although the visa application requirements are different. It requires the sponsoring company to be established and operating in Australia.
- *Business skills visas.* There are a number of these visas – most are temporary visas for four years and are not renewable. They require visa holders to establish or purchase a business in Australia (a small business is usually sufficient) and manage that business. If that business achieves certain business outcomes in terms of turnover, equity, staffing, etc, then the visa holder may apply for permanent residence.

These visas target people who have successfully run their own businesses over the last few years, or who have had very senior executive positions in large corporations (non-government), or who have themselves actively managed a portfolio of investments over a number of years and who have a high net worth.

For further information on Australian visas and entry rules, contact:

- Harriet Mantell, Registered Migration Agent No 9901517, BDO Migration Services Pty Ltd, 563 Bourke Street, Melbourne VIC 3000 (tel: +613 9615 8747, e-mail: harriet.mantell@bdomigration. com.au)
- Surekha Kukadia, Immigration Manager, BDO Stoy Hayward LLP, 8 Baker Street, London W1U 3LL (tel: +44 020 7893 2430, e-mail: sue.kukadia@bdo.co.uk).

Useful information

Financial year: The Australian financial year runs from 1 July to 30 June.

Electricity: Electrical goods should be checked with the maker to see if they will work in Australia, because the voltage systems differ (220–250 V, 50 Hz ac). Gas appliances are particularly tricky because of differences in pressure and gas composition. British TVs and video recorders do not function in Australia because of different signals and need to be professionally converted to be compatible with the Australian system.

Driving: A car, essential in Australia, is best bought there. If you import a car you will have to make sure that it meets the safety regulations of the state to which you are going. You can drive on a British licence for the first three months. After that you will have to take a local test, but this will only be an oral one if you already hold a British or international licence.

Transport: Interstate transport is usually by aeroplane, although there is also a large railway network.

Education: Education begins at the age of five or six and is compulsory up to age 15 or 16 (depending on the state). The school session starts early in February, not September as in the UK. It must be remembered that, in the southern hemisphere, the seasons are reversed; hence the Australian Christmas is in mid-summer. Tuition is free in government schools, but parents generally have to provide uniforms, books and other materials. As many as 25 per cent of pupils, however, attend private schools, particularly in the latter years of secondary education. Fees are reasonable because these schools are aided by government grants. Allow A$5,000–$8,000 a year for private secondary school tuition fees.

There are small tuition fees for university-level education, which is very well provided for in all states. Most Australians take a pass degree rather than honours. Standards are similar to those in the UK.

Useful contacts:
British High Commission, Commonwealth Avenue, Yarralumla, Canberra, ACT 2600 (tel: 612 6270 6666, website: www.uk. emb.gov.au)
Australian High Commission, Australia House, Strand, London WC2 (tel: 020 7379 4334)
Australian Tourist Commission (tel: 020 8780 2229, websites: www. aussie.net.au, www.australia.com)

Personal taxation

Residence

Australian tax residents are taxed on their worldwide income, while non-residents are taxed only on Australian-sourced income, subject to the operation of double taxation agreements, which override domestic tax law.

An individual will be an Australian resident for taxation purposes if they ordinarily reside in Australia or if any of the following tests is satisfied:

- the individual's domicile is in Australia and they do not have a permanent place of abode elsewhere;
- the individual has physically been present in Australia for 183 days or more in the financial year (1 July to 30 June) and does not have a usual place of abode outside Australia; or
- the individual is a member of certain Commonwealth government superannuation schemes.

A place of abode is the place where the taxpayer adopts a habitual mode of living. Where an individual is a dual tax resident, double taxation agreements may apply to demarcate the taxing right of each country in respect of the income derived.

Taxes on income

Taxable income for personal income tax purposes includes income from employment, business income, certain capital gains and passive income such as dividends, interest and rental income. Tax rates are progressive up to 45 per cent. The top marginal rate kicks in at A$133,560 of taxable income. A 'temporary' resident (one who holds a temporary visa, is not a resident within the meaning of the Social Security Act 1991 and does not have a spouse who is an Australian resident) is granted exemption for most foreign-source income and capital gains and for interest-withholding tax obligations associated with foreign liabilities.

Deductions and allowances

Generally, all non-cash fringe benefits provided to employees are subject to Fringe Benefit Tax (FBT), a tax payable by the employer. Business expenses are deductible if they are necessarily incurred in gaining or producing assessable income. Expenses of a capital, private or domestic nature are not deductible. Residents are allowed some tax rebates, including rebates for dependants and certain personal expenses.

Superannuation

Employers are required to withhold 9 per cent of gross salary and transfer the withheld amount into a superannuation fund of their choice to a maximum earnings level of A$38,180 per quarter. No contributions need to be made above this level of earnings.

Social security

Employers contribute to the mandatory superannuation pension scheme on behalf of their employees at 9 per cent of an employee's gross income or salary. In addition to income tax, a 1.5 per cent Medicare levy is payable on the taxable income of Australian residents including permanent residents and taxpayers from the UK, Northern Ireland, Italy, Malta, Sweden, the Netherlands, Finland or Norway. Relief is available to low-income taxpayers. A further 1 per cent surcharge may be imposed on taxpayers with taxable income exceeding A$50,000 (or A$100,000 for families) who have no private hospital cover.

Taxes on capital

Capital gains

Gains derived from the disposal of assets acquired after 19 September 1985 are included in assessable income. For assets acquired after 1 October 1999 and held for more than one year, individuals are taxed at their marginal rate on half the gain, setting a maximum effective capital gains tax rate of 22.5 per cent. For assets acquired before that date, individuals may choose between the new system and the pre-September 1985 system, under which they are taxed at their marginal rate on the whole gain, indexed for inflation. Indexation of the cost base of existing assets was frozen at 30 September 1999. Capital gains tax applies only to taxable Australian property disposed of by foreign investors as from 12 December 2006.

Real property tax

Land tax is assessed annually to the owners of real estate property or users of the land. The tax is imposed at state level, but there is an exemption from land tax for one's principal place of residence.

The states and territories impose stamp duty at varying rates up to 6.75 per cent on the transfer of real property.

Other taxes

There is no net wealth/net worth tax, inheritance/estate tax, capital acquisitions tax or capital duty.

Double taxation agreements

Australia has double tax agreements with more than 40 countries, including both the United States and the UK.

Filing and payment

Joint tax returns for spouses are not permitted. Every individual with assessable income in excess of the tax-free threshold of A$6,000 is required to file a tax return for each year ending 30 June by 31 October of that year, unless the individual is on a tax agent lodgement programme and is eligible for an extended deadline.

Penalties and interest may be applied for late filing, failure to file, failure to exercise due care, and tax evasion.

Source:
KPMG's Individual Income Tax Rate Survey 2009.

Canada

The economy

Canada is basically a very rich country, but its economy tends to follow relatively closely that of its neighbour, the United States.

Canada is one of the largest producers of valuable minerals and is also a major exporter of automotive, timber and paper products. Most trade is with the United States, particularly following the North American Free Trade Agreement (NAFTA) in 1993. In 2007, real GDP growth was 2.7 per cent (0.2 per cent down on 2006) but plunged to 0.5 per cent for 2008. The deep recession in the US, Canada's dominant trading partner, curtailed exports, and caused a parallel decline in GDP to −2.5 per cent for 2009. Shortages in hydro-carbon production capacity caused upsurges in the cost of energy, which have affected consumer confidence and spending. Unemployment in January 2010 was 8.3 per cent, up from 7.2 per cent in 2008. Consumer price inflation steadied at 1.3 per cent in December 2009 compared to 1.2 per cent a year previously. Canada registered a budget deficit of −3.1 per cent of GDP in 2009, down from a surplus of 0.3 per cent in 2008, and a foreign trade current account deficit of −2.8 per cent in 2009, compared to a surplus of just 1 per cent in 2008.

Working conditions

The general working atmosphere and corporate style in Canada closely resemble those of the United States, but Canadian society is more stable, with lower crime figures. If you go to Canada intending to stay more than three months, you have to register this fact on arrival. You cannot change your status from visitor while in-country. Applications for visas or permanent residency must be made abroad.

By and large, executive salaries are higher than in the UK, becoming more equal going down the scale. Professional groups that are in demand include mathematicians, sales and advertising personnel, chemists and physicists. It is also possible to immigrate if you have capital available or intend to run a business in Canada under the Business Immigration Programme. Other schemes include Temporary Employment Authorization and the Live-in Caregiver Program, as well as work opportunities for foreign students.

In the public services, preference is given to Canadian citizens and here, as well as in many private sector jobs, a knowledge of French is essential. It should not be assumed that the status of French in Canada is merely a nationalistic gesture. It is the mother language of many Canadian citizens. However, people who do not speak it may still enter public service, as provision will be made for them to learn the language subsequently.

People who want to exercise professional skills will have to apply to the appropriate professional bodies and institutes to make sure that their qualifications are recognized and that they possess the appropriate licence. In some cases where training to achieve the qualifications in question is substantially different in Canada, further examinations may have to be taken to achieve recognition. In all instances, though, documentary proof of degrees, etc should be taken with you, as well as such personal documents as birth and marriage certificates.

Anyone who is not a Canadian citizen or a permanent resident who wishes to work in Canada requires authorization. In certain cases an individual is authorized by virtue of the regulations, but in most cases the individual must obtain a work permit from Citizenship and Immigration Canada. A work permit can only be issued for a temporary position. In order to reside and work permanently in Canada, the applicant must qualify as a skilled worker.

Useful information

Climate: Canadian winters are much colder than anything one is accustomed to in temperate zones, although similar to those of Scandinavia. This is true even in the population centres in the southern part of the country. If you are to arrive in Canada any time between October and March make sure you have plenty of warm clothes. On the other hand, the summer (June to September) can be very warm, with temperatures averaging around 32°C in midsummer in southern places like Toronto.

Electricity: 120 V, 60 Hz; conversion from other voltages is not really possible.

Health care: Canada operates a national health insurance programme, which is administered by the provinces, for both hospital and ordinary medical (though not dental) care. In all provinces except Quebec and British Columbia, which impose a brief residence qualification (though in the case of Quebec only for hospital insurance), this is available to immigrants immediately on arrival, and you should be sure to obtain details of registration and premium payments as soon as possible. Many employers pay the employee's contribution as part of the remuneration package, and this is a point worth checking in any job offer.

Education: Education is compulsory from six or seven to 16 (15 in some provinces) and is free to the end of secondary schooling. Educational methods are progressive and similar to those in primary and comprehensive schools in the UK. There are also a small number of private schools. For registration you will need a birth certificate, visa, vaccination certificate and previous school records. In Quebec and French-speaking Canada the medium of instruction in many schools is French, and the teaching of French is an important part of the curriculum.

Post-secondary education is not free, but repayable loans are available from the province, and there are various other forms of monetary assistance including scholarships for able students. University fees vary but are mainly low.

Useful contacts:
British High Commission, 80 Elgin Street, Ottawa K1P 5K7 (tel: 1 613 237 1530, website: www.britainincanada.org)
Canadian High Commission, Macdonald House, 38 Grosvenor Street, London W1K 4AA (tel: 020 7258 6600, website: www.canada. org.uk)
Canadian Tourism Commission, 62–65 Trafalgar Square, London WC2N 5DV (tel: 020 7389 9988)

Personal taxation

Residence

Like many countries, Canada taxes on the basis of residence. Tax legislation does not specifically define residence, although it does include several rules under which an individual may be 'deemed' to be resident. Generally, residence is determined by common law principles. Under these rules, an individual is generally considered to be resident if they have a 'continuing state of relationship' with Canada, as evidenced by a dwelling held for year-round use, the presence of a spouse or other family members in Canada, or the maintenance of personal property or other social ties in Canada, such as bank accounts, furniture and club memberships. An individual is also deemed to be resident if they stay in Canada for 183 days or more in a calendar year.

Taxation of personal income

Canadian residents are subject to tax on their worldwide income. Taxation can also arise in respect of investments in foreign investment entities and certain non-residential trusts. Non-residents are subject to tax on income earned from Canadian sources. The federal tax rates rise progressively up to 29 per cent, which kicks in at CAD126,265 of taxable income. In addition, each province or territory imposes an income tax, with the maximum rate ranging from 10 per cent to 19.25 per cent.

Employment income (including most employment benefits), certain investment income and profits earned from a business or a profession are taxable at the individual's applicable personal tax rate. Dividends received from Canadian corporations are subject to a more favourable tax regime.

Social security

Employed persons, as well as their employers, are required to make employment and government pension plan contributions at rates from 6.68 per cent upwards. The maximum employee contribution is approximately CAD2,851.

Taxes on capital

Capital gains

One-half of capital gains realized are included in taxable income albeit the gain may be discounted by up to 50 per cent.

Real property tax

Municipal authorities levy taxes on the owners of real property, generally in the range of 1 to 2 per cent per year, of the assessed value.

Other taxes

There is no net wealth/net worth tax, formal inheritance or estate tax, capital duty, stamp duty or capital acquisitions tax in Canada.

Individuals are deemed to dispose of all property on ceasing Canadian residency. They are subject to Depart Tax, although there is potential relief.

Double taxation treaties

Canada has concluded more than 90 income tax treaties or conventions in force with other countries for the elimination of double taxation on income, including treaties with both the UK and the United States.

Filing and penalties

There are no family income tax returns in Canada. The tax year is the calendar year. The deadline to file an individual tax return and to pay the outstanding tax liability is 30 April of the year following. Individuals and their spouses or common-law partners who operate a business or profession have an extended filing deadline of 15 June, but the tax liability is still due by 30 April. Penalties are applied for late filing, and interest is payable on any late balance owing, compounded daily. In all provinces but Quebec, individuals file a single tax return with the federal government which collects both federal and provincial taxes.

Source:
KPMG's Individual Income Tax Rate Survey 2009.

The People's Republic of China

The economy

Continuing economic reforms since 1979 have brought the country step by step into line with other economies. Sustained foreign investment has enabled the construction of an industrial and communications infrastructure. In November 2001 China finally gained accession to the World Trade Organization (WTO) and committed itself to a firm programme of tariff reductions. Since then, China has enacted and amended many new laws in compliance with its WTO obligations. Many of the former barriers to investment and trade have been removed, with new standards of transparency. There are two stock markets, in Shanghai and Shenzhen, and Shanghai has emerged strongly as China's financial centre, although most of the large successful state-owned enterprises have preferred public flotation in Hong Kong.

The economy grew steadily at more than 10 per cent in recent years (more than 11 per cent in 2006 and 2007), with higher exports every year and soaring foreign investments. In 2008 however, China's exports began to be impacted by the early stages of the global recession and GDP growth declined to 9 per cent. The full force of the recession hit the economy in the first quarter of 2009, with rapidly rising unemployment. However, the government took rapid action with a massive programme of 'quantitative easing' through the state-controlled banks and the GDP growth rate for 2009 was maintained at 8.7 per cent. China has come out of recession more strongly than any other economy with GDP growth of about 10 per cent forecast for 2010 and an export recovery which has sustained a trade balance in excess of US$360 billion. By the end of 2009 foreign exchange reserves had passed US$2.1 trillion, the biggest in the world, much of which is invested in US bonds and securities. The current account surplus for 2009 is estimated at US$380 billion, representing 8.2 per cent of GDP.

By 2004, China had gained international recognition of its growing status as 'the workshop of the world', and in 2005 became the world's fourth-largest economy, overtaking France and the UK. In 2006 China overtook Japan to become the second-highest-spending country on research and development after the United States. In 2007 China was confirmed as the largest source of imports by the EU. By the end of 2009 China had overtaken Germany as the world's top exporter.

Working conditions

Office accommodation is scarce and very expensive. Many foreign companies still have their offices in hotels. It has been estimated by the *China Business Review* that it costs a company around £400,000 to keep a small, one-person office in China. Business hours are from 8.00 am until midday and 2.00 to 6.00 pm. Expatriates require a work permit to work in China. The employer must have permission in the form of a licence to employ a foreign individual. However, job opportunities in the mainland for Chinese-speaking managers are likely to increase as the restrictions on foreign investment in service sectors such as banking, insurance and retailing are removed from 2007 under the terms of China's WTO admission.

Useful information

Transport: Both imported cars and spares are still subject to high rates of duty, although reductions are scheduled. However, there is now a good choice of cars manufactured in China, mainly through joint ventures with European, Japanese and US auto-motive multinationals. Taxis are often the preferred mode of transport. If you have a car it is becoming increasingly possible to get around. You need a permit to travel, but this is generally granted without difficulty.

Health: Cholera and yellow fever inoculations are advisable. An AIDS test may be required.

Health care: Good medical care is available, although the equipment may not be the most modern, and proprietary medication may not be in full supply.

Education: There is an international school in Beijing and US schools in Guangzhou and Shanghai. The British International School Shanghai, in the Pudong area of Shanghai, is also recommended.

Accommodation: International-standard living accommodation can now be rented or purchased by foreigners in major cities, particularly Beijing, Shanghai and Guangzhou.

Useful contacts:
British Embassy, 11 Guang Hua Lu, Beijing 100600 (tel: 861 06532 1961)
Chinese Embassy, 49–51 Portland Place, London W1 (tel: 020 7299 4049)
Chinese National Tourist Office, 4 Glentworth Street, London NW1 5PG (tel: 020 7935 9787)
US website: www.cnto.org

Personal taxation

Residence

The People's Republic of China (China or the PRC) imposes individual taxes on the basis of residence and domicile. An individual is regarded as being domiciled in China if they usually or habitually reside in China owing to family relationships or because they are a registered householder with a personal residence record. An individual who lives abroad for reasons such as education, employment, work assignments, visiting relatives or touring, and who thereafter must return to China, is regarded as being domiciled in China. The extent to which individuals who are not domiciled in China are liable to income tax depends on their period of residence in China.

Personal income is liable to individual income tax (IIT). Individuals domiciled in China are liable to IIT in respect of their worldwide income. After five consecutive years of residence in China, a foreign individual will be subject to IIT on their worldwide income in the same way as a PRC domiciliary, starting from the sixth year. Subject to the approval of the tax authorities, foreign individuals who have resided in China for one to five years will be taxed on their PRC-source income and non-PRC-source income borne by a PRC establishment. Foreign individuals who have resided in China for less than one year are liable to IIT on their PRC-source income only.

A foreign individual who works in China for less than 90 days (or 183 days if from a tax-treaty country) during a calendar year is exempt from IIT if their income is paid by a foreign entity and is not borne by a PRC establishment.

Taxes on income

Wages and salaries are subject to progressive tax rates rising to 45 per cent, with the top marginal rate kicking in at RMB100,000 of monthly taxable income. Dividends, remuneration from manuscripts, royalties, income from leasing properties, income from transfer or assignment of properties and contingency income are taxed at 20 per cent. Interest income is taxed at 5 per cent. Income from personal services is taxed at progressive rates up to 40 per cent. The tax year-end is 31 December for those individuals earning more than RMB120,000.

Deductions and allowances

An individual is entitled to a fixed monthly deduction of RMB2,000 for expenses effective from 1 March 2008; an additional fixed deduction of RMB3,200 is granted to individuals who are not usually or habitually resident in the Chinese mainland and who derive wages or salaries from the mainland. For domestic individuals, personal basic contributions are deductible. These include payment to housing funds and for certain medical insurance, pensions and unemployment insurance.

Social security

A resident individual must contribute to basic endowment insurance, unemployment insurance and the house accumulation fund from taxable income on a monthly basis. Social security rates vary by city and are subject to annual change. Generally social security is assessed against salary with a maximum capped at three times the average city salary of the prior year.

Taxes on capital

Capital gains

There are no capital gains taxes as such in China. Capital gains derived by an individual are categorized as 'other income' for PRC

IIT purposes. Gains derived from the sale of property are subject to tax at a flat rate of 20 per cent and to land value added tax. Individuals who have occupied their sole private dwelling for five years are exempt from capital gains tax.

Real property tax

An individual who rents out their own property is subject to urban real estate property tax at varying rates set by local authorities.

Other taxes

There is no net wealth/net worth tax, inheritance/estate tax, capital acquisitions tax or capital duty in China. Stamp duty is levied on contracts, agreements and certain documents at 0.05 to 0.1 per cent.

Double tax treaties

China has more than 80 tax treaties in force with other countries for the elimination of double taxation on income, including treaties with the UK and the United States.

Filing

Each individual must file a separate return; joint filing is not permitted. All individuals must register with the Chinese tax authorities as soon as they become liable to IIT. Married couples file returns separately. Tax returns filing due date is 31 March after the close of the year.

Source:
KPMG's Individual Income Tax Rate Survey 2009.

France

The economy

The French economy suffered less than its eurozone neighbours in 2009 with a decline on GDP of –2.2 per cent. As France emerges from recession GDP growth of 1.6 per cent is forecast for 2010. However, industrial production was still falling by 2.3 per cent in December 2009 and unemployment stood at 10 per cent. In other respects France did less well then Germany, its principal EU partner, with a 2009 current account deficit of –2.1 per cent and a budget deficit of –7.9 per cent.

Although France is one of the largest industrial powers in the world, it is the world's second-largest agricultural exporter. Foreign companies accounted for more than 27 per cent of manufacturing output and 30 per cent of exports in 2008.

France is well off for natural resources, with coal, natural gas, iron ore, potash, bauxite and fluorspar. However, despite a strong nuclear power industry, the steep rise in the price of oil has impeded economic recovery. Trade is primarily with EU countries, headed by Germany, with the UK as its third-largest export market. Principal exports are food, wine and dairy produce, petroleum products, metals, steels, chemicals, cars, non-ferrous metals and a wide range of consumer goods. Fashion and luxury items and tourism are also important sources of revenue.

Industry is fairly evenly dispersed, though Greater Paris has the largest and most heterogeneous concentration, and some areas, such as Brittany and the south-west, are under-industrialized. Textiles, coal and steel have declined, but new technologically advanced and science-based industries, such as chemicals, electronics and nuclear engineering, have been developed, particularly in the Lyon–Grenoble region, the second most prosperous in

France, while in the south-west, based on Toulouse, the aeronautical industry flourishes alongside the new technology industries.

Agriculture, largely dominated by small family farms, is still of major importance and influence, even though the numbers working on the land have steadily fallen and there has been a drift to the towns and cities. Residential property values in rural areas are much lower than in the UK and in recent years, with improved air travel facilities, have been a major incentive for UK families to relocate to France. The recent significant increases in property values in those areas served by airports, particularly in the south-west since 2004, are likely to continue over the medium term.

Working conditions

European Union citizens do not require work permits. At the end of 2003 a law was passed by which residence permits were no longer required by EU citizens subject to certain conditions. The 35-hour week is standard, but this is under review. French workers are entitled by law to five weeks' annual leave. There are 11 public holidays. Many firms and offices are shut for much of August.

The level of managerial salaries is around 30 to 40 per cent higher than in the UK. Employers' contributions to social security are among the highest in Europe, but direct taxation is relatively low. Secretarial salaries are much the same as in the UK.

Most wages are fixed by collective bargaining at national level. Equal pay is theoretically obligatory – the gap between men's and women's pay is narrower than in most EU countries. There is also a minimum legal wage. Given the current economic problems, these areas are under a great deal of pressure for change.

Many fringe benefits are provided, and most employers have to contribute to housing and welfare. The practice of a 13th-month bonus is widespread, and most manual workers are now paid monthly, instead of fortnightly, and enjoy staff status. French workers attach as much importance to social security and fringe benefits as to money wages.

Useful information

Banking hours: 9.00 am to 4.30 pm weekdays (closed in the afternoon before a public holiday), some closed on Saturdays. May be closed for lunch in the provinces.

Post office: 8.00 am to 7.00 pm weekdays, 8.00 am to 12.00 pm Saturdays.

Shopping hours: 10.00 am to 7.00 pm Monday–Saturday, closed 1.00 to 3.00 pm and all day Monday outside Paris.

Electricity: 220 V (may vary).

Driving: Driving is on the right. Paris is congested and parking difficult, but the traffic flows. If you take your own car, you are obliged to have it fitted with seat belts back and front; yellow head-lamps are no longer compulsory for motor vehicles.

Transport: The main centres are linked by internal airways, and there are airports at Lyon, Marseille, Nice, Bordeaux, Strasbourg and Toulouse, as well as two in Paris: Charles de Gaulle and Orly. The railway network is highly efficient, with a number of express and TGV (260 km/h) trains. Fares are cheaper than in the UK. A direct rail link with the UK is via the Channel Tunnel. The roads are good, and there is a network of motorways, on which tolls are payable. These can be expensive on a long journey.

Health care: There was a reciprocal health agreement with the UK, but the French government has withdrawn benefits for UK expatriates domiciled in France from 2008. Medical attention is expensive, but 75 per cent of the fees for doctors and dentists working within the French sickness insurance scheme can be reimbursed. A proportion of the cost of prescriptions can be refunded (40–70 per cent), as well as outpatient hospital treatment (80 per cent), although this system is under review and may face cuts. Private treatment is costly. There is a British hospital in Paris, the Hertford, and a more expensive US one.

Education: Some expatriate parents send their children to local schools, which are of a high educational standard and where pupils can acquire a good knowledge of French. There is free compulsory education from 6 to 16, and for children below that age there are many crèches and nursery schools. Secondary education is in two cycles, from 11 to 15 and from 15 to 18. Those who complete the second cycle can take the baccalaureate examination, before proceeding to university or institutes of technology. US and British schools in Paris cater for children of diplomats and business people. The British School of Paris is geared to the UK system; it takes pupils from 4 to 18 and offers boarding facilities.

Directory enquiries: 12.

Emergency services: Police 17, fire 18, ambulance 15.

Media: Most provincial regions have their own newspapers, but some Paris papers, such as *Le Figaro* and *Le Monde*, circulate nationally. There is a wide range of weeklies, the best known being *Paris Match* and *L'Express*. TV is state controlled with limited advertising, though cable and satellite facilities are expanding rapidly. There are one state, four commercial and a number of local private radio stations.

Useful contacts:
British Embassy, 35 Rue du Faubourg St Honoré, 75383 Paris, Cedex 08 (tel: 44 51 31 00, website: www.amb-grandebretagne.fr)
French Consulate General, 21 Cromwell Road, London SW7 (tel: 020 7838 2000)
French Tourist Office, www.franceguide.com, www.maison-de-la-france.fr

Country information:
www.paris-anglo.com
www.parisfranceguide.com

Further information: Living and Working in France, by Genevieve Brame (published by Kogan Page, www.koganpage.com), provides in-depth information for expatriates living in France.

Personal taxation

Unless otherwise stated, all figures relate to 2008 income.

Territoriality and residence

An individual is considered to be French resident if one of the following three criteria is met:

1. The individual's permanent home (foyer) is in France or, if the permanent home cannot be determined, the individual's principal place of stay, regardless of permanency, is in France.
2. The individual carries out an occupation or employment in France, unless subsidiary to a main occupation carried out elsewhere.
3. The individual's place of economic interest (main investments and their management) or main source of income is in France.

A French resident is subject to French tax on their worldwide income, while a non-resident is subject to French tax only on French-source income.

Taxation of personal income

Individuals are subject to income tax on their annual taxable income. Taxable income is determined by adding together the various categories of income and deducting losses, expenses and relief.

Categories of income include:

- industrial and commercial profits;
- non-commercial profits;
- rental income;
- employment income;
- financial income;
- agricultural income.

The tax year for income tax purposes is the calendar year, and the yearly taxable income is determined for the whole household, that is, husband, wife and dependent children. Income tax is computed by the French tax authorities on the income of the preceding year (eg in 2010 taxpayers must complete and lodge their tax return for income received during 2009). Income tax is levied at progressive rates from 5.5 per cent. From 1 January 2009, the maximum rate was 40 per cent for 2008 income, to which miscellaneous social taxes must be added (including social security taxes), amounting to up to 22 per cent.

The top marginal rate kicks in at €69,505 for the single taxpayer (double if married) of net taxable income.

Employment income

Employment income includes all benefits in cash or in kind received by an individual. Professional expenses are deductible, with taxpayers choosing between a standard deduction of 10 per cent and a deduction of actual professional expenses. Pensions are taxed in the same way as employment income.

Social security

French social security covers obligatory health insurance, basic and complementary pension contributions, unemployment insurance and other charges, all deductible. The employee portion of social charges and surtaxes is between 18 and 22 per cent of gross income and varies from company to company and according to industry.

Financial income

Share dividends and bond interest are subject to income tax at the progressive rates.

Capital gains

Capital gains from the sale of securities and real estate property are taxed at a flat rate of 18 per cent plus a special social security surcharge of 12.1 per cent if the annual proceeds exceed the threshold (€25,730 for 2009).

Other taxes on capital

There is no capital duty or capital acquisitions tax. Transfers within a family are mostly exempt from inheritance/estate tax.

Net wealth/net worth tax

Households, rather than individuals, pay a wealth tax on worth more than €790,000 for 2009.

Real property tax

Owner-occupants are liable for tax on developed real property based on the rental value of the property assessed by the tax authorities.

Inheritance tax

Inheritance tax from 5 to 60 per cent is imposed, with different rates applied to the spouse's inheritance and that of the children.

Tax treaties

France has signed tax treaties with more than 110 countries, and this includes the entire developed world. There is a favourable tax regime for the inbound under certain conditions on which tax advice should be taken.

Filing and penalties

Married persons must file a joint tax return. The tax return must generally be filed by 1 March after the end of the tax year. In some cases the filing date can be extended to the end of May. Late payments and filing are subject to a 20 per cent penalty. Interest is charged at 9 per cent per year. Employment income of individuals is taxed by advance payments of tax.

Source:
KPMG's Individual Income Tax Rate Survey 2009.

Singapore

The economy

Singapore has no natural resources other than its natural harbour, its well-developed infrastructure and the skills and industry of its people. Despite the inherent disadvantages of a small domestic economy and lack of natural resources, Singapore has established itself as one of the best business destinations. It is recognized as one of the world's most competitive economies, supported by an increasingly globally competitive workforce.

International banks, insurance companies, ship operators, traders and professional consultants are an integral part of Singapore's business environment. The republic is also a leading financial centre with a strong and stable currency, no exchange control restrictions, low inflation and low interest rates.

The success of the economy is the result of the government's timely implementation of a policy of industrialization and diversification. The economy has been restructured to place emphasis on higher technological applications and skill-intensive, capital-intensive industries such as electronics and pharmaceuticals, and to promote Singapore as an important centre for such activities as international trading, warehousing, financial and business services, medical and dental services and computer services.

As the economy matures, Singapore has found it increasingly difficult to maintain the same rates of high growth experienced in the 1980s and 1990s. Manufacturing and services continue to be promoted as the twin engines of growth for the future. GDP growth in 2007 remained well in excess of 7 per cent but tumbled to 1.1 per cent for 2008. Echoing the effects of the financial crisis elsewhere, GDP shrank by –2.1 per cent in 2009 but is bouncing back with growth of 4.9 per cent forecast for 2010. Inflation jumped to 6.5 per cent in 2008 but had fallen back to 4.3 per cent at the year end and was reduced further to 0.2 per cent by December 2009. Unemployment was held down to 2.1 per cent in Q4 2009. To some extent, Singapore was insulated from any US and European economic downturn because 60 per cent of export sales are now to Asian markets, but the temporary decline of its Chinese, Japanese and South Korean trading partners hit hard.

Singapore's main trading partners are Malaysia, the United States, Japan, Hong Kong and China. Singapore has maintained massive foreign reserves, still amounting to nearly five months of imports and has extended its investment activities from other high-growth economies in Asia into Western assets through its sovereign fund, Temasek, in order to balance the more modest domestic growth rate. The foreign trade current account remained comfortably in surplus, running at 15.9 per cent of GDP in 2007, but moderated to 14.0 per cent in 2008 and to 12.3 per cent in 2009. Singapore's GNP per capita in US dollars stands at more than 15 times the regional average. In spite of the recessionary effects, a budget deficit of only –1.1 per cent was registered for 2009.

Working conditions

The British expatriate community is quite large – between 7,000 and 8,000. Jobs are advertised in the appropriate sectors of the overseas press and are usually on a contract basis with a salary plus fringe benefits, as indicated in the 'Personal taxation' section below. The major Singapore professional bodies are affiliated to, or otherwise closely connected with, their UK counterparts. People going to work in Singapore must have an employment pass, which has to be obtained by the prospective employer. Dependants must also obtain a pass that has to be applied for by the employer. There are various immigration schemes for those with proven technical, professional or entrepreneurial skills.

Useful information

Climate: Singapore is less than 137 kilometres from the equator and is hot and humid for most of the year.

Electricity: 230–250 V, 50 Hz ac. Three-square-pin plugs are common.

Transport: The importing of cars is discouraged, and there is a duty of 45 per cent on imported cars on top of a basic additional registration fee of 150 per cent of the value of any new car, imported or otherwise. Thus it is not advisable to bring a car into Singapore from abroad, even though buying one locally is very expensive. Second-hand cars are advertised for sale in the *Straits Times*. The government is trying to limit car ownership on the island, both by fiscal policies and by placing restrictions on the use of cars in the central business district. On the other hand, both taxis and public transport are correspondingly inexpensive, and indeed are among the world's cheapest.

Health: Singapore has a good health record, and the government wages a somewhat draconian cleanliness campaign, which includes hefty fines for dropping even a bus ticket in the street.

Health care: There are no free medical facilities, but treatment in government clinics is very cheap, though most expatriates prefer to use private doctors, who charge between S$25 and S$50 (specialists S$45–$80), depending on their qualifications and what sort of treatment is involved. Surgeons' and obstetricians' fees start at around S$2,100, and a private room in a hospital costs about S$180 a day. Medical fees, or insurance premiums to cover them, are often, in the case of expatriates, met by employers.

Education: As with many other jobs overseas, education can be a problem, and arrangements to send children to local schools should be made as soon as possible. Government schools are very cheap, with only nominal fees for the children of Singapore residents. There are three good British private primary schools. The Singapore American School takes all ages up to 18, and there is also the United World College of South East Asia, which has facilities for A-level teaching. There is an excellent university in Singapore, at which the standards of entry and the level of the courses are equivalent to UK universities. Fees vary depending on the nature of the course being taken.

Useful contacts:
British High Commission, 100 Tanglin Road, Singapore 247919 (tel: 656424 4200, website: www.britain.org.sg/)
Singapore High Commission, 9 Wilton Crescent, London SW1 (tel: 020 7235 8315)
Singapore Tourism Board, 1st Floor, Carrington House, 126–130 Regent Street, London W1R 5FE (tel: 020 7437 0033)

Expatriate contacts: www.expatsingapore.com

Information on Singapore tax: simonpoh@bdo.com.sg

Personal taxation

Residence

A Singaporean is tax resident if they normally reside in Singapore except for temporary absence. A foreigner is regarded as resident in Singapore if, in the calendar year preceding the year of assessment, they were physically present in Singapore or exercised employment in Singapore (other than as a director of a company) for 183 days or more.

Taxes on income

Singapore tax residents are subject to income tax on income accrued in or derived from Singapore. Since 1 January 2004, foreign-source income has been exempt from income tax in Singapore. Certain investment income derived from Singapore sources by individuals on or after 1 January 2004 is also exempt. Non-resident tax individuals are subject to Singapore income tax only on the income accrued in or derived from Singapore.

Taxable income includes gains or profits from a trade or profession and earnings from employment (including the value of employer-provided benefits). Residents are taxed at progressive rates ranging from 3.5 to 20 per cent. The top marginal rate is applied from S$320,000 of taxable income. Non-residents are taxed on employment income at a higher rate, at a flat rate of 15 per cent (without any deduction of personal reliefs and allowances). All other non-residents' income sourced in Singapore, including directors' and consultants' fees, is taxed at a flat rate of 20 per cent. A non-resident individual (other than a director) on short-term employment in Singapore for less than 60 days may be exempt from tax in Singapore.

Deductions and allowances

Personal reliefs and tax rebates against assessable income are granted only to resident individuals.

Social security

Only employees who are Singapore citizens or permanent residents are generally required to contribute to the Central Provident Fund (CPF), at a rate of 20 per cent of their ordinary wages, subject to an annual wage cap to S$54,000 (S$76,500 when additional wages such as bonus are included). Graduated rates may apply for the first three years, when the employee first attains permanent residence.

Taxes on capital

Capital gains

Singapore does not have capital gains tax.

Inheritance/estate tax

An individual domiciled in Singapore at the time of their death is liable to estate duty on all movable and immovable assets in Singapore and movable assets outside Singapore at 5 per cent on the first S$12 million and 10 per cent thereafter. A person neither domiciled nor resident in Singapore at the time of death is liable to estate duty only on immovable assets in Singapore.

Other taxes

There is no net wealth/net worth tax, capital acquisitions tax or capital duty.

Double taxation treaties

Singapore has signed 55 comprehensive tax treaties.

Filing and payment

There is no provision for joint filing, including married couples living together. The tax year is the calendar year. Individual tax returns and computations are due by 15 April each year following the end of the tax year, and an assessment is raised on the basis of this return. There is no system of deduction of tax from employment income. Penalties and interest are provided for late filing or failure to file although extension beyond 15 April is generally allowed if there are valid reasons.

Source:
KPMG's Individual Income Tax Rate Survey 2009.

Index

Index of advertisers